Executive's Treasury of Humor for Every Occasion

WILLIAM R. GERLER

PARKER PUBLISHING COMPANY, INC., WEST NYACK, N.Y.

Executive's Treasury of Humor for Every Occasion

Dedicated to

FRANCES MARIE BRUNNER GERLER

Executive's Treasury of Humor for Every Occasion
by William R. Gerler
© 1965 by Parker Publishing Company, Inc.,
West Nyack, N.Y.

Library of Congress Card Catalog Number: 65-25040

Printed in the United States of America
29451 B & P

WHEN AND HOW TO USE HUMOR

Humor has long been regarded as a fundamental ingredient in both formal and informal speaking. It adds savor to a speech just as a culinary spice flavors a cooking dish. And like a spice it must be selected with care, used in the right proportion, and added at the right time. Properly used, humor makes even the most carefully prepared and expertly delivered speech much more palatable to the listener.

George Jessel once said that good speeches, like good socks, depend on the yarn that is used.

This book is a private collection of contemporary humor that should provide executives, businessmen and others with a fresh source of humorous material for speeches, talks, introductions, and other day-to-day speaking activities.

Here you will find over 325 major classifications of humor, organized by subject matter and cross-referenced for handy use. There are short jokes, ancedotes, witticisms, epigrams, humorous stories and dozens of definitions; a zesty collection carefully selected to appeal to the modern tastes in humor by both men and women.

You have no doubt seen speakers use humor in a variety of different ways, from a few humorous definitions in a serious speech to the hundreds thrown at an audience at machine-gun rate by comedians for entertainment.

Generally, however, humor should be used only when it emphasizes a point in the message or when it can be injected comfortably in a talk to relax a tense audience or change a mood.

Never try to drag in a story just for the sake of telling it. Never begin by saying, "I understand that it is customary for speakers to begin with a story or two" and then tell something unrelated to your topic.

Care also should be exercised not to use humor to irritate or offend a person or an audience in any way. Prejudge the reaction of the joke before you use it. When in doubt, use yourself, your wife, or someone else you know will not be bothered by it.

How to Get the Most from This Book

While the jokes, stories and ancedotes can be used as printed here, to be most effective they should be personalized to the audience and the occasion and often to the locality where they are being told.

If you are serving, for example, as chairman of the membership committee of a Rotary Club and have to introduce as a new member a well-known physician, you would turn to the section on (Doctors-Medicine) and select a joke like this one:

Then there's the tale of a young doctor who hung up his shingle in a small town and waited for his first patient. Some days later one arrived—covered from head to foot with an angry-looking rash. The puzzled young medic hastily consulted his books but could find no help there.

Finally, he said to the patient, "Did you ever have this affliction before?"

"Oh, sure Doc," replied the patient. "I've had it twice before."

"Well," diagnosed the Doctor, "you have it again."

When using this joke in your Rotary Club introduction, it would be changed to something like this:

When our new member, Dr. Fred Jones, came to town 20 years ago and hung his shingle up on North Main Street, one of his first patients was Jack Thompson (a member). Jack was covered from head to foot with an angry-looking rash. So Doctor Jones hastily consulted his books but could find no help there.

Finally, he turned to Jack and said: "Did you ever have this affliction before?"

"Oh, yes," said Jack, "I've had it twice before."

"Well," diagnosed Doctor Jones, "You have it again."

Here's another suggestion on how this material can be used informally in conversation.

You are attending a national convention and are assembling early in the morning for one of the sessions after a strenuous evening of entertainment. You enter the room and join the group you were with the previous night. Usually some one in the party will ask you:

"Did you get home all right last night?"

"I got home all right," (you say) "but a funny thing happened to me. Just as I was turning the corner, someone stepped on my fingers."

ACKNOWLEDGMENTS

While this treasury of humor has been collected from many sources over the past 15 years, I especially want to acknowledge the many industrial editors throughout the United States whose publications I received while associated in various official capacities of the International Council of Industrial Editors.

Acknowledgement specifically goes to the editors of the following publications from whose periodicals much of this humorous collection has been compiled: KVP Philosopher, Parts Pups, Investment Dealers' Digest, PG&E Progress, Tim Burr Helps, The Workman, We Lumberman, Bagology (Chase Bag Company), Braun Brevities, Prints of Paris, Kreolite News, Navy News Magazine, Gilcrafter, Two Minutes With You, Pocketbook, Management Review, Nugget, Notes and Quotes, The Hoist, Cy-N-Peace, Butler Bee, Saturday Review of Literature, Bagpipe (Encyclopaedia Britannica, Inc.), Olethe Air Scoop, Blankie's Bulletin, Chevron, Union Signal, Westlake Bugle, Pathfinder, Bag-O-Fun, Annapolis Log, In-A-Nutshell, Seng Fellowship News, Quonset Scout, South Side Federal News, Mauk Talk, Chemical and Engineering News, Solar Flakes, Safety Broadcast, Arizona Grocer, Oklahoma Food Journal, Home Life, N.Y. Journal-American, Gas Flame, Journeyman Barber, Ohio State Sundial, Time Out, Carrier, Montrealer, Jax Air News, Columbian Crew, Gerber News, Highways, Dill Valve, Typing Tips, School Activities, Pipefuls, Great Northern Goat, Solar Flash, Advertiser's Digest, and Sales Review.

WILLIAM R. GERLER

Accidents—Auto, Home

A fast-driving motorist lost control of his car and ran into a telephone pole. When he came to, he was on the ground, clutching telephone wires. "Thank goodness," he murmured. "It's a harp."

> A dashing young fellow named Tim,
> Drove his car with a great deal of vim.
> Said he: "I'm renowned
> For covering ground."
> But, alas, now the ground covers him.

A woman was filling out an accident report. She had dented the fender of a parked car while trying to park her own. One question on the report was: "What could the operator of the other vehicle have done to avoid the accident?"
She wrote: "He could have parked somewhere else."

Talking to a lawyer, a man asked him to what activity he devoted the most of his time.
"The greatest part of my time is spent," he said, "investigating collisions between cars, each of which was on its own side of the road, each having sounded its horn, and each, at the time of the accident, being almost at a standstill."

Too many light heads believe the headlights cause accidents.

The reason there were fewer wrecks in the horse and buggy days was because the driver didn't depend wholly on his own intelligence.

"What's the matter," yelled the pedestrian at the driver, "Are you blind?"
"Blind? I hit you, didn't I?"

An old lady fell down the stairs and broke her leg. The doctor put it in a cast and warned her not to walk up or down the stairs. The leg was slow in mending. Finally, after six months, the doctor announced it was all right to remove the cast.
"Can I climb the stairs now?" asked the old lady.
"Yes," answered the medical man.

1

"Oh, I'm so glad," she chortled. "I'm sick of climbing up and down the drainpipe all the time!"

An aged gentleman, crossing the street, was knocked over by a racing St. Bernard dog. Seconds later a tiny compact car skidded into him, inflicting other damage. Helped to his feet by a passer-by he was asked if he were hurt. The old man replied, "Well the dog didn't hurt me very much, but the tin can tied to his tail nearly killed me!"

The purchasing agent had been given a bottle of rare old Scotch in honor of the holidays. On his way home, he tripped on a child's toy wagon that had been left on the sidewalk. He tumbled head over heels, landed on a patch of ice and ended up, head first, against a tree. Suddenly he felt something warm trickling down his leg. "Egad," he groaned. "I sure hope that it's blood."

A motorist was picked up unconscious after a smash and was being carried to a nearby filling station. Opening his eyes en route, he began to kick and struggle desperately to get away. Afterwards he explained that the first thing he saw was a "Shell" sign, and "some damn fool was standing in front of the 'S.'"

MAGISTRATE: "How did you happen to hit the other car?"
MOTORIST: "It was entirely my wife's fault. She fell asleep in the back seat."

The salesman had picked up a hitch-hiker just a few moments before a sleet storm blew up. In a short while the roads became slippery and the freezing moisture made vision extremely difficult.
The salesman stopped at an open highway stop sign and asked his passenger if he saw anything coming.
"No, man. Just a dog."
So the salesman put his car in gear and started up. Three days later he woke up in a hospital and saw his companion in the next bed. "Hey, you nut, I thought you said there was only a dog."
"Sure, man . . . a Greyhound."

The young bride had sad news for her husband when he returned from his day's work. "I feel terrible," she said with a sob. "I was pressing your best suit and burnt a hole in the seat of the trousers."
"Don't worry about it, dear," said the husband. "I have another pair of pants to that suit."
"Yes I know," was the reply, "and it's lucky that you have. I was able to use them to patch the hole."

"Haven't heard much out of Uncle Buckle lately."

"You won't either—for a while, anyway."

"What happened?"

"He was eating a piece of cheese when the trap slammed shut on his tongue."

Accountants

Old accountants never die—they just lose their balance.

Actors (see Motion Pictures)

A much-married Hollywood actor was confronted by a gay damsel.

"Hello there," she said, "don't you remember me? Ten years ago you asked me to marry you!"

"Really?" yawned the actor. "And did you?"

First Showgirl: "How would you act if the producer of this show kissed you?"

Second Showgirl: "I'd act in all his future productions."

Hollywood bride entering home with the new groom: "Jack darling, are you sure we haven't been married before? This house looks familiar."

Adolescence

Adolescence: When a girl's voice changes from no to yes.

Advertising

The wife of an advertising copywriter put her small son to bed and told him, "Now, Mickey, say your prayers."

"Oh, Lord," mumbled the little fellow, "please bless mama and daddy, and give us this day our slow-rising, oven-baked, vitamin-enriched bread."

A man appeared at a newspaper office to place an ad offering $500 for the return of his wife's pet cat.

"That's an awful price for a cat," the clerk commented.

"Not for this one," the man snapped. "I drowned it."

At the perfume counter the clerk was applying sales pressure. "This one has a delightful fragrance," she said to the customer. "Believe me, you can't go wrong with it."

"That's odd," murmured the young lady. "Most perfumes advertise that you can."

Ad in a weekly paper: "Lawn mower, push type. Used very little, and when used, pushed very slow."

Age (see Middle Age, Old Age, Adolescence)

Most people have no respect for age unless it be bottled.

Airplane–Air Travel

Two elderly women, about to board a plane for their first flight, approached the pilot. "Now young man," said one, "don't fly faster than sound. We want to talk."

A passenger in a plane sat relaxed at a window drinking in the spectacle of the heavens sliding by. Suddenly a parachutist appeared and drifted by.

"Going to join me?" cried the parachutist.

"Thank you very much," replied the passenger. "I'm very happy just where I am."

"Just as you like," called back the parachutist. "I'm the pilot."

A Navy pilot visited the office of the National Aircraft Show during a particularly busy moment when the telephone rang. All hands being occupied, he took up the phone and listened for a moment to the complaints of an irate resident of a nearby town.

"This is a dreadful thing!" she said. "These airplanes are making so much noise I can hardly hear myself think!"

"Are they Russian planes?" the pilot asked.

"Certainly not! They're American planes. I can see them."

"Thank God!" said the Navy flier and hung up."

A country boy went for an airplane ride. When he came down he said to the pilot, "Thanks for the two rides."

"Two rides?" asked the pilot. "You had only one."

"No, sir, two," he replied. "My first and my last."

A man walked up to the ticket agent and asked for a ticket to the moon.

"Sorry, sir, all flights are cancelled."

"Bad weather?" asked the customer.

"No," the agent replied. "The moon is full right now."

Professors are supposed to be absent-minded but a prominent general of one of the smaller nations allied with us during World War II was more than a match for the professor.

During an inspection of one of the allied bases in the Mediterranean, he was invited to try out a new flying boat. The general considered himself quite a flyer and everything went well until his host saw that the general was inland and about to bring the boat down on a flying field.

"Excuse me, General," the host said, "but it would be better to come down at sea. This is a flying boat."

"Of course," replied the pilot. "I don't know what I was thinking of."

He swung back out to sea and soon landed the boat safely on the water. Rising from his seat, he turned to his host and said, "I greatly appreciate the tact with which you drew my attention to the incredible blunder I nearly made."

Then he opened the door and stepped into the sea.

A salesman growing nervous about traveling by air went to see a statistician one day.

"Can you tell me," he asked, "what the odds would be against my boarding an aircraft on which somebody had hidden a bomb?"

"I can't tell you until I've analyzed the available data," the statistician replied. "Come back again in a week or so."

"Well," the worried salesman asked on his next visit, "do you have the answer?"

"Certainly," the statistician said. "The odds are one million to one against your getting on an aircraft with one bomb on it."

"Those are good odds," the salesman mused, "but I'm not sure they're good enough for me. I travel a good deal."

"Well, if you really want to be safe," the statistician said, "carry a bomb with you. The odds are one billion to one against your boarding an aircraft with two bombs on it."

Our Dumb Blonde went out with a young airman the other day when the familiar sound of aircraft engines overhead made them look up.

"That's a mailplane," announced the airman.

"Beats me how you can tell at this distance," said the D.B.

Ambition

The average man's ambition nowadays is to be able to afford what he is spending.

In this country every little boy, no matter how humble his circumstances, can grow up and become a taxpayer.

America

America: A place where we jump traffic lights to save seconds, and wait patiently for hours on the first tee.

When the white man discovered this country, the Indians were running it. There were no taxes, there was no debt. The women did all the work. And the white man thought he could improve on a system like that!

'Tis said that this country was founded partly to avoid taxation. Our founding fathers should take a look now!

Anatomy

An eminent surgeon attended the unveiling of a bust of himself at the University. After the ceremony a young woman came up to him.

"I hope you appreciate," she said, "that I have come fifty miles to see your bust unveiled."

Whereupon, with a bow, the doctor replied, "I would go a hundred miles to see yours."

The human body is very sensitive. Pat a man on the back and his head swells.

A little old lady riding on a bus was anxious not to pass her destination. She poked the driver with her umbrella and asked,

"Is that the First National Bank?"

No, madam," he replied. "That's my rib."

Introduction of a chairman at club meeting:

"Ladies and gentlemen, in China there is an ancient custom that parents must kiss their offspring on that part of their anatomy through which they hope the children will become famous.

"If they want their child to be a philosopher, they kiss him on the forehead. If they want him to be an orator, they kiss him on the mouth. If they hope he'll be a singer, they kiss him on the throat.

"Now, I don't know on what part of his anatomy Mr. Smith's parents kissed him . . ." and the twittery mistress of ceremonies paused an instant for effect . . . "but he certainly makes a wonderful chairman."

SMALL BOY: "Dad, there was a man here to see you this morning."

DAD: "Did he have a bill?"

SMALL BOY: "No, just a regular nose."

In a night club one evening a very pretty girl was wearing around her neck a thin chain from which hung a tiny golden airplane. One of the young men in the party stared at it so that the girl finally asked him: "Do you like my little airplane?"

"As a matter of fact," he replied, "I wasn't looking at it. I was really admiring the landing field."

Ancestry

A woman was trying to impress her friends at a party one afternoon.

"My family's ancestry is very old," she said. "It dates back to the days of King John of England."

Turning to a woman sitting nearby she said condescendingly: "How old is your family, my dear?"

"Well," replied the woman with a smile, "I really can't say. All of our family records were lost in the flood."

Some families can trace their ancestry back 300 years but haven't the slightest idea where their children were last night.

A miser isn't much fun to live with, but he sure makes a wonderful ancestor.

"That sergeant! I've never heard a man talk so fast in my life."

"Why shouldn't he? His father was a tobacco auctioneer, and his mother was a woman."

Animals—Miscellaneous (see also Farms—Farming)

"Goodness, what a remarkable act! How did you ever get that bear to play the piano?"

"How does anyone learn to play the piano?" snapped the trainer. "He took lessons."

It seems that a scientist crossed a porcupine with a gorilla. When asked what he got, he answered: "I don't know what it is, but it sure gets a seat on the bus!"

A lion got loose at the circus and ran toward a man in the audience. The man broke and ran, quite frightened. "Don't be afraid," the trainer said. "That lion hasn't got any teeth!"

"Maybe not," the fellow shouted from a safe distance, "but I'm not going to stand here and be gummed to death."

PAPA KANGAROO: "Annabelle, where's the baby?"
MAMA KANGAROO: "My goodness! I've had my pocket picked again!"

Two ducks were gaping at another duck who had just left them. "Doesn't she simply slay you?" said one. "She walks just like a woman wearing tight slacks."

All the animals had left the ark except two snakes lying over in a corner.
"Why don't you go forth and multiply?" asked Noah.
"We can't," answered one. "We're adders."

The owner of a circus was being pestered by a clown to engage him and his pet mongoose.
"My partner is very clever," he said. "He can talk, sing and dance—he is positively human."
"If that's the case," exclaimed the circus owner, "why is he on a leash?"
"Because," confessed the clown, "he owes me twenty bucks!"

"I just saw a couple of elephants go into that bar across the street," said Luke, "and I'm waiting to see what a couple of drunk elephants will do."
"Oh, those elephants don't drink," said Mac. "They just went in for the peanuts."

A man visited the city zoo one day and was greatly mystified by a baby deer.
"What kind of an animal is that there?" he asked an attendant.
"You mean you don't know?" the keeper replied. "Why, my goodness man, what does your wife call you every morning?"
"Well, whadda ya know," the dope exclaimed. "So that's a skunk!"

The two cats were watching a tennis match. One was obviously quite bored with the whole proceeding while the other was watching avidly, swiveling his head back and forth as he followed the ball.
"Say," said the bored cat, "I notice that you are quite interested in this game. You must be a real fan."
"Oh, no," replied the other. "It's not that at all. You see, my old man's in the racket."

The worried leopard walked into the optometrist's office and said: "Doc, you'd better examine my eyes. Every night when I come home to my wife, I see spots before my eyes."

"What's so odd about that?" asked the optometrist.

"The thing is," said the leopard, "I'm married to a zebra.'

The rabbit wouldn't let his dentist give him Novocain—because he was an ether bunny.

A man owned a parrot that had a bad habit of swearing. He decided to break the parrot of this habit, so he gave it quite a lecture on the evils of profanity and at the conclusion of his remarks said: "It's a nice day, isn't it?"

The parrot replied: "Damn fine day."

The man jerked it out of its cage and whirled it around his head, then dunked it in a pail of water until it was nearly drowned. He then restored it to its cage, and while the parrot was still gasping and shaking itself, asked in a severe tone of voice: "Now, then, nice day isn't it?"

To which the parrot replied, "Yes, sir. But where the hell were you when the typhoon struck?"

A kangaroo walked into a bar and in clear, well-modulated tones asked the bartender for a Martini. The bartender was amazed, but concealed his surprise and mixed and served the drink to the kangaroo. The latter drank it quietly and eventually asked how much he owed.

"$1.75," said the bartender.

The kangaroo paid the check and was about to walk out when the bartender, no longer able to restrain his curiosity, remarked: "We've never had the pleasure of serving a kangaroo here."

To which the kangaroo politely and promptly replied: "And at these prices, it will be a mighty long time before you serve another one."

A baby rabbit had been pestering its mother all day. Finally the exasperated parent replied, "You were pulled out of a magician's hat—now stop asking questions."

Anniversaries

A couple celebrating their golden wedding anniversary were obviously still very happily married and enjoyed each other's company. A young couple, much impressed, asked their recipe for happiness.

The old gentleman, with a twinkle in his eye replied: "Well, Sonny, I've always tried to treat Ma in such a fashion that if I should have died, it would have taken more than a hot water bottle to replace me."

The old couple had just celebrated their golden wedding anniversary. Now all the guests were gone and they sat by the open fireplace, hand in hand, with her head on his shoulder, and reminisced.

"Mary," he said tenderly. "You're still my sweetheart. In fact, I've never had another sweetheart because I never found anyone as sweet and beautiful as you."

"Henry," she replied "you're as big a liar as ever, and I believe you just the same."

On their golden wedding anniversary, the old lady was asked: "In all these years have you ever thought of divorce?"

To which she replied: "No, only of murder."

On their golden wedding anniversary, the husband remarked: "Well, dear, it's been many years and I haven't deceived you yet."

"No, John," the wife declared, "but it's not from lack of trying."

GREEN: "What are you doing this evening?"

WHITE: "Celebrating my wife's fifth anniversary."

GREEN: "Wedding anniversary?"

WHITE: "No, fifth anniversary of her fortieth birthday."

When the husband started about his business as usual the morning of his 25th wedding anniversary the wife was rightfully annoyed.

"Don't you realize what day this is?" she asked.

"Sure I do," he replied.

"Well, let's celebrate by doing something unusual."

He meditated for a moment, then he suggested quietly, "How about two minutes of silence?"

"Dear," said the wife, "do you know what day this is?"

"I sure do," said the husband. "It's our wedding anniversary."

"Our wedding anniversary," repeated the wife, sounding somewhat miffed. "Did you remember to get me something?"

"I sure did," says the hubby. "I spent hours trying to think of something that would be unusual, of real appeal, and useful—something I felt sure you'd be proud to own."

By this time the wife was all ears. "What," she inquired, "is it?"

"I got for your anniversary present," the husband announced, "a fine family plot in the exclusive Restwell Gardens cemetery."

Knowing her stuff, the wife let on to be pleased and allowed that a family plot was a wonderful idea.

Next year on the same date, the couple again sat over the second coffee following breakfast.

"Do you know what day this is, dear?" she asked.

"Yep," he said, looking at the newspaper. "Our anniversary."

"Did you get me anything?" she asked coyly.

"Did I get you anything?" the husband burst out. "Why, you haven't used the present I got you last year!"

Antiques

Antique: An object which has made a round trip to the attic.

Sign seen in a well-known Boston center for antiques: "The Den of Antiquity."

Appointment

SALESMAN: "I've been trying to see you all week. When may I have an appointment?"
BIG SHOT: "Make a date with my secretary!"
SALESMAN: "I did—and we had a swell time. But I still want to see you."

Arrest

"Okay, lady, pull over," shouted the traffic cop.
Mrs. Black's blood froze. This was the second time in two days she had a brush with the law—and since her husband was in the habit of going over her check book, she was at a loss to itemize the latest ticket on the stub. Finally, she had an inspiration.
"One pull over," she wrote, "ten dollars."

COP (*to lady driver parked illegally*): "Lady, can't you read?"
LADY: "Why, certainly. The sign says fine for parking."

Art—Artists

The gentleman was gazing rapturously at "Spring," a large oil painting of a shapely girl dressed in a few leaves. Suddenly the voice of his wife snapped, "Well, what are you waiting for—autumn?"

A modernistic painter was robbed. In order to assist the police in catching the thief, he drew a sketch of the culprit. Guided entirely by this sketch, the police rounded up a TV aerial, three can openers, a hearse, and two pairs of boots.

ARTIST: "Well, to make a long story short, it took me ten years to finally realize that I had absolutely no talent for painting."
FRIEND: "So you quit."
ARTIST: "Oh, no, I couldn't. By that time I was too famous."

The young daughter of a well-known painter danced in glee on hearing that one of her mother's paintings had been purchased by a famous museum.

"Oh, Mama," she exclaimed joyfully, "that makes you an Old Mistress, doesn't it?"

Two men were discussing the work of a renowned artist.

"He painted a spider's web on the wall which was so realistic that the maid spent two hours trying to wipe it down," said the first.

"That's too fantastic to believe," replied the second.

"But artists do things like that," insisted the first.

"Maybe so," conceded the second, "but maids don't."

"Can you make a good portrait of my wife?"

"Can I? I'll make it so realistic that you'll duck every time you look at it."

Automobiles

It's not a cheaper car that people want. It's an expensive car that costs less.

The young couple decided to buy a compact car, but when they entered the showroom and saw the suggested price they were astonished. "Why that's almost the same price as a big car," the husband complained to the salesman.

"That's right," replied the salesman. "If you want economy, you got to be willing to pay for it."

The wife was trying to get her husband to purchase a new automobile, but he didn't seem to like the idea.

"What?" he roared. "Me buy a new car? Do you think automobiles grow on trees?"

"Of course not, silly," replied his wife calmly. "Everybody knows they come from plants."

Nothing deteriorates your car so fast as your neighbor's buying a new one.

PROSPECT (*who was being given a demonstration in a used car*): "Say, what makes it jerk so when you first put it in gear?"

SALESMAN: "Ah, that proves it to be a real car. It's anxious to start."

SALESMAN: "This car goes 180 m.p.h. and stops on a dime."

BUYER: "Then what happens?"

SALESMAN: "A little putty knife comes out and scrapes you off the windshield."

Classified ad for a used car: "Owner—young fellow—used mostly for parking."

"What's the matter, lady?" asked the garage man.

"They say I have a short circuit. Can you lengthen it while I wait?"

A woman confronted her butcher in a raging voice. "Just how do you explain these pieces of rubber I found in this hamburger you sold me?"

The butcher shrugged his shoulders helplessly: "I guess it's just another instance proving the automobile is replacing the horse, Ma'am."

An alarmed motorist stopped hurriedly when he saw a young man standing beside an overturned small sports car. "Anybody hurt in the accident?" he inquired.

"There wasn't any accident," replied the young man calmly. "I'm changing a tire."

OFFICER: "Hey, you, is that your car?"

CULPRIT: "Well, Officer, since you ask me, considering the fact that I still have fifty payments to make, owe three repair bills, have not settled for two new tires, and don't know when I will be able to, I really don't think it is."

Bucket seats don't always fit the bucket.

Bachelor (see Husbands, Wives, Marriage, Courtship)

"Jones never completed his education, did he?"

"No, he lived and died a bachelor."

"What would you call a man who has been lucky in love?"

"A bachelor."

A bachelor is a college man who did not have a car when he was young.

The question that bothers every married man is: why aren't all bachelors rich?

A bachelor is a man with no children to speak of.

A sweet little old lady spent days working on a pair of men's pajamas which she contributed to the Red Cross.
"I made them myself," she said proudly.
They were perfect in every detail except that there was no opening in the front of the pants. The inspector hated to hurt her feelings, but he explained the error to her.
The dear old soul's face fell. Suddenly, however, she brightened. "Couldn't you give them to a bachelor?" she queried.

A bachelor is a fellow who is crazy to get married—and knows it.

A bachelor is a fellow who comes to work every morning from a different direction.

A bachelor is a fellow with no buttons on his shirt—or on his lip.

"So Kim's a confirmed bachelor, is he?"
"He is now. He sent his picture to a Lonely Hearts Club, and they sent it back to him with a note saying, 'We're not that lonely.' "

A bachelor is a man who looks but never leaps.

The reason so many men remain bachelors is that they've learned that women switch quickly from "I do" to "You'd better."

The difference between a married man and an unmarried man is that when a bachelor walks the floor with a baby, he's dancing.

It's been said that all men are fools. That's not true. Some are bachelors.

The bachelor's attractive new housekeeper tiptoed into the study and asked apologetically:
"Sir, shall I clean your stove and sweep your porch now?"
"Margie," said the bachelor, "in this house we are all for one and one for all. You do not say 'your stove' or 'your porch' or 'your chair.' Instead you say 'our stove,' or 'our porch,' or 'our chair.' "
That evening Margie served a splendid dinner to the bachelor and his boss and the boss' daughter, whom the bachelor was anxious to impress.
Margie was late in serving the last course and she rushed into the dining room and excitedly announced:
"I'm sorry I was late, sir, but I was upstairs chasing a mouse from under 'our bed.' "

Two fellows met at a bar. "Say," said the first, "what does your wife say when you're out this late?"

"Nothing," replied the other. "I'm not married."

The first fellow pondered for a moment, and asked, "Then why do you stay out as late as this?"

What's worse than being a bachelor? Being a bachelor's son!

A bachelor is a fellow who can get into bed from either side.

> The bachelor's a cagey guy,
> And has a lot of fun;
> He sizes all the cuties up
> And never Mrs. one.

A bachelor is a fellow who knows enough not to go on a hayride with a grass widow.

Bankers—Banking

Old bankers never die, either. They just lose interest.

On his 75th birthday, the hard-bitten president of the small town bank was interviewed by the community's one reporter. "Everybody here knows pretty much everything about you," the newsman said, "but how did you get started on a banking career?"

"T'wasn't nuttin'," shrugged the local Croesus. "Long about the time I come into my brains, I hung up a sign that sez 'Bank.' Pretty soon a feller strolls in and deposits 50 dollars. A while later, another stranger mosies by and deposits a hundred dollars. This kept up until I got so confident I put in 10 dollars of my own money!"

STRANGER: "Can you tell me what a joint account is? My wife and I wanted to open one."

CASHIER: "Well, in that case, a joint account is one where you put money in and your wife takes it out."

A clerk at the local bank informs us that a joint checking account is never overdrawn by the wife. It's just under-deposited by the husband.

Mrs. Upstart walked importantly into the bank and addressed the cashier. "I want to open an account in your bank," she announced.

"Do you want a savings account or a checking account?" he inquired.

"Neither," replied the caller. "I want a charge account, like I have at the department store."

The bank cashier told his new assistant to "Count this pack of bills to make sure there are one hundred."

The new employee counted up to "54, 55, 56," then threw the package in the drawer, remarking to the man next to him, "If it's right this far, it's probably right all the way."

A bank president, extremely sensitive about his baldness, wore his hat much of the time inside and out. One day, while the porter, an employee of long standing, was sweeping out his office the president asked jokingly, "Sam, why is it after all these years you don't have an account with us?"

"Because, Boss, you always look like you're about to go somewhere!"

BANK CLERK: "You forgot to dot an 'i' in your signature."
PATRON: "Would you mind dotting it for me?"
CLERK: "I'm sorry, but it has to be in the same handwriting."

CITY BANKER (*visiting the farm*): "I suppose that's the hired man."
FARMER (*who has visited banks*): "No, that's the first vice president in charge of cows."

"Our bank has just gone through a reorganization."
"What was the matter?"
"Nothing, except we discovered we had more vice presidents than depositors."

"A banker," said Mark Twain, "is a fellow who lends you his umbrella when the sun is shining and wants it back the minute it begins to rain."

HUBBY: "The bank has returned that check."
WIFE: "Isn't that nice of them! What can we buy with it this time?"

The bank robber shoved a note across to the teller which read: "Put the money in a bag, sucker, and don't make a move."

The teller pushed back another note: "Straighten your tie, stupid. They're taking your picture."

Bankruptcy

Sign on store housing bankrupt business venture: "Opened By Mistake."

Barbecue

A man who owned a hand-operated rotisserie was barbecuing a chicken in his back yard when a beatnik walked by.

"I don't want to bug you, dad," said the character, "but your music has stopped and your monkey's on fire."

Barber

A barber shop customer was complaining about the price of haircuts. "I'm just back from London," he said. "Over there I was able to get a good haircut for 65 cents."

"Yeah," retorted the barber. "But look at the fare."

Barber Brooks had just finished shaving a customer. "Would you like your neck shaved?" he asked.

"No," said Jack Fraser. "Just scrape it, too. It's no better than my face."

A man rushed into the barber shop and addressed the barber at the first chair, "How many ahead of me?"

"Two haircuts," responded the barber. The man rushed out but didn't come back. The next Saturday, the same thing was repeated. The third Saturday, when the fellow dashed in with his inquiry, the barber said, "Three ahead of you. Say . . ." but the fellow was gone.

"Follow that man and find out who he is," the barber instructed the shine boy. "This is the third Saturday he has run in here, asked how many ahead of him, then ran out and not come back."

A few minutes later the shine boy returned. "Boss," he said. "Ah doan' know who dat fella is, but ah sho' know where he went!"

"Where?" asked the barber.

"To yoah house, suh!"

BARBER (*whispering to new helper*): "Here comes a man for a shave."
APPRENTICE: "Let me practice on him!"
BARBER: "All right, but be careful and don't cut yourself."

The barber asked, "Are you taking a vacation this year?" and the man in the chair said, "Yes. In fact, my wife and I are flying to Rome tomorrow for a couple of weeks."

BARBER: "How are yor going?"
CUSTOMER: "By Pan-Am."
BARBER: "Don't go by Pan-Am. The service is poor, the food is

lousy, the stewardesses are ugly and it'll be rough all the way. Where are you staying in Rome?"

CUSTOMER: "At the Hilton."

BARBER: "Don't stay there, you won't like it. The food's no good, the beds are hard and nobody'll pay any attention to you. You can find a better place to stay than that. What're you going to do in Rome?"

CUSTOMER: "We thought we'd try to get an audience with the Pope."

BARBER: "Take my advice—don't waste your time. You'll never get near him. There'll be ten thousand Italians milling around the square smelling like garlic. You'll wish you never went near the place."

The fellow paid his bill and walked out. Three weeks later he was back.

BARBER: "Did you get to Italy?"

CUSTOMER: "Yep."

BARBER: "How'd you go?"

CUSTOMER: "We went by Pan-Am. It was a wonderful trip, smooth sailing all the way. The food was excellent, the service was great and the stewardesses were 20-20 visions. Couldn't have been better."

BARBER: "Where'd you stay?"

CUSTOMER: "At the Hilton. It's a beautiful place. The food was terrific, the beds were the best I've ever slept in and everybody was marvelous. Wonderful accommodations!"

BARBER: "Did you get to see the Pope?"

CUSTOMER: "Yes, we did. We had a good half hour with him. There were only about a half dozen people and we didn't have to wait over five minutes. It was one of the highlights of the trip."

BARBER: "Well, what'd he say?"

CUSTOMER: "As I knelt at his feet to receive his blessing, he looked at me and said, 'For Pete's sake, man! Where'd you get that miserable haircut?'"

A man, accompanied by a small boy, entered a barber shop and asked for a haircut. When the barber had finished with him, the man said,

"I'm going next door for a beer while you cut the kid's hair."

The barber gave the boy a haircut, then waited for the man to return. Finally he turned to the kid and asked, "Where in Pete's sake did your father go to?"

"Oh," said the boy, "that ain't my father. He's a man who stopped me in the street and asked if I'd like a free haircut."

ROBINSON: "Who was that man you just raised your hat to?"

GREEN: "That? Oh, that was my barber. He sold me a bottle of hair restorer a month ago, and whenever I meet him I let him see what a fraud he is."

Baseball

An American soldier in Germany was leaning against a tree on a Berlin street reading his home town paper. A German citizen walked by and politely inquired, "Vos Sachs Do?"

The soldier looked up from the sports page and said, "They lost six to four."

Ball players will never have a union, because no ball player wants to be called out on strikes.

The teacher had asked the class to list, in their opinion, the nine greatest Americans. After a while, she stopped at one desk and asked, "Have you finished your list yet, Bobby?"

"Not yet, teacher," Bobby replied. "I can't decide on the shortstop."

FIRST BASEBALL PLAYER: "You didn't do so well with that millionaire's daughter, hey?"

SECOND BASEBALL PLAYER: "Terrible! No hits, no runs, no heiress!"

A boy and his very slow girl friend finally arrived at the baseball game. It was the 7th inning and the score was 0 to 0.

"See?" said the girl. "We didn't miss a thing!"

Bathing Suits

"That's quite a bathing suit you have on. With no straps, what keeps it up?"

"A city ordinance."

MOTHER (*to daughter*): "If I'd had a bathing suit like that when I was a girl, you'd be six years older."

"Young lady, I'll bet your mother would be angry if she saw you in that skimpy bathing suit."

"I'll say she would! It's hers!"

MAN (*to small boy dragging top half of a bikini bathing suit along edge of the beach*): "Now show Daddy exactly where you found it."

"Arrested for wearing a French bathing suit?"

"Yes!"

"Shocking! What excuse did the young woman have for exposing her person like that?"

"Ah! You should have seen her excuse!"

There are two sides to everything except, of course, a Bikini bathing suit.

Beauty

She had just come from the hairdresser's.

"Why, Joan," exclaimed her friend, Doreen, "what have you done to your hair? It looks like a wig!"

"It is a wig," replied Joan.

"Well, my goodness," exclaimed Doreen, "I'd never have known it!"

"You say she inherited her beauty?"

"Yes, her uncle died and left her a drug store."

Bigamist

Bigamist: A man who has taken one too many.

"Young lady, you've married five men without getting a divorce. That's bigamy."

"Big of you? Don't you think it was pretty generous of me, too?"

"Not guilty of bigamy," said the judge. "You may go home."

"Thanks, judge. Which one?"

Recently a man in Alaska was arrested for bigamy. It was discovered that he had a wife in Nome. And another wife in Fairbanks. And still another in Juneau. The judge looked down at the culprit and sternly remarked, "How could you do such a thing."

And the bigamist gently replied, "Fast dog team."

Birds

A stork is a bird with many things charged against it which should be blamed on a lark.

When the man asked for a good singing canary, the pet store owner said, "You've come to the right place. This one sings like Sinatra, and he's only $1,000."

"Pretty steep," said the customer, "but if he's that good, I'll take him."

"Not so fast, sir. To get him, you'll have to take that other bird, too."

The customer looked at the second bird, an old and ruffled parrot, with rings under his eyes.

"Why do I have to buy him?"

"Because he's the arranger."

We hear that the bird with the largest bill is not the pelican, but the stork.

A formation of birds was flying south for the winter, and one bird near the back asked another, "How come we always follow that same idiot leader?"

The other replied, "He's got the map."

Leader of a flock of geese to the bird following: "Stop that infernal honking—if you want to pass, pass!"

How do the birds know you have just polished your car?

Breeding

The ladies met on a train. I'm from Boston," haughtily remarked one. "There, breeding is everything."

"Well, I'm from St. Louis," the other replied. "We like it there, too, but it's not everything."

Budget

Budget: An attempt to live below your yearnings.

Budget: Mathematical confirmation of your suspicions.

The time to start economizing is before you run out of money.

Burglar—Burglary

In the dark of the night two safebreakers entered a bank. One approached the safe, sat down on the floor, took off his shoes and socks, and started to turn the dial of the safe with his toes. "What's the matter with you?" said his pal. "Let's open this thing and get out of here."

"Naw, it'll take only a minute longer this way and we'll drive them fingerprint experts nuts."

Then there was the bashful burglar who, upon finding the lady in the shower, covered her with his revolver!

The burglar's wife was nagging him for money.
"Okay," he said. "I'll get you some as soon as the bank closes."

"I'll carry this to the highest court in the land, but in the meantime, you'd better try to escape."

Business—Businessmen

"Business is terrible," complained the man on the next stool. "In February we lost $10,000; in March our losses were $15,000; in April over $20,000 went down the drain."

"You think that's bad," was the reply. "You know that $500,000 building I put up? Well just as the finishing touches were being completed, a workman's torch started a fire and the whole thing burned to the ground. And I didn't have a bit of insurance. What could be worse than that?"

Lost in his own thought, the first complainer answered: "May."

JOHNNY: "How's business, Cortez?"
CORTEZ: "Good! I got a $1500 order day before yesterday."
JOHNNY: "I don't believe it!"
CORTEZ: "It's true. I can show you the cancellation that came this morning."

"We claim to be the second best printer in town."
"Second best? Who claims to be first?"
"All the others."

The sales manager was urging his men to go after increased volume from their accounts.

"Once upon a time," he said, "a Sultan had twenty beautiful wives. He would sit on his throne and when he had picked out a wife he wanted, he'd send a 10-year-old boy, called a 'runner,' after her. Now, as time went on, the Sultan lived to be 121 years old, while the 'runner' died at 40. Gentlemen, business never hurt anyone—it's the running after it that wears men out!"

Mr. Bouncer, an American manufacturer who had obtained an interview with the Pope, was overheard to offer $1,000,000 to the Pope in return for a favor. But the Pope said, "No," with amazement and indignation.

When the American had gone, the Cardinal, thinking that $1,000,000 could achieve a great amount of good, asked the Pope why he had refused.

"Oh," said the Pope, "he wished me to change two words in the Lord's Prayer."

"Only two words?" exclaimed the Cardinal.

"Yes," replied the Pope. "He wished me to change 'daily bread' to 'Bouncer's Wheat-flakes.'"

A businessman stood gazing silently and wonderingly at the crib where his firstborn lay gurgling.

After watching the tender scene for a moment, his wife tiptoed over and put her arm through his.

"A penny for your thoughts, dear," she whispered.

"I can't get over it," he answered. "How the devil can they turn out a crib like this for only $29?"

The only one who watches the clock during the coffee break is the boss.

Maybe historians will refer to the present era as "The Age of Chiselry!"

Two partners took a day off to shoot a round of golf. On the third tee, one partner suddenly exclaimed, "My goodness, I think I forgot to take the cash box."

"So what," said the other, "we're both here aren't we?"

Requisition: Necessary to issue a purchase order.
Purchase Order: An involved document requiring correction.
Cancellation Order: The only way to clear up the mess.

The electronic computer saves man a lot of guesswork, but so does a Bikini bathing suit.

A man who takes his wife to a convention is like a hunter who takes the game warden on a hunting trip.

Back in the depression days circumstances made for cold blooded business methods. When an eastern firm received word its salesman had been found dead in San Francisco, it wired as follows:

"Send samples back by freight and search the body for orders."

A woman was shocked by the language used by a couple of workmen repairing a roof, so she wrote a letter to the roofing company. The manager asked the foreman on the job for an explanation. He made this report:

"Well, me and Joe O'Mara was on the job. I was on the roof with the blowtorch and accidentally let a hot spark fall on Joe. It went down his neck. Joe turned and looked up at me and said: 'Really, Richard, you must try to be a little more careful.' "

Boss *(to secretary)*: "If the Sunshine Club, bowling league, basketball pool and office gift collection committee can spare you, I'd like you take a letter."

The production manager was looking over the specifications for some new equipment which had been ordered by one of his firm's largest customers. Attached to the papers was a coded note saying, "MILTDD-41" and signed by the salesman on the account.

These specifications were not familiar to the production man and he spent several fruitless hours searching various technical journals. Finally he gave up and called the salesman. "Hey, Joe," he asked, "what kind of specs are 'MILTDD-41?' "

"The customer wanted me to be sure to put those on," answered the salesman. "They mean, 'Make it like the damned drawings for once.' "

Nobody ever got hurt on the corners of a "square deal."

Recession—a period when sales are down 5 per cent and staff meetings up 25 per cent.

Then there is the definition of a white collar worker: One who carries his lunch in a briefcase instead of a lunchbox.

Theory: A hunch with a college education.

Businessmen who have no weaknesses are a sorry lot—there's no way of taking advantage of them.

Assistant: The fellow who can't get off.

A sale without a profit is not a sale—but a donation.

Cannibalism

MISSIONARY: "Why do you stare at me like that?"
CANNIBAL: "I'm the food inspector."

A castaway from a wrecked ship was captured by cannibals. Each day a vein in his arm was punctured by a dagger and the natives would drink his blood. Finally one day he called for the native king:

"Look, Buster," he said, "I don't care if you kill me and eat me, but I'm getting mighty tired of being stuck for the drinks all the time!"

As the airliner passed over a South Sea Island, the little Cannibal looked up and asked his mother, "Mother dear, what is that?"

"That," answered the cannibalistic lady, "is something like a lobster; you only eat what's inside."

First Cannibal: "The chief has hay fever."

Second Cannibal: "Serves him right. I told him not to eat that grass widow."

Cards–Card Playing

Lou: "So you taught your wife to play poker?"

Don: "Yes, it was a swell idea! Last Saturday I won back nearly a third of my salary."

If looks could kill, a lot of people would die with bridge cards in their hand.

Al: "What kind of bridge does your wife play?"

Bill: "From the cost, I'd say it must be toll bridge."

Celebration

Too much celebrating has kept many a man from becoming celebrated.

"I refused to marry Joe three months ago and he's been drunk ever since."

"That's what I call carrying a celebration too far."

After his wife had quadruplets, he went out and bought a fifth.

The father had obviously been celebrating the birth of his latest offspring. He wove into the local courthouse and called out, "Gentlemen, I want to report the birth of twins."

"Why do you say 'gentlemen,'" asked the clerk. "There's no one here but me."

"The heck you say," said the father. "I'd better go home and have another look."

Chaperone

A chaperone is an elderly woman who accompanies young women to see that they do not indulge in any of the things she would have indulged in if she hadn't been chaperoned when she was a young women.

Character

An Irishman was charged with a petty offense.

"Have you anybody here who can vouch for your character?" asked the judge.

"Yes, your Honor, the sheriff there can."

"Why, I do not even know this man," exclaimed the sheriff.

"Observe, your Honor," said the Irishman triumphantly, "that I've lived twelve years in this county and the sheriff doesn't even know me."

Charity

It takes a hunk of remembering to remember back when charity was a virtue instead of an industry.

Friend of ours recently made a sizable contribution to the Home For Unwed Mothers. But he says next time he intends to give money.

There is a lot more begging done on expensive letterheads than with tin cups.

The little box with a slot in the top, appearing on the storekeeper's counter, and bearing the sign "For the Blind," drew plenty of money from his customers who, with commendable sympathy for the unfortunate, contributed generously of their change.

After a month the box was missing.

"What happened to collection box for the blind?" asked a customer.

The storekeeper chuckled and pointed to the window. "Oh, I collected enough," he said. "There's the new blind."

It's better to give than to lend, and it costs about the same.

Chemists—Chemistry

The ardent motorist animal lover was most distressed because he had run over a hare and saw it lying in the road taking its last gasps.

He stopped his car and went back to put the animal out of its misery when another motorist stopped to offer help. A chemist, the latter fetched a bottle of tonic from his car and placed it under the nostrils of the hare. In a few seconds the hare revived and bolted through the hedge and across the field.

"That's wonderful stuff," said the animal lover. "What on earth is it?"
Came the modest answer: "Hair restorer."

Regardless of how smart chemists are, they can't seem to get the bugs out of fresh paint.

Children

The behavior of some children suggests that their parents embarked on the sea of matrimony without paddles.

Little Willie is at the awkward age—too young to leave home alone and too old to trust with baby-sitters.

HUSBAND, *pacing the floor with howling baby, to wife:* "Isn't it about time to take him back to the doctor for a thousand mile check-up?"

The tycoon's wife delighted on putting on airs. One evening during a party the pattering of tiny feet was heard on the stairs. She raised her hand for silence. "Hush," she gushed, "the children have come to deliver their goodnight message. It always gives me such a feeling of reverence to hear them. Listen!"
There was a few moments of silence. Then from the hallway came a small voice: "Mama, Willie found another bedbug."

Little Susan's mother had caught cold and resorted to that old-fashioned remedy, a glass of hot whiskey and water. A bit later Susan was going to bed. When her mother came to kiss her goodnight, the child looked at her strangely. "You've been using Daddy's perfume," she said solemnly.

NEIGHBOR: "Your baby looks very pretty in that dress. Where are you taking her?"
MOTHER: "To her grandmother's house for a general over mauling."

DOOR-TO-DOOR SALESMAN: "Do you have children, madam?"
HOUSEWIFE: "Two small boys."
SALESMAN: "Ah, then you will be interested in our new Space Soap, especially concocted to remove rocket grease, interplanetary smudge, comet grime and stellar dust."

The carpenter's children were hammering nails into the dining room table.

"Isn't that rather expensive?" asked an amazed visitor.

"Oh, it's not too bad," replied the carpenter, "You see, I get the nails wholesale."

The following is told about a woman who divorced her husband and obtained custody of their 12-year-old son. When she remarried after a year or so, her ex-husband, being somewhat concerned about the boy, asked him the first chance he got, "How do you get along with your step-father?"

"Fine," said the youngster. "He takes me swimming every morning. We go out to the lake, and he rows me out to the middle, and then I swim back in."

"Isn't that a pretty long swim for a boy your age?" asked the father.

"Not too bad. Really, the only tough part of it is getting out of the sack he puts me in."

One of those benign lady settlement workers stopped a hard-looking youngster and asked where his father was.

"Ain't got no father," said the kid.

"And your mother?"

"Ain't got no mother."

"Ah, too bad. When did she pass away?"

"I never had no mother."

"Then how were you born?" the lady settlement worker asked in dulcet tones.

"Some bum played a dirty trick on my aunt!"

Getting the baby to sleep is hardest when she's about eighteen years old.

Two small boys were swinging on a gate together, passing the time of day. In the course of their conversation one asked the other, "How old are you?"

"Five," came the reply. "How old are you?"

"I don't know," said the first.

"You don't know how old you are?"

"No."

"Do women bother you?"

"No."

"You're four."

Everything in the modern home is controlled by switches except the kids.

Childbirth

EXCITED FATHER: "Quick! Tell me! Is it a boy?"
NURSE: "Well, the one in the middle is."

The telephone rang in the hospital and when the nurse answered, an excited male voice on the other end blurted out: "This is Patrick O'Crosby. I'm on my way. That is, I'm bringing my wife in to have a baby!"

"Now, sir," soothed the nurse, "slow down and let me have a little information. Is she having any pains?"

"Yes. This is Patrick O'Crosby, and my wife is having . . ."

"Is this her first baby?" asked the nurse.

"No," came the reply. "This is her husband!"

DORA: "I see where a young wife presented her 85-year-old hubby with a baby boy. What do you think of that?"
JACK: "The same as you."

Aunt Mandy had just given birth to her sixteenth child. A rather prim young social worker was remonstrating with her over the size of her family in relation to her economic status. Aunt Mandy was having none of it.

"Yes, ma'am, ah understands," said Aunt Mandy, "but that birth control is all right for you single folks . . . I'se married."

The excited nurse rushed up to the young man pacing the hospital corridor, and exclaimed: "It's a boy! It's a boy!"

"Good," said the father, and started to leave.

"But you haven't asked how the mother is. Aren't you interested?"

"Not much," he replied. "I'm mad at her. We haven't been on speaking terms for a year."

"B—B—But . . . the baby?"

"Oh, we didn't get *that* mad!"

Christmas

"Lulu, put a bigger piece of cheese in the mousetrap—it's Christmas time."

A small boy was asked by his father, a well-known industrialist, what he would like to have for Christmas. "A baby brother," replied the boy.

"But it's only two weeks to Christmas," objected the father, "and that doesn't give me enough time."

"I know," said the boy. "But can't you put more men on the job?"

Let's Save a Bit of
Christmas Cheer
For the other 364
Days of the Year.

At Christmas time people don't worry about the past or the future—
all that matters is the present.

Here's a Tip (So You Won't Be Surly),
Do Your Christmas Hunting Early.

Church (see Preachers, Religion, Prayers)

The head of a civilian defense corps looked up the parish priest.
"We're planning on simulating a bombing, Father. How many people
could sleep in your church if they were bombed out of their homes?"

"I don't know how many could lie down and sleep, but every Sunday
about 900 persons sleep here sitting upright!"

Did you ever think that Church is a wonderful place to get a beauty
treatment? There, if anywhere, can you get your faith lifted.

Pray for the best but be prepared for the worst. Note that even
churches are equipped with lightening rods.

The Sunday school teacher was reviewing a lesson. "Who led the
children of Israel out of Egypt?"
No answer. So she pointed to a small lad at the back of the room.
"Wasn't me, ma'am," he answered. "We just moved here from Tulsa."

A wealthy farmer decided to go to church on Sunday. After services
he approached the preacher with much enthusiasm. "Reverend, that was
a damned good sermon you gave, damned good!"
REVEREND: "I'm glad that you liked it, but I wish you wouldn't use
those terms in expressing yourself."
FARMER: "I can't help it Reverend. I was so impressed that I put a
hundred dollar bill in the collection basket."
REVEREND: "The hell you did!"

A backslider whose riotous Saturday night escapades had brought him
fame of a kind began faithfully attending church on Sunday mornings.
The pastor was highly gratified and told him, "How wonderful it makes
me feel to see you at services with your good wife."
"Well, preacher," said the prodigal, "it's a matter of choice—I'd
rather hear your sermon than hers."

A minister of our acquaintance believes the only way our churches will ever have peak attendance is for a Constitutional amendment to be passed prohibiting attendance!

A salesman was taking an evening off to sell tickets for a church benefit. At one house the prospect said, "I'm sorry I have a very important engagement that evening, so I won't be able to attend. But I will be there with you in spirit."

"That's fine," said the quick-thinking salesman. "Would your spirit like to sit in the $3 or the $5 section?"

"The poor will always be with us," said the Preacher as he tallied the collection on Sunday.

MINISTER *(announcing a special attraction):* "Come early, if you want a back seat."

There was a time when church collection plates got most of the money the filling stations now get on Sundays.

The church is a hospital for sinners, not a club for saints.

One Clergyman who's very well tuned to the spirit of the times has tacked a poster to his church bulletin board which reads:
"Redemption Center; No Stamps Needed."

Josiane and her mother were in the village church when the little girl suddenly began to feel ill.
"Mama," she whispered, "I have to throw up."
"Hurry around to the little garden behind the church."
Josiane left but was back again in two minutes.
"Were you there and back already?" asked her mother.
"I didn't have to leave the church building. They have a little box on a stand next to the church door."
"What!!!?"
"Yes, they do! It has a sign 'For the sick.' "

A poor widow and her flock of children moved into North Carolina. The folks at the Methodist Church were moved to compassion by her plight and took up a collection to buy clothes so that she and her children could attend Sunday services.
When Sunday came, everyone was on hand at the Methodist Church to see the new family in its finery. But they didn't show up. Thinking the children might be ill, a delegation called on the widow that afternoon. They found her rocking on the front porch.

"How are the children?" she was asked.

"Oh, they're jes' fine," enthused the widow, "and I want to thank you for all those lovely clothes. When I got the young 'uns all dressed up this mornin', they was so pretty, I took them to the Episcopal Church!"

The couple was leaving church. "Did you see that new purple hat Mrs. Lambert was wearing?" the wife asked.

"I'm afraid not," the husband replied.

"What did you think of that orange velvet dress Mrs. Frawley had on?" the wife asked.

"I didn't notice it either," the husband said.

"Oh, for goodness sakes," snapped the wife, "a lot of good it does you to go to church!"

The retiring usher was instructing his youthful successor in the details of his office. "And remember, my boy, that we have nothing but good, kind Christians in this church—until you try to put someone else in their pew."

Sign on a bulletin board in front of the church in a small Wyoming town: "Subject for this Sunday: 'Do You Know What Hell Is?' Come and hear our new organist."

A tavern keeper owned a parrot whose perch was upon the piano. One night the tavern burned down and the parrot flew into a nearby church, and perched on the organ. Next morning when the organist arrived, the parrot replied, "Ha, new pianist." When the congregation came in the parrot replied, "But all of the same old faces."

Civilization

Civilization: A system under which a man pays a quarter to park his car so he won't be fined a dollar while spending a dime for a cup of coffee.

Clothing–Dress

On clothes she spends her legal tender;
Because this truth she's found—
A dress can make a girl look slender,
And a hundred men look around.

"Clarice is certainly wearing a daring gown, isn't she?"
"Yes, it's daring every man in the room."

"Honey, Ah loves yo' bathin' suit!"
"Sho' nuff?"
"It sho' does!"

The wives of two prominent business tycoons were talking things over in the hotel lobby.
"Does your husband confide his business troubles to you?" asked one.
"Oh, yes, indeed," replied the other. "Every time I come home with a new dress."

Nowadays when a girl says her new evening gown is really nothing, she means it.

Lady's Dress: Something that should be tight enough to show she is a woman and loose enough to show she's a lady.

HE: "That's a flimsy dress you're wearing."
SHE: "That's a flimsy excuse for staring."

A robust matron asked a fashion expert her opinion of the purple dress she was wearing.
"What colors should I wear?" she inquired.
"Madam," the expert said, "when God created butterflies, He made them with brilliant colors. But when He made the elephant, in His wisdom, He made it gray."

The salesgirl explained it this way: "If you remove the bodice, you will have a playsuit. If you remove the skirt, you will have a sunsuit. If you remove anything else, you'll have a lawsuit."

In a nightclub, a girl wearing an extremely low-cut gown was pointed out to an out-of-town visitor. "That girl is wearing a $1000 gown."
"That may be true," gasped the wide-eyed visitor, "but her heart isn't in it."

SHE: "How did you get such a lovely expensive fur coat on your salary?"
HER: "Oh, I got it for a song."
SHE: "Looks more like an overture to me."

A customer, astonished at the high price on a new hat, commented, "Why there's nothing to this hat. Why should it cost so much?"
The saleswoman replied, "Madam, nowadays you must pay for the restraint."

SALESLADY *in hat store to customer:* "Now here's a number that will never go out of style. It will just look ridiculous year after year!"

HUSBAND: "Darling, what has happened? Why do you have that plaster over your eye?"
WIFE: "Plaster? That's my new hat."

CONFUCIUS SAY: "She who wear strapless gown worry not about cost but upkeep."

CO-ED *(on shopping tour):* "Where can I get some silk covering for my settee?"
FLOOR WALKER: "Lingerie—next aisle and to the left."

"Where did you get that dress?"
"Do you like it?"
"Yeah."
"It's really nothing."
"That's why I like it."

Then there is the woman who bought a gown for a ridiculous price, while her husband thought she got it for an absurd figure.

If Mother Nature could have foreseen bermuda shorts, she surely would have done a better job on the male knee.

Getting ready for the club's annual hike, the rather hefty lady asked her husband what he thought would go well with her red slacks. His advice was an ankle-length coat.

The young lad watched, worried and anxious, while his father changed from a business suit into a tuxedo. Finally, the boy could hold it no longer.
"Dad," he pleaded, "please don't wear that suit. It always gives you a headache the next day."

Maybe you can't make a silk purse out of a sow's ear—but many a woman has gotten a mink coat out of an old goat!

You don't see a woman with hind-sight wearing slacks.

. . it hasn't been so long ago that women dressed on the beaches as they now do in supermarkets.

Two beauties were admiring a fur coat in a swank shop.

"It's gorgeous," said one, "but who would be fool enough to pay $12,000 for it?"

"I don't know," replied the other, "but I'll find him."

Clubs

One Thursday noon a member of the exclusive Bonehead Club of Atlanta walked in and was shocked to see women at the luncheon table for the first time.

"We've decided to let members bring their wives to one luncheon meeting a month," the Chief Bonehead informed him.

"But I'm not married," complained the member. "Could I bring a girl friend?"

The Chief thought for a minute and replied: "I suppose it might be all right, provided she's the wife of a member!"

An applicant for membership in an exclusive club passed all social, mental and financial requirements and was asked to bring in a specimen of his wine. A day or so later he showed up with a saucer-full. When asked if he had walked all the way from home with it, replied, "No, I came in on a bus."

A woman's club, says Lulu, is a place where they knock after they enter.

"Daddy isn't home," said Junior, answering the parson's knock on a Sunday afternoon. "He went over to the golf club."

Then, noting the expression on the parson's face, he added, helpfully, "Oh, he isn't playing golf, of course. He just went over for a few highballs and poker."

The difference between the old saloon and a modern night club is that in the old-time saloon a wistful little girl would pull on your sleeve and whisper, "Daddy, dear Daddy, come home with me now," and you paid no attention to her.

In a night club now a wistful little girl pulls at your sleeve and whispers, "Daddy, dear Daddy, come home with me now," and you do!

College (see Education, Student)

There was a knock on the door of the room of the dormitory.

"May I come in?" said a male voice. "It's the room I had when I went to college here. Yes, sir," he continued in reverie. "Same old room. Same old furniture. Same old view of the campus, same old closet."

He opened the closet door. There stood a girl terrified, half clothed.
"That's my sister," said the student.
"Yes, sir," the old grad replied. "Same old story."

"Dear folks! Please send me $400 at once. The school is bankrupt and each student has to make a contribution to keep it going. Please make the check out to me."

"A fine sort of welcome!" said his father. "I'm no sooner out of the train and you ask for money."
"Well, Dad," said the son, "you must admit the train was 20 minutes late."

Many a college boy who appears to be ill is merely suffering from co-ed in the head.

A father passing through his son's college town late one evening thought he would pay his son a surprise visit. Arriving at the son's fraternity house, he rapped on the door but was unable to rouse anybody. Then from a second floor window came a voice:
"Whadda ya want?"
"Does Charlie Jones live here?" asked the father.
"Yeah," replied the voice, "carry him in!"

"What is College Bred, Pop?"
"College bread is a four year loaf made from the flavor of youth and the old man's dough."

Fashion notes: The most popular shades this spring are those left up in the dorm window.

A young man just received his college degree and rushed out saying, "Here I am world; I have an AB."
And the world replied: "Sit down, son, and I'll teach you the rest of the alphabet."

Several years ago Harvard broke off football relations with Princeton. Soon afterward a Princeton alumni luncheon was held in a midwest city.
Each guest rose and gave his name, his class, occupation, whether married or single, and number of children.
One man rose and declared himself as follows:
"Smith, class of 1905, lumber broker, unmarried, two sons—both at Harvard."

A small college decided to go co-educational. Having only one dormitory, they assigned one wing to the boys and the other to the girls and painted a white line over which no one was to stray.

The first night a boy got over the line and was hauled before the dean. The dean informed the lad that his first offense would cost him a fine of $5, a second offense would be $10, a third $15, and so on.

"Do you understand?" asked the dean.

The boy replied that he did and the dean asked:

"Are there any questions?"

"Yes," replied the boy. "How much will a season ticket cost?"

A lobbyist opposing a large appropriation for a state college approached a legislator who boasted of his self-education.

"Do you realize," asked the portly lobbyist gravely, "that up at the state college men and women students have to use the same curriculum?"

The legislator looked startled.

"And the boys and girls often matriculate together?"

"No!"

The lobbyist came closer and whispered, "And a young lady student can be forced at any time to show a male professor her thesis?"

The legislator shrank back in horror. "I won't vote 'em a danged cent!"

Prof: "I will not begin today's lecture until the room settles down."

College Freshman: "Why don't you go home and sleep if off?"

Student: "I hear the Board of Trustees is trying to stop necking."

Co-ed: "That so? First thing you know they'll be trying to make the students stop, too."

We're not trying to discredit colleges—my, no! But when Luke's beefy brother, Lawrence, won his letter, somebody had to read it to him.

Visitor: "Can you tell me the name of this school?"

Young Man: "Sorry, I'm just a football player here."

Committee

Most jobs are done by committees of one.

Committee: A group of people who squander hours and keep minutes.

A giraffe is an animal designed by a committee.

Communications

A tourist spotted an Indian sending up smoke signals in the desert with a fire extinguisher strapped to his side.

"What's the idea of the fire extinguisher?" asked the tourist.

The rugged redskin explained, "If me misspellum word, me erasum."

Companionship

"Do you enjoy my company?"

"What company are you with?"

Conference

A conference is a gathering of important people who singly can do nothing, but collectively decide that nothing can be done.

. . . a conference is a meeting where people talk about things they should be doing.

As an experienced executive recently put it, "A conference is the confusion of one man, multiplied by the number present."

Confession

A man was sitting beside the deathbed of his partner. The partner knew he was doomed and said with a sigh of repentance: "I've a confession to make, partner. I robbed the firm of $500,000 and sold the blueprint of the secret formula for $250,000. I stole the letters from your desk that got your wife a divorce, and . . .

PARTNER: "Oh, don't worry, old chap. I poisoned you."

HE: "Girlie, I have a confession to make. I'm married man."

SHE: "Gawd! I thought you were going to say this car didn't belong to you!"

Confidence

Confidence: the feeling you have before you know better.

Congressman (see Politics, American)

The conscientious Congressman held his job uppermost in his heart and mind, even while at home. One night his wife nudged him from his slumber and whispered, "Sam, I think there are burglars in the house."

Sam raised up on one arm, squinted, and replied, "No, my dear. There may be a few in the Senate, but in the House? Never!"

The reason some Congressmen were so anxious to get re-elected is that they knew they couldn't make a living in private business under the laws they passed while in Congress.

Conscience

Conscience gets a lot of credit that belongs to cold feet.

SHE: "I've been misbehaving and my conscience is bothering me."
RECTOR: "Should I give you something to strengthen your will power?"
SHE: "No, give me something to weaken my conscience."

The little voice inside used to be conscience. Now it's a pocket radio.

Conscience: That something which prompts a man to tell his wife before someone else does.

Cooking

Jimmy Porter read aloud a recipe for roast ham. "Place the ham in a pot," it directed. "Soak it one day in bourbon and cook it for a while. The third day, add a bottle of port wine, and the fourth day some fine rye whiskey."
Jimmie asked his old Negro cook.
"I dunno about the ham," was the reply, "but it sure sounds like the makings of a mighty powerful gravy."

Cooperation

Cooperation would solve most problems. For instance, freckles would be a nice coat of tan if they'd get together.

Cosmetics

Cosmetics are a woman's means for keeping men from reading betweeen the lines.

"Jim, what are all those jars and bottles there on the dresser?"
"Those are my wife preservers!"

PERFUME SALESGIRL: "Just a word of advice. Don't use this stuff if you're only bluffing!"

Courts—Laws (see Politics, Congressmen, Diplomacy)

A Chinese thus describes a trial in the English law courts:
"One man is quite silent, another talks all the time and 12 men condemn the man who has not said a word."

JUDGE: "Couldn't this case have been setlled out of court?"
DEFENDANT: "Your Honor, that's exactly what we were doing when a couple of policemen butted in."

JUDGE: "I sentence you to twenty years each on six counts, or a total of 120 years. However, I don't want to be too harsh, since you're already middle-aged. You don't have to serve all 120 years—just do as much as you can."

CALLER: "I would like to see the Judge, please."
SECRETARY: "I'm sorry, sir, but he is at dinner."
CALLER: "But my errand is important."
SECRETARY: "It can't be helped, sir. His honor is at steak."

JUDGE: "Have you anything to offer the court before sentence is passed on you?"
PRISONER: "No, Judge, I had fifty dollars but my lawyer took it."

"Why do you want a new trial?"
"On the grounds of newly discovered evidence, your honor."
"What is the nature of it?"
"My client has dug up $400 I didn't know he had."

CLIENT: "You charge me 10 bucks just for looking up something in that law book? Why, I can buy the same book and save money."
LAWYER: "You paid me, not for owning the book, but for knowing what page to look on."

"Do you have a criminal lawyer in town?" a tourist asked an oldtimer.
"Well, we think so," the old man said, "but we can't prove it."

A man about to be electrocuted phoned his lawyer from the death chamber. "They're ready to put me in the electric chair. You're my lawyer —what do I do now?"
The lawyer thought a moment, then said, "Don't sit down."

At a 25th anniversary party the husband seemed very morose, so a friend tried to console him. The husband explained, "On our fifth anniversary I wanted to kill my wife but my lawyer told me I'd get 20 years. Just think! Today I could be a free man!"

Then there was the not-too-successful prize fighter who only won battles with his wife, whom he had punched around every day for almost 20 years. Finally, the poor woman couldn't take it any longer and swore out a warrant for his arrest. When the case came up in court she told the judge about the repeated batterings.

"Well, what do you have to say about this?" asked the judge.

"Don't pay any attention to her," answered the pugilist. "She's punch-drunk."

French lawyer pleading for an attractive transgressor:

"Gentlemen of the jury, shall this charming young lady be cast into a lonely cell, or shall she return to her beautiful little room at 33 rue Neuve, telephone 88-39-54?"

JUDGE: "You are sentenced to four years of hard labor and then deportation. Have you anything to say?"

ACCUSED: "Yes, I would like to do the deportation part of the sentence first."

"Honest, Jedge," said the defendant, "I hope de good Lawd will strike me daid if I stole dem chickens."

"Well," replied the judge, "you stand over there in the corner, and if you aren't struck dead in thirty minutes, I'm going to give you thirty days."

JUDGE *(after charging jury):* "Is there any question you would like to ask before considering the evidence?"

JUROR: "A couple of us would like to know if the defendant boiled the malt one or two hours and how did he keep the yeast out?"

The judge's expression seemed understanding as he leaned over the desk and addressed the little man before him.

"So you're a locksmith," said the judge. "And what was a locksmith doing in that gambling dive?"

The meek little man took courage and grinned, "Your honor, I was making a bolt for the door."

Nobody ever made a law that will prevent a man from making a fool of himself.

A wife has a perfect right to pour castor oil in her husband's whiskey, according to the Kentucky Court of Appeals, because "it is a wife's right to try to reform her husband."

We wonder if the ruling would hold good if the same husband tried to reform his whiskey-spoiling wife by giving her a strong, retaliatory clout on the head!

Thirty days hath September, April, June, and Uncle Jeff for speeding.

SHERIFF: "Say, young lady, there ain't no swimmin' allowed in this lake."

BEAUTIFUL: "Well, why didn't you tell me before I undressed?"

SHERIFF: "Well, there ain't no law agin that."

A lobbyist was browsing through an encyclopedia the other day when he came upon this stunning idea.

In ancient Greece, in order to prevent idiot statesmen from pressing stupid laws upon the people, at one point in Greek history lawmakers were asked to introduce all new laws while standing on a platform, a rope around their neck.

If the law passed, the rope was removed. If it failed, the platform was removed.

Courtship

Old Batch, the thrifty mountaineer, had long been dividing his attention between skinny Elvira and buxom Matilda, the village spinsters. One day a loafer asked: "When are you going to make your mind up between them two gals, Batch?"

"Cain't say," replied the thrifty bachelor. "Matilda's bigger and can do more work. On the other hand, it only takes three yards of calico to make Elviry a dress."

MECHANIC: "I sure had a big night last night. My girl let me kiss her for the first time. But first she made me take the top down, and boy I had that top down in 17 minutes."

TRUCK DRIVER: "What's so wonderful about that? I can put a convertible top down in three minutes."

MECHANIC: "Yeah, but we wasn't in a convertible."

HE *(making the time-worn excuse):* "I'm afraid we'll have to stop the car for a while. The engine is overheated."

SHE: "You guys are such liars. You always say the engine."

They had just had a lovers' spat, and as the youth was leaving his girlfriend's house he encountered her kid brother. "Your sister's a little spoiled, isn't she?" he commented.

"No," was the kid brother's reply. "That's just the perfume she's wearing."

Then there was the good little girl who had been saying "no" so long that she almost loused up her wedding cermony.

"If I broke off our engagement," said a wealthy man to his glamorous sweetie, "would you take it to heart?"

"No, darling," she replied sweetly, "to court."

Back in the Roaring Twenties, Lulu's Aunt Effie spent so much time in parked cars that they started showing her on road maps.

When some men aren't chasing jack, they're running after Jill.

"You will shortly meet a tall, dark man who will sweep you off your feet," the fortune teller told the eager blonde. "He will shower you with gifts and take you to breath-taking night spots, and you will drink a toast to everlasting love."

"Has he got a lot of money?" asked the girl excitedly.

"He is president of a large firm and heir to a $900,000 estate."

"Gosh," exclaimed the girl. "Now just tell me one more thing."

"What is that, dear?" asked the fortune teller, visualizing many pieces of silver crossing her palm.

"Just what happens to my husband and the three kids?"

A man who had been keeping company with a girl for a number of years took her out one night to a Chinese restaurant. They began studying the menu and he inquired, "How would you like your rice—fried or boiled?"

She looked up at him and said, "Thrown."

A girl can always tell when the right man comes along—he notices her.

Courtship is that period during which a girl decides whether or not she can do any better.

SHE: "The man I marry must be entertaining, be musical, tell jokes, sing and dance, stay home, drop no ashes, be no trouble and shut up when I want him to."

HE: "Lady, you don't want a husband. You want a television set."

Sometimes it's just as hard to find a husband after marriage as before.

"I've decided not to marry Harvey."

"How come?"

"I saw him in his swim suit and he looks so different without his wallet."

Which recalls to mind the single girl who came into her office and passed out cigars and candy—both with blue ribbons. Somewhat puzzled, her co-workers asked what the occasion was.

Proudly she displayed a solitaire on her left hand and announced:

"It's a boy—six feet tall and 185 pounds!"

Sam wanted to get married but didn't want to have his wedding on the Tuesday his fiancee had selected. Asked about it point blank by his future father-in-law, Sam explained:

"If we get married on a Tuesday we'd celebrate our silver wedding anniversary on a Friday night—and Friday is my bowling night."

Courtship is the short interlude between lipstick and mopstick.

GIRL: "I'm sorry I can't marry you, Bill, but circumstances over which I have no control prevent me."

BILL: "What circumstances?"

GIRL: "Yours."

"Now that I've told you about my past, do you still want to marry me?" she asked.

"I sure do," he replied.

"And I suppose you'll expect me to live it down?"

"Down, nothing. I'll except you to live up to it!"

A sailor, just home from a long cruise, rushed to a phone to call his girlfriend. In a few minutes he came out of the booth looking bewildered.

"She's gonna get married," he told his pal.

"Aw, forget her," advised the pal. "There's lotsa girls."

"Yeah," replied the sailor, "but she's gonna marry me!"

"I had a date with an absent-minded professor last night."

"How do you know he's absent-minded?"

"Cause he gave me a zero this morning."

One sweet thing to another: "I like men who make things. Like Mr. Porter. He made $50,000 last year.

Girls who try to be talking encyclopedias should remember that reference books are never taken out.

A man's downfall wasn't the apple but a peach. Someone made a mistake.

"I said some foolish things to my boy friend last night."
"Yes."
"That was one of them."

A boy and girl were riding horseback out in the country. As they stopped for a rest the two horses rubbed necks and noses affectionately.
"Well, well," said the guy. "That's what I'd like to do."
"Go ahead," said the girl. "It's your horse."

They were huddled together about a close as they could get.
"What are you thinking, my sweet?" he whispered into her mouse-like ear.
"The same thing you are, my darling," she coyly replied.
"Good!" he replied. "I'll race you to the refrigerator."

"Why doesn't your boy friend take you to the movies any more?"
"One evening it rained and we stayed home."

"My boy friend has cold feet," said the sweet young thing.
"Gracious," exclaimed her grandmother. "In my day we didn't learn that until after we were married."

"I don't like Bill," confided a co-ed to her roommate. "He knows too many naughty songs."
"Does he sing them to you?" asked her friend.
"Well, no," she replied. "But he whistles them."

GIRL'S FATHER: "Young man, we turn out the lights at 10:30 in this house."
BOY FRIEND: "Gee, that's darn nice of you."

"Darling, I've lost all my money. I haven't a cent in the world."
"That won't make any difference, dear. I'll love you just as much even if I never see you again."

CHARLIE: "What do you mean, the dates you had with Susy were like pearls?"
RAY: "Neckless, brother, neckless!"

"You know," confided Nell, "you'll be surprised how many men will be wretched when I marry."

"Heavens," replied her friend. "How many are you going to marry?"

Strolling through the field with his sweetheart, Paddy spied a bull rushing toward him. Quick as a flash he beat a hasty retreat.

"Why Paddy, you were afraid," she said when they reached safety. "And you said you would face death for me."

"I know I said that," said Paddy, "but the bull wasn't dead."

The girl was complaining about her boy friend. "Tom is just hateful sometimes," she told her friend. "Last night when we went out to that party he said I looked like a million dollars—after taxes."

SHE: "You're the kind of man a girl cannot trust."
HE: "Haven't we met before? Your faith is familiar."

"What's home without a mother?" asked the good-looking young man.
"Well," replied the sweet young thing, "tonight I am."

GIRL: "I don't want to be easily won. But if I say 'no' now you won't get angry and never ask me again, will you?"

CARL: "Betty, may I take you home? I like to take experienced girls home."
BETTY: "But, Carl, I'm not experienced."
CARL: "You're not home yet, either."

A wolf is like a good dry cleaner: He works fast and leaves no ring.

SON: "What is puppy love?"
FATHER: "Just a prelude to a dog's life."

SEAMAN: "May I take you home?"
GIRL: "Yes, where do you live?"

The subject of kissing was debated with much earnestness by a girl and the young man calling on her. He insisted that it was always possible for a man to kiss a girl against her will, even though she resisted. She was equally firm in her contention that it was not possible. They decided that the only thing to do was to test it.

So, they clinched and the battle was on. After a sprightly tussle, they broke. The girl had been kissed ardently for many minutes. Her comment showed her undaunted spirit:

"Oh, well, you really didn't win fairly. My foot slipped. Let's try it again."

HE: "Do you ever expect to find the perfect girl?"
JOE: "No, but it's sure a lot of fun finding they're not."

Credit

You can get almost anything for 5 bucks down and 12 uneasy payments.

Probably the bluntest dun ever written was as follows: "Dear Sir: You have been on our books for a year. We have carried you longer than your mother did."

INSTALLMENT COLLECTOR: "Do you know that you are seven payments behind on your piano?"
CUSTOMER: "But your company advertises that you pay as you play. And I play very poorly."

Charge Account: What you use to buy today what you can't afford tomorrow while you're still paying for yesterday.

ANGRY WOMAN *(to credit manager):* "But you people were the ones who said the payments would be easy!"

The salesman was urging a small storekeeper to carry his full product line in the store.
"I can't afford it," the retailer protested. "I owe everyone in town now."
The salesman insisted, "But you owe it to yourself to carry a line like ours which can bring you greater profits."
"I know it," agreed the prospect, "but I ain't pushing myself like my other creditors are."

SON: "Dad, the bill collector's here."
FATHER: "Fine, give him the pile on the table."

My wife is just like Teddy Roosevelt's Rough Riders. Everywhere she goes she yells "charge!"

Customer

IRATE SALESGIRL *(to disagreeable customer):* "Go easy, madam: the days when I used to insult customers are still fresh in my mind."

OWNER: "What's the dispute about? Remember, in this store the customer is always right. What did the man say?"

CLERK: "He said you were the toughest old bird in town."

The young fellow was new in the store which was having a drive to get customers to open a charge account. When a woman came in and began to look at merchandise as if she were going to buy something, he asked, "Have you an account here, ma'am?"

"No," the lady replied, "but I would like to talk to the credit manager."

He led her into the credit manager's office and announced, "A no-account lady to see you, sir."

Deaf—Deafness

"What's that man washing his hands so thoroughly for?"

"He's a deaf and dumb guy and he's just finished telling a dirty story!"

A gentle old lady on a suburban bus watched for some time, with the kindliest interest, a young soldier sitting next to her. The fellow was chewing gum vigorously. Finally, she leaned across and patted him on the knee and said,

"I'm awfully sorry, but it simply isn't any use trying to talk to me, young man. I'm completely deaf!"

An old lady traveling on the train in Michigan with her nephew, suddenly told him: "Why, there's Bill Smith across the aisle. I helped raise him back in El Dorado. He is very hard of hearing, but I will see if I can make him understand."

She went over and hollered loud: "Aren't you Bill Smith from El Dorado, where I knew you?"

SMITH *(finally):* "Yes."

Then in an ordinary tone of voice she said: "I've pinned many a diaper on you."

HE *(not hearing the last):* "You wouldn't know the place. It's all growed up."

The old gentleman was getting quite deaf. One day while driving his car he crossed a bridge over a railroad track. A huge locomotive sped beneath and let out a shrill whistle.

"Hm!" muttered the old man happily, "first robin I've heard all spring."

Debt

Running into debt isn't so bad. It's running into creditors that hurts.

SHE: "It isn't my fault I get so deep in debt."
HE: "No, it's all owing to other people."

A car dealer in Graham, Texas, who was having trouble collecting installments, wrote a customer: "What would your neighbors think if I repossessed the car?"
Two weeks later he received this reply: "All the neighbors think it would be a lousy trick."

A salesman, visiting a country fair, was amazed at the sight of one of his customers riding the merry-go-round. The customer, whose penny-pinching tendencies were known far and wide, looked as if he was having anything but a good time. What's more, as the merry-go-round stopped, the little miserable-looking man made no attempt to get off.
After several "trips," the salesman's curiosity finally got the best of him. The next time the carousel stopped, he walked over to his customer and greeted him. "Tell me," he asked, "do you enjoy riding this thing?"
The little man grimaced. "I hate it," he replied, "but the man who owns this contraption owes me $3.25, and this is the only way I can get my money out of him."

Bill collectors always call at the most inopportune time—when you're at home.

Dentist

A fellow who came into a dentist's office to have a tooth pulled was so frightened at the prospect that the dentist sympathetically offered him a shot of whiskey. Then the fellow asked for another shot and gulped it down. The dentist then asked kindly:
"There, young fellow. Do you feel any braver? Got your courage back?"
"Yeah," snarled the man, "and brother, I'd like to see anybody touch my teeth."

"I'm sorry," said the dentist to the patient, "but I can't give you an appointment this afternoon. I have eighteen cavities to fill."
Whereupon he picked up his golf bag and left for the course.

Depression

Depression is that period when people do without what their parents never had.

Diplomacy

Diplomacy: The art of being able to say "Nice doggie" until you have time to pick up a rock.

Diplomat

A diplomat is one who can bring home the bacon without spilling the beans.

Disappointment

The most disappointed woman is one who buys fancy underwear for a doctor's examination and then finds he only looks at her tongue.

Discipline

Boy *(about to be spanked):* "Dad, did grandpa spank you when you were little?"
FATHER: "Yes, son."
"And did grandpa's father spank him?"
"Yes, son."
"And did great-grandpa's father spank him, too?"
"Yes, son."
"Well, don't you think it's about time to stop this inherited brutality?"

Discretion

JOEY: "Pa, what is 'discretion'?"
PA: "It's something, son, a feller learns after it's too late to do him any good."

The age of discretion comes when you are too young to die and too old to have any fun.

Distrust

The brothers, Uncle Grover and Uncle Jeff, don't and won't trust each other.
For instance: The other day Grover lost a dollar bill. He remarked later that if Jeff hadn't helped him look for it, he might have found it.

Divorce (see Marriage, Wives, Husbands, Courtship)

Just heard of another marriage ending in divorce. He lost his capital and she lost her interest.

A Las Vegas, Nev., lawyer was sitting in his office one day when a woman entered unannounced and without preliminaries declared she wanted a divorce.

"On what grounds?" asked the attorney.

She replied that she did not think her husband was faithful.

"And what makes you think he isn't faithful?"

"Well," the lady replied. "I don't think he's the father of his son."

There's the girl who has been married and divorced so many times that her wedding gown has become her native costume.

"I'm going to get a divorce. My wife hasn't spoken to me in six months."

"Better think it over, John," his friend advised. "Wives like that are hard to find."

Some guys learn the high cost of leaving when they desert the bride.

"Now that you have your divorce, how do you feel?" asked a friend of a woman who had just come back from Reno.

"I feel like a new man," came the reply.

Divorce is likely to result when a husband decides he's too good to be true.

The judge looked at the man seeking a divorce. "You claim false pretense?" he asked. "Misrepresentation is a rather curious reason to want a divorce. What's your reason?"

"Well, your Honor," said the man readily. "When I asked this woman to marry me she said she was quite agreeable. Well, she wasn't."

Today when word gets around that a wife is planning to leave her husband and seek a divorce and return home to her mother, the person who is really scared is mother.

"Give a reason why so many wives are opposed to divorce."

"They don't like the idea of sharing their husband's money with a lawyer."

GERRY: "I took the first step toward divorce yesterday."
BERRY: "What happened?"
GERRY: "I got married!"

The word "alimony" comes from a Latin word meaning "sustenance" and a word meaning "to nourish" so when a woman in a divorce case is given alimony she really gets a "meal ticket."

The old Indian was suing for divorce on the grounds that his wife was untrue to him. The judge told him if he could prove his charges he would grant the divorce; otherwise, he would not.

"Me prove him all right," said the chief. "When me plant corn, me get corn. When me plant wheat, me get wheat. When me plant potatoes, me get potatoes—this time me get China Boy!"

Doctors—Medicine (see Dentists)

"Have you been to any other doctor before you came to see me?" asked the grouchy doctor.

"No, sir," replied the meek patient. "I went to a druggist."

"That shows how much sense some people have!" growled the doctor. "And what sort of idiotic advice did he give you?"

"He told me to come to see you."

John is so successful that he's made enough money to occasionally tell a patient there is nothing wrong with him.

DOCTOR: "I don't like to mention it, but the check you gave me has come back."

PATIENT: "Well, that sure is funny, Doc. So did my lumbago."

"Have you ever had appendicitis?" asked the doctor.

"Well, I'm not sure," replied the patient. "I was operated on—but I've never been quite certain whether it was appendicitis or professional curiosity."

Then there's the tale of a young doctor who hung up his shingle in a small town and waited for his first patient. Some days later one arrived—covered from head to foot with an angry, dangerous-looking rash. The puzzled young medic hastily consulted his books but could find no help there.

Finally he said to the patient, "Did you ever have this affliction before?"

"Oh, sure, Doc," replied the patient. "I've had it twice before."

"Well," diagnosed the doctor, "you have it again."

The executive was just buttoning up his coat after a physical examination.

"Doctor," he said, "if there's anything wrong with me, don't try to hoodwink me by giving it a long scientific name. Just tell me in plain English, what's the matter with me."

"Well," the doctor replied hesitantly, "to be perfectly frank, you are just plain lazy and need more exercise."

"Thank you, doctor," murmured the patient. "Now please give me the scientific name so I can tell the people at the office."

"Paw," said the farmer's boy. "I want to go to college and learn to be a doctor. Think I'll study obstetrics."

"Likely you'll be wasting your time, son. Soon as you learn all about this obstetrics, somebody'll find a cure for it."

DOCTOR: "I'll examine you for $5."
PATIENT: "Okay, if you find it, I'll split with you."

You meet the craziest people on the subway. One day a fellow sitting next to me kept saying, "Call me a doctor. Call me a doctor."

"What's the matter?" I asked. "Are you sick?"

"No," he answered. "I just graduated from medical school."

PATIENT: "Doc, my head feels like a pipe and my chest feels like lead."
DOCTOR: "You don't need a doctor, you need a plumber."

BUSINESSMAN (to his physician): "I can't my bill, Doc. I slowed down just like you told me to . . . and I lost my job."

A consulting physician is a doctor they call in at the last minute to share the blame.

PATIENT: "This is my first operation and I'm terribly nervous."
YOUNG SURGEON: "I know just how you feel. It's my first, too."

A woman used to go to a doctor to see if she could have children—now she goes to her landlord."

ORTHOPEDIC SPECIALIST: "The girls at these Florida beaches have beautiful legs, don't they?"
LUNG SPECIALIST: "I hadn't noticed. I'm a chest man, myself."

What's the sense of paying the doctor to tell you you need a vacation you can't afford?

The nice old lady had a problem for her doctor. She had difficulty in going to sleep.

"And when I finally drop off, I have such a strange dream," she reported. "Always the same dream about a handsome young man chasing me."

The doctor, properly sympathetic, grave her a pill, saying: "It is a harmless little pill to make you slip into a prompt dreamless sleep."

The little old lady thanked him and departed with her medicine.

However, in less than a week she was back in his office with a small complaint.

"Doctor, those pills you gave me are fine. But doctor, could you give me something now to make me dream only just a little? You see, I miss that young man!"

YOUNG M.D.: "I'm afraid I made a mistake in filling a death certificate."

OLD M.D.: "How was that?"

YOUNG M.D.: "I absentmindedly signed my name in the space left for the cause of death."

Ethel was shapely but shy, and visited a doctor for the first time. He ushered her into his private office and said:

"And now my dear, please get completely undressed."

Ethel blushed and replied: "Okay, doctor, but you first!"

"Why, doctor, " the elderly woman screamed, "you probably don't remember me, but 10 years ago when I came to your office you told me to go home to bed and stay there until you called back. But you never called again!"

"Didn't I?" the doctor said. "Then what are you doing out of bed?"

A doctor had just finished checking over a not-so-young patient. "Well, old man" he said with a laugh. "I can't seem to find a thing wrong with you, but I do recommend you give up half your love life."

After a pause and deep thought the patient replied, "Doctor, which half do you recommend I give up, thinking about it or talking about it?"

There ain't much fun in medicine, but there's a good deal of medicine in fun.

"What's my trouble, doc?" asked the patient.

"I'm not sure what's wrong with you," replied the Doctor. "But, if you were a building, you'd be condemned."

"Just dropped in to tell you how much I've benefited from your treatments," said the young man.

"But, you're no patient of mine," said the physician.

"No, but my uncle was and I'm his heir."

"Tell me doctor, what is my husband's trouble?"

"He has a severe case of voluntary inertia."

"My goodness. And I had been thinking all along he was just plain lazy."

"I can't find too much wrong with you. I think it's due to drinking."

"Okay, Doc. I'll come back when you're sober."

A young surgeon received a telephone call from a colleague who invited him to make a fourth at bridge.

"Going out, dear?" asked the wife suspiciously.

"I'm afraid so," was the brave reply. "It's a very important case. There are three doctors there already."

SERVICE STATION ATTENDANT: "Your doctor is outside with a flat tire. What shall I do?"

STATION OWNER: "Diagnose it as a deflation of the perimeter and charge him accordingly."

A man recovering from an anaesthetic became very romantic. His wife turned to the Doctor and said: "I haven't heard him talk like that since our honeymoon. Where do you buy the stuff?"

The doctor stood by the bedside and looked gravely down at the sick man. "I cannot hide from you the fact that you are very ill," he said. "Is there anyone you'd like to see before you go?"

"Yes," said the sufferer, faintly.

"Who is it?"

"Another doctor."

"Frankly," the doctor said, "I must warn you that this is a most serious operation. Four out of five patients do not survive. But I'll do my best. Is there anything I can do for you before I begin?"

"Yes," the patient replied hurriedly, "Help me on with my pants."

"That doctor of mine has a lot of nerve."

"How is that?"

"Listen to this item on the bill: 'For waking up in the middle of the night and thinking of your case—$5.00.'"

The young doctor was taking his wife out one evening when a pretty girl smiled and spoke to him. The wife, scenting an earlier love affair, inquired: "Who is the lady, dear?"

"Oh, a girl I've met professionally."

"No doubt," replied the wife, "but whose profession—yours or hers?"

A tired medical man got his wife to answer the phone by the bed, say he was out, and give advice which he whispered to her.

"Thank you very much, Mrs. Simpson," said the voice, "but I should like to ask you one thing. Is that gentleman who seems to be in bed with you fully qualified?"

The country village doctor's two children were considered the prettiest little girls in the district.

While out walking one day, two small boys passed the little girls. "Hey, who are those girls?" asked one, a visitor for the day.

"They are the doctor's children," replied the village boy. "He always keeps the best for himself."

I had been sitting in the doctor's waiting room for a long time. Every chair was filled and some patients were standing. There was desultory conversation, but after a while a silence fell and we sat waiting—waiting—waiting. Finally an old man stood up wearily and remarked, "Well, guess I'll go home and die a natural death."

DOCTOR: "What are you taking for your cold?"
PATIENT: "I don't know, make me an offer."

The doctor came out of the bedroom and spoke to the anxious wife. "Frankly," he said, "I don't like the way your husband looks at all."

"Well," replied the wife, "neither do I, but he's nice to the kids."

The patient had complained for months about stomach pains. Finally the doctor decided to operate.

Inside the poor fellow was found a beautiful bouquet of American roses.

"Now how in hell did those get in there?" exclaimed the doc.

"I don't know," said the patient. "Let's look at the card and see who they're from."

One of the main reasons an obstetrician is so busy and successful is because he has so many men working for him.

If he still has his appendix and his tonsils, 10 to 1 he's a doctor.

DOCTOR: "How is the boy who swallowed the half dollar?"
NURSE: "No change yet, Doctor."

And then there was the doctor who said: "The best thing for you to do is to give up drinking and smoking, get up early every morning, and go to bed early every night."

And the patient replied: "Doctor, I don't deserve the best. What's second best?"

The conceited young man, in the hospital for some time, had been well looked after by the pretty nurse.

"Nurse," said he, "I'm in love with you. I don't want to get well."

"Don't worry," replied the nurse, cheerfully, "you won't. The doctor is in love with me, too, and he saw you kissing me this morning."

DOCTOR: "Is your cold any better?"
LUKE: "Naw."
Doc: "Did you drink the orange juice after the hot bath?"
LUKE: "Naw. After drinking the hot bath, I couldn't get the orange juice down."

An Indian had gone to see the doctor, who, after examining him, told him to be careful about what he ate—in fact, not to eat at all until he got an appetite. Meeting the Indian a few days later, the doctor asked how he felt.

"Oh, I feel fine now," he replied. "I wait one day, appetite no come, wait two days, appetite no come, wait three days, appetite no come, get so hungry I eat anyway."

A new resident in the backwoods community was on his way to the hospital to visit his wife who had been stricken with tularemia, called "rabbit disease" by the natives of the area.

An acquaintance stopped him to inquire the nature of his wife's illness.

"She is suffering from 'rabbit disease,'" the husband explained.

"Ah!" beamed the other. "Congratulations! Boy or girl?"

"Your wife used to be so nervous. Now she's as calm and cool as a cucumber. What cured her?"

"The doctor. He just told her that her kind of nervousness was the natural result of advancing age."

"My good woman," said the doctor after a thorough examination of the feminine patient, "there's only one thing wrong with you: you are going to have a baby."

"But, doctor, that's not possible. I'm not even married. I don't know anything about having babies. I've led a very sheltered life."

"Nevertheless, it's going to happen," said the doctor.

"Oh, my," said the patient, with a sudden light in her eyes. "That dirty fireman! He told me that was artificial respiration!"

At the time the Medicare bill was being discussed in Congress, a survey was taken by a newspaper to see what the public's reaction was to it.

A sweet old lady of 71 was asked, "What do you think of Medicare?"

She replied: "I don't know, myself, but I have a friend that tried it and lost 21 pounds."

Dogs (see Animals, Horses)

On answering the doorbell, a man found an old friend and a large dog standing on his porch.

"Come in! Come in!" he said.

His friend came in and sat down while the dog put the man's cat to flight, knocked over a bridge lamp and several vases, and finally made himself comfortable in his best chair.

When the guest rose to leave, the host said with a touch of sarcasm in his voice, "Aren't you forgetting your dog?"

"Dog? I have no dog. I thought he was yours."

Two old coon hunters were swapping tall stories about their dogs.

"Why," said one of them. "I had a yaller hound once and every time just before I went hunting, I'd whittle out a board in the shape of a coon hide stretcher, just to show him the size of the one I wanted. Then I'd sit outside where he could see it. Well, sir, one day my wife set the ironing board outside and that critter ain't back yet!"

A women went to buy a drinking trough for her dog and the shopkeeper asked her if she would like one with the inscription, "For the Dog."

"It really doesn't matter," she replied. "My husband never drinks water and the dog can't read."

The reason the dog is man's best friend is probably because he gives no advice, never tries to borrow money, and has no in-laws.

A man dropped in to pay a friend an unexpected visit and was amazed to find him playing chess with his dog. The man watched in silence for a few minutes, then burst out with:

"That's the smartest dog I ever saw in my life!"

"Oh, he isn't so smart," was the answer he received. "I've beaten him three games out of four."

This fellow loved bulldogs. The uglier and meaner the better. The last one he owned was a blue ribbon winner, and meaner and stronger than a middle-sized gorilla.

When he took this dog for a walk he was literally pulled along the street.

One day this mean, ugly bulldog was dragging his "master" down the street when they met a little colored boy who was being followed by a yellow cur-looking "mongrel."

The bulldog leaped to the attack.

Was he ever surprised—his owner, too! With one snap of his jaws, this "yellow cur" crushed the bulldog's head, leaving him bloody and very dead.

With an oath, the man shouted, "Your mongrel has just killed the meanest and most valuable bulldog in the world. What kind of a dog is he, anyway?"

"I don't rightly know, Mister," said the little colored fellow, "but befo' I cut off his tail and painted him yeller, he wuz a alligator."

A dog wins friends and influences people without reading books.

On a trip in town, seven-year-old Janie took her new collie into a grocery store.

"My, that's a fine dog you have there, Janie," the grocer remarked. "If she has puppies, will you save one, please?"

"I'd love to," replied Janie, "but Lady won't have any puppies. She's already had her tonsils out."

A man had his new dog out for a walk when he came to a river. He threw a stick in for the animal to fetch. To his astonishment, instead of plunging in the water, the dog walked out on the surface of the river and retrieved the stick. Not believing his eyes, the man threw the stick again. Again the dog walked across the water and fetched it.

"Where did you get that dog?" asked a passerby.

"I bought him for one hundred dollars," said the owner.

"Well, you'd better get your money back," said the stranger. "You've been taken. That dog can't even swim."

LITTLE GIRL: "I'd like to buy a puppy. How much do they cost?"
"Ten dollars apiece."
LITTLE GIRL: "But I want a whole puppy, not a piece of one."

He calls his dog his loyal "American Legion" pooch because he stops at every post.

Sign in a pet shop window: "Boxer puppy for sale. Housebroken, faithful, will eat anything. Especially fond of children."

He was hopelessly lost and hip deep in snow. Just as he was about to give up hope, he saw coming toward him a big St. Bernard with a flask tied around its neck.

"At last!" he gasped. "Here comes man's best friend and a dog!"

"Madam, for a dog that's so careless and unhousebroken as yours, I suggest a lethal chamber."

"Oooh, but do you think he'd use it?"

"They had to shoot poor Fido today."

"Was he mad?"

"He wasn't any too pleased."

Since eating so much chlorophyll food, all dogs do now is shake hands.

"My dog is a neurotic."

"Why don't you take him to a psychiatrist?"

"He's not allowed to get up on a couch."

Fellow walks into a saloon and asks for a Scotch. Suddenly he looks up and realizes that, there tending bar, apron, bar-rag and all, is a horse. He does a double-take.

"Whatsa matter?" says the animal. "Haven't you ever seen a horse tending bar before?"

"It's not that," says the guy, "it's just—what happened to the dog? Did he sell the place?"

A young woman returned to the village after a run-away match and dropped in at the local newspaper office.

"I suppose my elopement was the talk of the town, eh?" she said to the editor.

"Well, not exactly," he replied, scratching his head, "you see, old man Higgins' dog went mad that same day."

Drinks—Drinking (see Drunks)

Card Table Cocktail: One drink and your legs fold up.

Housemother: "I know the girls don't drink when they go out, because they're so thirsty in the morning."

Not all gentlemen prefer blondes; some we know prefer blends.

CUSTOMER *(to bartender):* "Give me a straight shot before the fight starts." Downing the drink he said, "Quick, give me another before the fight starts."

Giving him the second drink the bartender asked, "Where's this fight you're talking about and when will it start?"

CUSTOMER: "Right here, and the rest depends on you. I don't have any money to pay for these drinks."

A thirsty man entered a bar and said to the bartender: "Make me a very dry Martini, please—twenty parts gin to one part Vermouth."

The bartender obliged and as he was about to serve the cocktail to the customer, he said, "Do you wish me to squeeze a little lemon peel in it, sir?"

"Say," he barked, "if I wanted a lemonade, I'd have asked for it."

Overheard at the convention: "Do you drink?"
"Nope."
"Swell. Here, hold the bottle while I tie my shoe."

Some people have a veneer that comes off with a little alcohol.

JOE: "Did you get home from the party last night? You were pretty high."

HARRY: "I got home all right except that as I was turning into my street, some idiot stepped on my fingers."

CONDUCTOR: "Did you get home all right last night?"
REGULAR PATRON: "Why of course! Why do you ask?"
CONDUCTOR: "Well, when you got up to give that lady your seat, there were only two of you in the car."

A somewhat inebriated gentleman was walking down State Street and did not know his location. He turned to a passerby and said: "Mister, where am I?"

The passerby answered: "You are at the corner of State and Madison Streets."

The inebriated gentleman said: "Never mind the details. What city?"

"Jones, I understand you really made a spectacle of yourself last night at the convention. They tell me you were pushing a wheelbarrow down the street, singing at the top of your voice. Now, what do you have to say for yourself?"

"Well, boss," answered Jones, "I guess I did. Maybe I had a little too much to drink."

"That's no excuse," said the boss. "Look at the loss of prestige you may have brought on the whole organization. What about that?"

"Yes. But I thought it didn't make much difference, since you ordered me to give you that ride in the wheelbarrow."

Two finishes for automobiles: lacquer and liquor.

A man returned to his office one Monday morning showing the signs of a very strenuous week-end. One of his good friends sauntered over after seeing his friend sitting at his desk with his head buried in his arms.

"How did you spend the week-end?" asked the friend.

"Fishing through the ice," was the reply.

"Fishing through ice? For what?"

"Olives," was the answer.

"My husband," a woman told her friend, "had an accident on his vacation. He drank a whole glass of gasoline, thinking it was gin."

"Didn't it make him deathly sick?" the friend inquired.

"No," came the reply. "But now instead of hiccupping, he honks."

"I resent your remark, sir," hiccupped a steady drinker at a local bar, "and I'll give you just five seconds to take it back."

"And if I don't take it back in five seconds?"

The drunk eyed him warily. "Well," he said, "how much time do you want?"

SHE *(coyly):* "You bad boy, don't kiss me again!"

HE: "I won't. I'm just trying to find out who has the gin at this party."

Husband to wife at cocktail party: "Honey, you better not drink any more. You're getting a little fuzzy around the edges."

> We eavesdropped for years
> But never yet
> Have we heard the order
> Martini—Wet!

Nowadays an old-fashioned girl is one who prefers them to martinis.

"Well, you can't say I made any noise coming in last night."

"No, but the men carrying you did."

Drink Metrinis. Composed of four parts Metrecal to four parts gin. Your pink elephants are thinner.

A guy who goes for the cup that cheers somewhat too much was finally cornered by his wife in a bar where he was dreamily contemplating a slug of rye. Being in a genial mood, he offered her a sip, but when she took it she gagged and spluttered, finally coming out with: "How can you ever drink that horrible stuff?"

"See?" said the husband. "And all the while you thought I was having a good time!"

Pat was determined to pass his favorite tavern on his way home. As he approached it he became somewhat shaky, but after plucking up courage, he passed it. Then, after going about 50 yards, he turned, saying to himself: "Well done, Pat my boy. Come back and I'll treat ye."

A hillbilly came to town carrying a jug of liquor in one hand, a shotgun in the other. He stopped a man on the street saying: "Here, friend, take a drink outa my jug."

The man protested he didn't drink and the hillbilly leveled his gun at him saying, "Drink."

The stranger drank, then shuddered, shook, shivered and coughed. "Gad, that's awful stuff," he gasped.

"Ain't it?" said the hillbilly. "Now hold the gun on me while I take a swig."

Slowly, her eyes glowing softly, the beautiful debutante raised the glass on high, exulting, "Port wine to me is the nectar of the gods, the very exilir of life." Said she, "When I imbibe its amber fragrance, my very soul begins to throb. The music of a thousand muted violins whispers softly in my ear and I'm transported to a make-believe world of magic. On the other hand, beer makes me burp."

"Don't mix alcohol and gasoline!"
"I won't—I don't like gasoline!"

> The Frenchman loves his native wine,
> The German likes his beer.
> The Englishman his 'alf and 'alf
> Because it brings good cheer.
> The Irish likes his whiskey straight
> Because it gives him dizziness.
> The American has no choice at all—
> So he drinks the whole damn business!

One friend said to another, "Say, how did you get that scar across the bridge of your nose?"

"From glasses."

"Well, why don't you get contact lenses?"

"They don't hold enough beer."

TEACHER: "Now spell 'straight.' "

PUPIL: "S-t-r-a-i-g-h-t."

TEACHER: "Correct. Now, what does it mean?"

PUPIL: "Without water."

The tiny little wife dragged her drinking husband into court and demanded a divorce instantly. Trying to pacify her, the judge asked if her husband ever tried Alcoholics Anonymous.

The frail woman dabbed at her eyes and said, "I guess so, your honor. He'll drink anything."

There's a new drink called "The Delegate." Two of 'em and you're speaking from the floor.

During the physical exam, the doctor noticed the patient's hands shaking demonstrably. "You drink a lot, don't you?" he asked.

"Nope," replied the man. "Spill most of it."

Alcohol: An excellent liquid for preserving almost anything but secrets.

Intoxication: Feeling sophisticated without being able to pronounce it.

The man entered the barroom and, sitting at the bar, slowly began weaving his head back and forth and mumbled "tick . . . tock . . . tick . . . tock . . . tick . . ."

Although the bartender had seen much in his day he was curious and finally asked, "Okay, what are you?"

"Can't you tell?" answered the drunk. "I'm a clock.

"If you're a clock," asked the barkeep, "what time is it?"

"It's six-thirty."

"That's where you're wrong," answered the bartender, looking at his watch. "It's seven o'clock."

"Gee whiz," was the reply. "I must be slow. Ticktockticktockticktockticktockticktock . . ."

Mint Julep: A depth bomb with a southern drawl.

"I never felt so punk in all my life."

"Do any drinking last night?"

"Yes, and when I went to bed I felt fine. When I woke up I felt terrible. It must have been the sleep that did it."

"Every morning I wake up feeling terrible," the store owner confided to his know-it-all friend.

"I'll bet you drink milk before going to bed," said the friend.

"That's right, I do. What has that got to do with it?"

"That's your whole trouble," replied Mr. Know-it-all. "You drink the milk, go to bed and toss and turn from side to side. The milk turns to cheese, cheese turns to butter, butter turns to fat, fat turns to sugar, sugar turns to alcohol, and the first thing you know, you wake up with a terrible hangover."

Two distillers of moonshine were discussing their operations.

"When Ah take my stuff into town," one of them explained, "Ah always drives mightly slow—about 20 miles per hour."

"Skeered o' the law?" the other jeered.

"Nope," retorted the first. "Gotta age the stuff, hain't ya?"

Sign in bar: "If you're drinking to forget, pay in advance."

WALTER: "Do you serve women at this bar?"

BARTENDER: "Nope, gotta bring your own."

Driving—Drivers (see Accidents)

A woman motorist jumped out of her car after a collision with another auto and shouted at the driver, "Why don't you people ever watch where you're driving? You're the fourth car I've hit this morning."

Nothing improves your driving like having a police car following you.

Lulu says she likes to drive but doesn't like that noisy crash when she backs into a parking space.

Mrs. Anklam doesn't park the family car—she abandons it.

TRAFFIC COP: "Use your noodle, Lady! Use your noodle!"

LADY: "My goodness! Where is it? I've pushed and pulled everything in the car!"

Did you know more auto accidents are caused by pickled drivers than by traffic jams?

Lost on a back road in Alabama, a motorist asked the way to Montgomery. An old farmer, sitting on a fence, looked down the road scratched his head, and gave directions.

Half an hour later the motorist found himself back at the starting point. The farmer was still sitting, in placid contemplation of the landscape.

"Hey, what's the idea?" the motorist shouted. "I did just what you told me and look where I wound up!"

"Wal, young feller," the farmer explained, "I didn't aim t' waste my time tellin' you how to get t' Montgomery till I found out if you could follow simple directions."

Mother had taken over the driving of the family car. Suddenly young Bill announced: "Isn't it queer that when Mom is driving we never see any blathering idiots, but when Dad is driving we see a lot of them!"

YOUNG SON: "Dad, Mom just backed the car out of the garage and ran over my bicycle."
DAD: "Serves you right for leaving it on the front lawn."

A woman driving 70 miles an hour noticed a motorcycle cop tailing her and thought she could shake him by speeding up to 80. When she looked again she saw two cops behind her. Suddenly she spotted a gas station and pulled up to a screeching stop in front of it, leaped out and dashed into the room marked "Ladies."

When she came out the cops were still there. Without batting an eye the lady said coyly, "I'll bet you thought I wouldn't make it."

An Englishman, driving through our country for the first time, read a highway sign which said: "Drive Slowly—This Means You!"

"By Jove!" he exclaimed. "How did they know I was here?"

Huge truck with two signs on the rear tells motorists: Left, passing side—Right, suicide.

It was on Highway 89. A man in a low slung car was cruising along at about 90 miles an hour. A motorcycle policeman stopped him and growled: "Say Buddy, didn't you see the speed limit back there?"

"Why, yes, officer," replied the speeder. "I thought it said 89 miles an hour."

"Brother," the cop sighed. "I'm sure glad I caught you before you turned onto Highway 101."

One cold night a man with reputedly poor eyesight was driving a friend home. The frost was thick on the windows, so bad that it was impossible to see through them.

After a couple of near accidents, the friend tactfully suggested that it might help if they stopped and cleaned the windshield.

"What's the use?" the driver replied. "I left my glasses at home."

"How are you getting along with your driving?" inquired an interested friend of a new driver.

"Oh, fine," she said. "Yesterday I went 50 miles an hour and tomorrow I'm going to try opening my eyes when I pass another car."

Fellows who drive with one hand are usually headed for a church aisle. Some will walk down it—some will be carried.

A woman motorist was driving along the country road when she noticed a couple of repairmen climbing telephone poles.

"Fools," she exclaimed to her companion. "They must think I never drove before."

DRIVER DOING EIGHTY: "It's great to be speeding along like this. Don't you feel glad you're alive?"

NERVOUS PASSENGER: "Amazed is the word I would have used."

A motorist is a person who, after seeing a wreck, drives carefully for several blocks.

TRAFFIC OFFICER: "When I saw you come around that curve, I said to myself, 'Forty-five at least.'"

WOMAN DRIVER: "Well, you're wrong. This hat just makes me look old."

When you're driving, keep this in mind, sir: "Wind can't go through your windshield, but you can."

A policeman walked over to a woman driver who had stalled at an intersection and was holding up a long line of cars.

Irritated over the back-up of cars on his corner, he said: "What's the matter, lady? Haven't you seen a color you like best?"

"Didn't you hear me yelling at you to stop?" asked the irate cop.

"Yes, I did hear someone yelling," the woman driver replied.

"Then why didn't you stop?" he asked.

"Why, I thought it was someone I had run over."

Drunks (see Drinking)

A drunk finally finds the keyhole and enters the house, stumbling around looking for the lights. Wife pipes up: "That you, Henry?"

No answer. A big crash of glass.

WIFE: "Henry! What in the world are you doing?"

HENRY: "Teaching your goldfish not to bark at me."

Two drunks staggered out of a bar and immediately noticed a large shining object in the sky. "Moon sure is bright tonight," said one.

"That ain't the moon; that's the sun," said the other.

They began to argue until another man, similarly conditioned, came shuffling by. "Say, fellow," asked one. "Is that the sun or moon up there?"

Peering up where they pointed, the newcomer hesitated a moment, then replied: "Don't ask me. I don't live in this neighborhood."

A priest walked up to a young man hanging on a lamp post.

"Shame on you! What have you been drinking?"

"Three Fathers, Feather."

The two guys were walking off the effects of a big party when they accidentally found themselves stumbling along a railroad track. After trudging along for some time, one commented. "This is the longest set of stairs I ever tried to climb."

"Sure is," complained his companion. "And I wonder why they made the bannisters so low?"

Nothing can hold liquor as well as a bottle.

A drunk was standing on a corner mumbling to himself. A policeman came up. As he did he heard the drunk say, "It can't be done. It can't be done."

"What can't be done," said the officer.

"Look at that sign over there," answered the befuddled topper. "It says, 'Drink Canada Dry.'"

They promised to meet in the same bar at the same time ten years later.

So when ten years came, one of them walked in diffidently and sure enough, there was his pal seated on a stool.

"I never thought," he said, "that day when we left that I'd really see you here."

"Left?" he said. "Who left?"

A drunk was doing his best to spear an olive with a toothpick at a bar. Time after time the olive eluded him. Finally a man nearby became annoyed, took a toothpick and said, "This is the way to do it," and speared the olive on the first try.

"Sure! Sure!" replied the drunk. "After I got him so tired he couldn't get away."

A man entered a cocktail bar and from each martini he extracted the olive and deposited it in a little bottle.

"Whata nut," said another drinker to the bartender. "Really peculiar."

"What's peculiar about that?" replied the bartender. "His wife sent him out for a bottle of olives."

Old Slush drinks only on special occasions such as sunsets and week days.

The passenger with the beer breath fumbled a folded transfer from his pocket to the bus driver's hand. The driver straightened it out, took a quick look and said: "This transfer's no good, Mac."

"Oh, yeah? Why not?" demanded the passenger.

"It's a Saturday transfer; today's Monday."

"So what?" the drunk insisted. "Is it my fault you're two days late?"

BARTENDER TO BARFLY: "Don't you think you've had enough to drink?"

BARFLY: "Misshen, lister. I only had tee martoonies and I'm not as much under the affluence of inkahol as some thinkle may peep, and the drunker I stand here the longer I get."

A drunk was wandering around and got into a graveyard. Stumbling here and there he fell into a freshly dug grave. As he was trying to get out, another drunk came by. Picking up a shovel, the second drunk began to heave earth on the fellow down in the hole.

"Hey," hollered the first drunk, starting to sober up. "Help me out of here. I'm freezing."

"Sure you are," consoled the second, continuing to shovel like mad. "You're all uncovered."

A drunk fell from a two-story window and hit the pavement with a terrific impact. A crowd gathered and as the drunk staggered to his feet someone grabbed him by the arm and asked, "What happened?"

To which the drunk replied: "I dunno, I just got here."

A tipsy commuter followed a New Yorker into the subway.

About a half-hour later he emerged miles away to meet a friend.

"Where ya been?" the friend asked. "I got tired of waiting."

"Down in some guy's cellar," he replied. "And boy, has he got a set of trains."

There's a new social group in town called AAA-AA. It's for people who are being driven to drink.

A drunk staggered home and made his way unconsciously through the house, winding up in the stall shower of his bathroom. As he groped about, he turned on the water, deluging himself and making a racket which brought the Little Woman to the scene.

Taking in the details, she called him all kinds of a so and so, winding up with a none too flattering estimate of his past, present and future.

"That's right, honey," admitted the shuddering sot. "I'm everything you said—and worse. But let me in, won't you? It's raining something awful out here."

The boys from the office did a little too much celebrating during the convention, and on the way home they wandered into a zoo. After staggering around, they ended up in front of a lion's cage just as the animal let out a roar.

"C'mon, let's go," said one of the men.

"Naw," replied one of the others, "you guys go ahead if you want to, but I'm gonna stay for the movie."

An inebriate staggered into a bar and placed a big live lobster in front of him.

After downing a martini, he said:

"Shay, you make the best martinis in town and I'm going to give you Ethelbert, my pet lobster."

"Fine," says the bartender, "I'll take him home for dinner."

"No, no, don't do that! He's had dinner. Take him to a show."

A drunk boarded a two-decker bus and sat near the driver whom he pestered with endless remarks. To get rid of him the driver suggested that he would get more air on the upper deck. The drunk clambered up but soon returned.

"What's the matter?" asked the driver. "Didn't you like it up there?"

"S'fine," replied the souse, "but it ain't safe—no driver."

Early Bird

Let's face it—it's the early bird that gets the garden seeds.

Education (see College, Student)

The mountain youth returned from college on vacation.

"Whatcha larnin' son," inquired his pa.

"I'm learning algebra, Pa," replied the son.

"That's fine, son," replied his father. "Say something in algebra."

Not wanting to disappoint his father, the youth proclaimed solemnly, "Pi-R-Square."

The old man exploded. "If that's what they're larnin' ya, ya kin stop right now! Everybody knows pie are round!"

"A telegram from George, dear."

"Well, did he pass the examination this time?"

"No, but he is almost at the top of the list of those who failed."

A mountaineer took his son to school to enroll him.

"My boy's arter larnin. Whadya have?" he inquired.

"We offer English, trigonometry, spelling and all of the various subjects listed here."

"Well, give him some of that trigonometry, he's the worst shot in the family."

The teacher was explaining to the class that a number of sheep is called a flock and a number of quail is called a bevy.

"Now," she said, "What is a number of camels called?"

A nine-year-old lad had a quick answer: "A carton!"

The most absent-minded of absent-minded professors is the one who forgot to write a $5.00 book to sell to his class.

It costs more to amuse a child now than it used to cost to educate his father.

A Red professor was lecturing on insects at the university of a satellite country, bent on indoctrinating the youth.

"On my right hand," he told his students, "I have a flea. I now order him to jump over to my left hand. As you see, the flea obeys me.

"Now," he continued, "I remove the legs of the flea and order it to jump. You note it does not jump. Therefore gentlemen, we have scientific proof that a flea whose legs are removed becomes deaf."

SMALL BOY *(to his father):* "I'm supposed to tell you there's going to be a small PTA meeting tomorrow night."

"Well, if it's going to be a small one, do I have to go?" asked the father.

"Oh, yes," answered the son. "It's just you, me and the principal."

A young woman working for her doctor's degree married a professor in the middle of her second year.

"But, Edith," protested one of her friends, when she announced her engagement, "I thought you came here to get your Ph.D."

"So I did," replied Edith. "But I had no idea I would get him so soon."

"I can't get my report card back," said the boy to his teacher. "You gave me an A in something and they're still mailing it to relatives."

A boy came home from school with a terrible report card.

"My goodness," said his father when he saw it. "What happened?"

"Oh, nothing special" the boy answered. "You know how it is. Things are always marked down after the holidays."

The teacher asked the class to name all the states. One small boy responded so quickly and accurately that she commended him for it.

"You did very well," she said, "much better than I could have done at your age."

"Yes," he replied, "and there were only 13 states then."

A youngster returning from his first day of school was greeted at the door by his mother.

"Did you learn anything at school today?" she asked.

"You bet I did," he replied. "All the other kids get allowances but me."

It takes more than a sheepskin to keep the wolf away from the door.

SALESMAN *(to farmer):* "Do buy an encyclopedia now that your boy is going to school."

FARMER: "Not on your life. Let him walk like I did!"

Efficiency Expert

An efficiency expert is a man who waits to make up a foursome before going through a revolving door.

FIRST WOMAN: "What does your husband do?"
SECOND WOMAN: "He's an efficiency expert."
FIRST WOMAN: "Efficiency expert? What are his duties?"
SECOND WOMAN: "It's hard to say exactly, but if women did it, they'd call it nagging."

An efficiency expert walked up to two clerks. He asked the first clerk: "What do you do here?"

The clerk, fed up with red tape, buck-passing, forms, office politics, and above all, efficiency experts, answered, "I don't do a thing."

The efficiency expert nodded, made a note, then asked the second clerk: "What's your job here?"

"I don't do a damn thing either," answered the second sufferer.

The efficiency expert's ears perked up. "Hmmmm," he said, "duplication."

Egotist

One of the hardest secrets for a man to keep is his personal opinion of himself.

The pompous business tycoon was loudly telling his companions about his accomplishments. "I tell you I started with nothing," he proclaimed. "I am completely a self-made man!"

One sad little man looked up and said: "I sympathize with you. I'm no good at those do-it-yourself projects either."

Elevator Operator

One of the frustrations of the elevator operator is that he never hears the ends of stories.

All day long the weary elevator operator had been patiently answering questions the department-store shoppers had thrust upon him. Just before closing time a voice from the rear of the crowded car asked, "Suppose the elevator cable broke, would we go up or down?"

"That, my dear lady," snapped the weary operator, "depends entirely upon the kind of life you have lived!"

ELEVATOR GIRL: "I'm sorry. Did I stop too quick?"

PASSENGER: "Oh, no. I always wear my pants down around my ankles."

An old man from the hill country took his first trip to a large city. Walking into one of the skyscrapers he saw a doorman standing by a special kind of door. An old lady stepped in, a light flashed red and she was gone. A moment later the elevator descended, the door opened and out stepped a beautiful young girl.

"Begorra!" said the old man, blinking his eyes. "I should have brought the old woman with me."

Embezzlement

The most common causes of embezzlement, according to a survey company, are slow horses and fast women.

Employees

"Boss," said the dock foreman, "the men on the dock are a little leery of the new freight loader you hired yesterday."

"Why so?" asked the terminal manager. "He checked out well."

"Maybe so," replied the dock foreman, "but this morning he stubbed his toe on a crate of iron castings and said, 'Oh, the perversity of inanimate objects.' "

Two employers were discussing the dumbness of their employees.

"I've got the dumbest," said the first. "Watch this." Calling Elmer, he said, "Here, take this $5 bill and go buy me a Cadillac." Elmer took the money and departed without a word.

"That's nothing!" said the second boss. Calling his accused dumb one, he said, "Luther, go over to the club and see if I'm there." Luther also left the room without a word.

Outside he met Elmer. "Boy, ain't we got some dumb bosses?"

"Yeah," said Elmer, mine gave me $5 to buy a Cadillac but the jerk didn't tell me what color he wanted."

"He's right bright compared to my boss," said Luther. "He asked me to go over to the club and see if he was there—when he could have picked up the phone and found out for himself."

Employer

A boss is a man who, when you get to work early, comes in late, and when you are late, comes early.

Employment Applications

The young man was seeking his first job. At the employment office of a large firm he was presented with a multi-page employment application. In considerable confusion he pondered each question. Finally his face broke into a smile. In answer to the query, "What machines can you operate?" he wrote confidently: "Slot and Pin Ball."

PERSONNEL MAN: "Your application says you left your last job because of illness. What was the nature of the ailment?"
APPLICANT: "Well, the boss just got sick of the way I was doing things."

It was undoubtedly the same young lady who, when filling out an application form, puzzled over the line, "Are you a natural born citizen of the United States?"
Finally she answered: "No . . . Caesarean."

Engineer

Engineer: A person who passes as an exacting expert on the basis of being able to turn out with prolific fortitude inane strings of incomprehensible formulae calculated with micromatic precision from vague assumptions which are based on debatable figures taken from inconclusive experiments carried out with instruments of problematical accuracy by persons of doubtful reliability and questionable mentality for the avowed purpose of annoying and confounding a hopeless chimerical group of fanatics referred to all too frequently as Engineers.

The host brought an eager young man across the room to introduce him to a buxom young thing in a strapless gown, saying: "Miss Bulger, I'd like to introduce Mr. Bridges. Mr. Bridges is a construction engineer and he has a question to ask you."

"We can't hire you," said the personnel manager of an engineering firm, "only college graduates can handle the kind of work we do around here."
The young man protested that his experience could, indeed, qualify him, even though he lacked a diploma.
"Yes, but—well, look—just as an example of what our people have to do, can you tell me what steps you would take to determine the height of a building with an aneroid barometer?"

"Sure," replied the applicant. "I'd lower the barometer on a string from the roof of the building, and then I'd measure the length of the string."

Entertainment

A salesman was passing through a small town and had several hours to while away. Seeing one of the natives, he inquired: "Any picture-show in town, my friend?"

"Nope, not one, stranger," was the answer.

"Any poolroom or bowling alley?"

"None of them, either," came the reply.

"What form of amusement have you here?" asked the salesman.

"Waal, come on down to the drugstore. Thar's a freshman home from the university."

The country dance floor was jammed and after one number a gallant youth said to a young lady beside him, "Thanks so much for the dance."

"Dance? Dance?" she queried aghast. "Why I was just pushing through the crowd to reach the refreshment stand."

"Well, how was the burlesque show?"

"Abdominal."

BOARDER: "It's disgraceful! Two rats were fighting in my room last night."

LANDLADY: "Well, whatcha want for ten bucks a week—a bull fight?"

The male half of a new dance team was pleading with a producer.

"You never saw anything so sensational," the dancer raved. "At the finish of our act I take my partner by the hair and whirl her around for exactly 20 spins. Then I wind up the whole thing by heaving her through an open window."

The producer paled.

"Heave her through an open window?" he repeated incredulously. "Do you do that at every performance?"

The young man shrugged.

"Nobody's perfect," he admitted. "Sometimes I miss."

A member of the Russian staff was the guest of the chairman of a large motor company in Detroit. He was very much impressed with all that he saw. As he was about to leave he asked his host if he might speak to one of the workers. The reply being in the affirmative, the Russian went over to one of the men working on an assembly line and introduced himself.

"Tell me," he said. "Are you a Capitalist or a Communist?"

"I reckon I'm a Capitalist," the man replied.

"Why is that?"

"Well," said the man, "I look at it this way. I leave here at the end of my shift and there's the boss, waiting on the parking lot in his auto. 'Hello, there!' he might say. 'What about a drink?' So I'd go in the car and we'd have several drinks. Then maybe he'd say: 'What about coming home to my place for dinner?' So we'd go home and have a few more drinks. Then we'd have dinner. Then, maybe, some more drinks and he'd say: 'Look, it's late. Why don't you stay here the night?' So I'd stay the night, and he'd drive me back to the works in the morning. That's the sort of treatment that makes a Capitalist!"

The Russian was astonished. "Has that happened to you?" he asked.

"No," said the worker, "not exactly. But it's happened to my sister several times."

Ethics

"Business ethics," the father explained to his son, "is something you couldn't do without. Take today for instance. A man comes in and pays me a hundred dollar bill to clear up his account. After he leaves, I find two bills stuck together. He has paid me two hundred instead of one. Now, son, here comes the question of ethics. Should I tell my partner or shouldn't I?"

Europeans

Young thing returning from Europe: "They're rich over there. Almost everybody drives a foreign car."

Executive

An exec is a businessman who wears out several suits to every pair of shoes.

A great executive is a fellow who's always annoying the help with his bright ideas.

An executive may be described as one who makes an immediate decision and is sometimes right.

An executive is a man with a worried look on his assistant's face.

Except for wrestlers, no really big man ever throws his weight around.

"They say a good poker player can hold any kind of executive job."
"What would a good poker player want with a job?"

Every time a man gets to thinking that he is a big gun, somebody fires him.

EXECUTIVE: "Get my broker right away, Miss Jones."
SECRETARY: "Yes, sir. Which one—stock or pawn?"

The executive had left for a trip to Great Britain just before a customer phoned him at his office. "I'm sorry," said the exec's secretary. "He's gone to the United Kingdom."
There was a short pause at the other end of the line. "This is terrible," the caller said sorrowfully. "Is it too late to send flowers?"

Expedite

Expedite: To bring a normally slow operation to a complete standstill.

Expense Account

She was "Honey Chile" in New Orleans,
The hot spot of the bunch;
But on the old expense account,
She was gas, cigars and lunch.

Boss: "What's this big item on your expense account?"
SALESMAN: "My hotel bill."
Boss: "Well, don't buy any more hotels."

Experience

Experience is what you have when you are too old to get a job.

About the time one makes good marks in the school of experience he is old enough to retire.

Experience is a wonderful thing! It enables you to recognize a mistake when you make it again.

Extravagance

Extravagance: The way other people spend their money.

Eyes–Eyesight

LUSH: "What's that crawling on the wall?"
LUKE: "A lady bug."
LUSH: "Gad! What eyesight."

The man who visits a swimming pool and passes a pretty girl in a bathing suit without turning around may not necessarily be blind . . . he may be with his wife.

Fairy Tale

This is a fairy tale about a king with three daughters. One had a pretty face with an ugly figure. Another had a pretty figure with an ugly face. The last one had a pretty face and a pretty figure.
Question: Which daughter did the Prince marry?
Answer: None of them. He married the King.

Family

DAD: "Here's an article that says a smart father is often a stumbling block to his son."
MOTHER: "Thank goodness our Jimmy has nothing to worry about."

Little Susie's hair cracked as her mother was combing it.
"Why does it crack?" the child asked.
"Because it has electricity in it."
"Gee," ejaculated the little miss, "we're sure in the groove. I got electricity, Grandpa's got gas on his stomch, and Daddy's lit up."

"Good Heavens, Mother!" cried Whistler when he saw the aged lady scrubbing the floor. "Have you gone off your rocker?"

Farms–Farmers

A small girl from the city was making her first visit to the country and on her first night to the farm, went to the barn to see the cows milked.

The next morning, the hired man came running with the news that one of the cows had been stolen.

"Don't worry," said the city girl. "She won't get far. We drained her crankcase last night."

A stranger, dining with a farm family, asked for cream for his coffee.

"Haven't had any milk since our dog died," the farmer drawled, then added, to the startled stranger's relief, "A good dog. He brought in the cows."

The irate farmer walked up to the man in the car.

"Your car is on my land," he said, waving back of him.

"Well," sighed the motorist, "your land is on my car. I'm stuck here."

A farm is a hunk of land on which, if you get up early enough mornings, and work late enough nights, you'll make a fortune—if you strike oil.

Said the bull as he picked up a lost glove in the middle of the pasture: "Hmmm. One of the girls must have lost her bra."

Definition of a farmer: A man outstanding in his field.

Farmer Brown staggered home early one morning from a grade A bender, fell into bed and scarcely closed his eyes when the rooster awoke him at dawn.

Hoisting his hangover, he went down to the barn to milk the cow.

"You look terrible," Bossy said. "Those circles under your eyes droop to your knees."

"I know," the farmer groaned. "And milking you is just the beginning of my chores—I'll have to slave on this durned farm the whole blessed day."

"Well," volunteered the cow, "I'll help all I can. You just hold on tight and I'll jump up and down."

FARMER'S WIFE (*showing enormous sow to a six-year-old city child*): "Big, isn't she?"

CITY CHILD: "And no wonder! I saw her yesterday and she had 10 little ones blowing her up."

An old farmer was an incurable grumbler. One fall he had the best apple crop for miles around. One neighbor stopped to congratulate him. "Well, Hiram, you sure ought to be happy now. Yours is the finest apple crop ever raised in these parts."

"Well, I suppose so," he groaned. "But where's the rotten apples for the hogs?"

There was the farmer who had such a beautiful hired girl that he just couldn't keep his hands off her. He finally fired the hands.

In the United States today, the farmer is the only man who can lose money every year, live well, educate his children, and die rich.

The instructor in atomic warfare asked his class of fire fighters: "What's the difference between 'radiation' and 'contamination'?"
The neophyte, fresh from the farm, thought for a moment and then came up with a 100 per cent answer.
"Radiation," he drawled, "is when you smell manure. Contamination is when you step in it."

A city girl was telling her friends about her brother-in-law's farm which she had just visited. "It's one of those experimental farms," she explained, "where the cows have calves without any bulls around. They call it artificial inspiration."

A tourist stopped where a farmer was erecting a building.
"What are you making?" he asked.
"Wal," answered the farmer, "I ain't sure yit. If'n I can rent it, it's a rustic cottage, and if'n I can't, it's a cow shed."

A young student from the agriculture college was in having a conversation with an old farmer. "Do you know," observed the young man, "that your farming methods are so far behind the times that I'd be surprised if you get $50 worth of oats out of this field."
"So would I," was the farmer's reply. "It's barley."

An Australian sheep farmer, having drawn a huge wool check, bought a Rolls-Royce. When he brought it back for servicing, the salesman asked if he was thoroughly satisfied with it.
"Oh, yes," said the farmer. "I especially like that glass partition between the front seat and the back."
"Why?" asked the salesman.
"Well," said the farmer, "it keeps the sheep from licking the back of my neck when I'm taking them to the market."

"Why do they call him a 'gentlemen farmer'?"
"Because he raises his hat!"

An old man's cow got loose, visited a neighbor's still, and ate so much sour mash that she died. The old man put in a claim against the neighbor for the cost of the cow.

"I'll never pay it," said the neighbor. "My whiskey didn't kill your cow. She gave eggnog, and you milked her to death."

A tractor salesman driving along a country road saw a farmer plowing his field with his bull dragging the plow.

Stopping along the fence he said, "Why don't you get a tractor? It will do twice the work in half the time."

"Got a tractor," replied the farmer, "but I don't want to use it."

"Why not?" asked the salesman.

"Well," drawled the farmer, "I want this bull to learn that life ain't all romance."

MOTORIST: "I'd like a dozen eggs."

FARMER: "I haven't a dozen. I've only got ten."

MOTORIST: "Well, are they fresh?"

FARMER: "That's right. They're so fresh the hen hasn't had time to finish the dozen."

A neighboring farmer leaned on the rail fence, watching his old friend plow. "I don't like to butt in," he finally said, "but you could save yourself a lot of work by saying 'gee' and 'haw' to that mule instead of just tuggin' on them lines."

The old-timer pulled a big handkerchief from his pocket and mopped his brow. "Yep, I know that," he agreed, "but this mule kicked me 6 years ago, and I ain't spoke to him since."

Two little boys discussing their future:

1ST LITTLE BOY: "I'm gonna be a streetcar motor man when I grow up. What are you going to be?"

2ND LITTLE BOY: "I'm gonna be a farmer."

1ST LITTLE BOY: "You can't be a farmer."

2ND LITTLE BOY: "Why not?"

1ST LITTLE BOY: "Cause you don't have a daughter."

A teacher was giving the 6th grade an arithmetic test.

"Jack," she quizzed, "if a farmer had 5,000 bushels of corn to market at $1.20 a bushel, what would he get?"

Came the prompt response: "A government loan!"

Fate

Fate is often blamed for what fools do.

Father (see Family, Mother, Son-In-law, Wives, Children)

During a bad electrical storm, a mother thought her young son would be frightened, so she tiptoed into his room to stay near him.

The child opened his eyes and mumbled, "What's Dad doing to the television set now?"

"When I was a boy of 14, my father was so ignorant I could hardly stand to have the old man around. But when I got to be 21, I was astonished at how much the old man had learned in seven years."

Father: A guy with snapshots in his wallet where money used to be.

Fathers should not get too discouraged if their sons reject their advice. It will not be wasted; years later the sons will offer it to their own offspring.

A father and son were posing for a picture at the time of the young man's graduation from college.

"Stand a little closer to your father," said the photographer, "and put your hand on his shoulder."

"I think it would be more appropriate," said the father, "if he stood with his hand in my pocket."

"What's your birthstone, Daddy?"
"I think it's the grindstone, son."

JUNIOR: "The Lord gives us our daily bread, doesn't He, Mother?"
MOTHER: "Yes, dear."
JUNIOR: "And Santa Claus brings the Christmas presents?"
MOTHER: "Yes, dear."
JUNIOR: "And the stork brings babies?"
MOTHER: "Yes, dear."
JUNIOR: "Then why do we need Pops around?"

JUNIOR: "Dad, did you go to Sunday School when you were a little boy?"
DAD: "I sure did. Never missed a Sunday."
JUNIOR: "See, Mom, it won't do me any good either."

"Grandma," asked the small boy, "I ain't ever seen pictures of angels with whiskers. Does that mean my daddy won't be an angel? He's got whiskers."

"Maybe, darlin'," the grandma replied, "but it'll be by a close shave."

"Ma, where does the fire go when it goes out?"

"That, son, is one of the inscrutable mysteries about fire and your father."

Faults

Women have their many faults,
Men, they but two—
It's everything they have to say,
And everything they do.

Her head is just as vacant as the breakfast room at Niagara Falls.

Fear

A shy little man was frightened by his boss. One day he told a fellow worker he was sick but was afraid the boss would fire him if he went home.

"Don't be silly. He'll never know. He's not even here today."

Finally the man went home. When he got there he looked in the window and saw his boss kissing his wife. He raced all the way back to the office. "A fine friend you are!" he said to his co-worker. "I nearly got caught."

"Sambo, wha' time in yoah life was you scared the worstest?"

"When ah was callin' on a married gal and her husban' came in and caught me. Was I scared!"

"How are you shuah dat was de worstest time?"

"Cause her husban' turned to Mandy an' says, 'What's dat white man doin' here?'"

VISITOR: "Doctor, what can you say to a girl who's so scary she jumps into the arms of a man every time she's frightened?"

DOCTOR: "Boo!"

Financial Genius

"Father," asked Junior, "what is a financial genius?"

"A financial genius, my son," replied his father thoughtfully, "is a man who can pay his family's Christmas bills in January."

First Aid

A young matron of our acquaintance, taking first-aid training, has reached the resuscitation stage. One evening recently, returning from a

Red Cross meeting, she observed a man on a darkened side street, sprawled face downward.

"Aha," though the matron, "providence has sent me hither to minister to this poor unfortunate." Parking her car nearby, she rushed over and began giving the treatment for resuscitation.

Presently the man stirred, looked up, and spoke with great difficulty: "Lady," he said, "I don't know what you're up to, but I wish you'd quit tickling me. I'm holding a lantern for a guy workin' down in this manhole."

Fishing

"Did you have any luck on your fishing trip?"
"I'll say I did! I caught four inside straights!"

FIRST FISHERMAN: "Havin' any luck?"
SECOND FISHERMAN: "Nope. Can't get the cork out."

A very talkative woman buttonholed an angler who was minding his own business and said, "Aren't you ashamed of yourself? A big fellow like you might be better occupied than in cruelly catching poor little fish."

"Maybe you're right," said the angler, "but if this fish had had the sense to keep his mouth shut he wouldn't be here."

ARTHUR: "I hooked a fish last week so big that it pulled the boat out to sea, and I couldn't get back to shore for two days."

MAC: "A mere minnow. I caught one so heavy that when we pulled him in he sank the boat."

GRAYSON: "I was standing on shore one day when I caught one that was really big. We had to pull him in with a wrecking truck winch, and when we got him ashore the whole island sank."

A fisherman was hauled into court charged with catching two more black bass than the law allows.

"Guilty," said the fisherman.

"Ten dollars and costs," said the judge.

After paying the fine, cheerfully, the defendant asked, "And now, your Honor, if I may, I'd like several copies of the court record to show my friends."

After several hours' fishing little Patty suddenly threw down her pole and exclaimed, "I quit!"

"Why, Patty, what's the matter?" asked her mother.

"Well, Mother," she answered. "I just can't seem to get waited on!"

Two men who had never been ice fishing were going to go for the first time. They found a cabin near a lake on a resort and had to borrow an ice chisel from the resort owner. They went out early in the morning to try their luck.

When they got back the resort owner asked, "Did you get any fish?"

"Did we get any fish!" the men exclaimed. "We barely had time to get the boat in the water!"

Nothing changes the line of a man's thoughts quicker than spading up a fishing worm while digging in the garden.

"You've been watching me three hours," said the angler. "Why don't you try fishing yourself?"

"I haven't the patience," he replied.

The salesman didn't know a thing about fishing, but when the purchasing agent invited him along on a fishing trip, he thought it might be good customer relations, so he accepted. He was fitted with the necessary tackle by his host and settled in a likely spot a short distance away to try his own luck.

A few moments went by and the salesman called out, "Hey, Joe, how much do those floats cost?"

"Oh, about a dime, I guess," was the reply.

"Well, I owe you a dime," said the novice. "Mine just sank!"

Flood

A traveler one night found himself obliged to remain in a small town on account of a landslide on the railway, caused by heavy rain which was still falling in torrents. The traveler turned to the waitress with: "This certainly looks like the flood."

"The what?"

"The flood. You've read about the flood, and the ark landing on Mount Ararat, surely."

"Mister," she returned, "I haven't seen a paper for three days."

Food

The shoemaker was explaining to a complaining customer the reason for the poor quality of his soles. "All the good leather," he said, "is going into steaks."

The apple is well-known in history. COMMENT: Sure it is, but the grapefruit stays in the public eye.

CUSTOMER: "I don't like the looks of that haddock."
GROCER: "Well, Madam, if it's looks you're after, why don't you try goldfish!"

A modern mother and her young son were shopping in a supermarket. The child, trying to help, picked up a package and brought it to her.

"No, no, honey," protested the mother, "go put it back. That has to be cooked."

Feed Store: The only place in town where you can get a chicken dinner for 10 cents.

There's not much point in ordering a "sizzling" steak, Grandpop, if your hearing aid is out of order.

The kiddie party was just about over and Bucky's mother was bringing in the dessert, a heaping platter of gelatin. As she placed it on the table, it quivered and shook. Most of the youngsters shouted with delight, but one pudgy, towheaded boy got up and started to leave the table.

"None of that stuff for me," he said. "It ain't dead yet."

Football

The football coach, dejected because his team is losing, looks down his bench of substitutes and yells: "All right, Jones, go in there and get ferocious."

Jones jumps up with a start and says: "Sure, coach, what's his number?"

A reporter boarded the train carrying the Notre Dame team to the Southern Methodist game. Thinking to get a new slant on a story, he asked for the student manager.

"I understand," he said, "that you carry a chaplain to pray for the team?"

"Yes, that's right," said the student.

"Would you mind introducing me to him?"

"Be glad to. Which one do you want, the offensive chaplain or the defensive?"

The football season is when you watch the numbers on sweaters instead of what's in them.

It was a cold November day and the football stadium was jammed. High up in the stands an alumnus kept standing up and calling, "Hey, Gus," and each time a man down in the third row would ceremoniously stand up and doff his hat.

After many calls of "Hey, Gus," the gentleman in the third row shouted back in a thick, stammering voice, "Now quit calling me. I'm tired of standing up . . . and besides my name ain't Gus."

The wife of one of the defensive tackles on the professional football team recently remarked: "It's really exciting to be married to a professional football tackle. Every time he comes home he looks like a different person."

COACH: "Joe, I'll let you play end, guard and tackle."

JOE: "How can I play all three positions?"

COACH: "Sit on the end of the bench, guard the water bucket, and tackle anyone who comes near it."

In the Rose Bowl football game a few years ago, the Southern California Trojans were being clobbered by a Big Ten team. In the course of the third quarter the Trojans' left halfback ran into a little trouble. It seemed that the entire opposing team was centered on stopping him. While over 100,000 people in the Bowl watched, he tried to make a plunge off his left tackle and was buried under a mound of heavy tacklers. It took the officials a long minute to get him uncovered. Finally he staggered to his feet, shook his head and, looking up groggily, saw the thousands in the stands.

"Gosh!" he exclaimed to a teammate, "How did all those people get back up there to their seats so quickly?"

Fraternal Orders

"My Dad is an Eagle, a Moose, an Elk, and a Lion," boasted one youngster.

"Yeah?" gasped his wondering companion. "How much does it cost to see him?"

MOSE: "Does this lodge yo' belong to have any death benefits?"

REMUS: "Yessuh! 'Deed it does. When yo' dies, yo' don't have to pay no more dues."

During a cold snap in the East, it got so cold that a 32nd degree Mason went down 10 degrees.

Friends

A Russian soldier arrived home after an absence of four years at war. He found his wife with a newborn baby, whereupon he began to question her: "Was it my friend Ivan?"

"No."

"Was it my friend Nicolas?"

"No."

"Maybe my friend Petrov?" But all she could say was "no." "Well, then, who was it?"

She answered, "Don't you think I have any friends of my own?"

MARINE: "Say, pal, will you lend me a dime to call a friend?"

SAILOR: "Here's two dimes; call all your friends."

The late John Barrymore was out walking one afternoon when he saw a certain notorious snob approaching. He tried to avoid the man, but the other singled him out with a hearty greeting: "Good afternoon, Barrymore. You are positively the only person I've met today worth stopping to speak to."

"Really," rejoined Barrymore. "Then you're much more fortunate than I am."

"So you lost your best friend. I'm very sorry; tell me how it happened."

"Vell, he was keelt by a weasel."

"Killed by a weasel? That's very unusual. What happened?"

"Is driving his hotomobul. Is coming to a railroad crossink, and din't hear no weasel."

It is fine to have a friend you can trust, but is finer to have one who will trust you.

Fringe Benefits

"I like the sound of the job, but the last place I worked paid more."

"Did they give you rest periods?"

"Yes."

"Furnish life insurance?"

"Yes."

"Vacation with pay?"

"Yes, and a $100 holiday bonus."

"Gad, man, why did you leave there?"

"The company went into bankruptcy."

Fun

A chorus girl showed her friend a check given her by a "sugar daddy" and returned from the bank marked "Insufficient Fun."

Funeral

At the baseball game, the boss suddenly came in behind his office boy and tapped him on the shoulder.

"So this is your uncle's funeral?" he demanded of the startled youth.

"Looks like it," the quick-witted youngster replied. "He's the umpire down there."

And then there was the boss who cornered the office boy, "My boy," he asked, "do you believe in life after death?"

"Yes, sir."

"Then that makes everything just fine," the boss answered tenderly. "About an hour after you left yesterday afternoon to bury your grandfather he came in to see you."

Future

FORTUNE TELLER: "You'll be poor and unhappy until you are forty."

CLIENT (*hopefully*): "Then what?"

FORTUNE TELLER: "You'll get used to it."

How little we know of what the future has in store for us. Little did I know when I carved my initials in a campus tree I would some day grow up and fail to become famous.

Gambling

In Las Vegas the odds are you won't get even.

Charged with passing four counterfeit $100 bills, a gambler in Louisville testified he had won the money with crooked dice.

"I hear your boss made a killing in Las Vegas," said the purchasing agent to a visiting salesman.

"I suppose some people would call it that," answered the salesman with a smile. "He left in a $7,000 Cadillac and came home on a $75,000 Greyhound bus."

A lovely young damsel wearing a mink coat walked up to a dice table at a Reno gambling hall and waited for her turn with the dice. When her turn came she took off the coat, revealing that she was clad only in a Bikini bathing suit, and picked up the dice. She bet $1,000, rolled the dice once, rolled them again, and exclaimed, "Made it!"

She collected her winnings, put on her coat again and left.

"By the way," one of the house men asked the other, "What was her point?"

His partner shrugged his shoulders and said, "I didn't notice either."

It was at a fast-moving table in the gambling town where a stranger picked up the dice, rattled them, then made his pass. To his horror, three dice rolled out on the green table instead of the two he had picked up. There was an ominous silence.

Finally, the houseman in charge of the table reached over and picked up the odd die which had dropped from the stranger's sleeve. Without batting an eye, he placed it in his rack, turned to look at the stranger, and commented: "O.K., your point's 16."

A gambler died. The funeral was well attended by his professional friends. In the eulogy, the minister asserted: "Spike is not dead. He only sleeps."

From the rear of the chapel came the interrupting words: "I got $100 says he's dead!"

Bandage-covered Joe lay in the hospital bed and spoke dazedly to his visiting pal: "Wh-what happened?"

"You absorbed too much last night and then made a bet you could fly out the window and around the block."

"Why didn't you stop me?" screamed the patient.

"Stop you? I had $25 on you."

The two tycoons were commenting on a friend's bad luck at the race track. "It's funny," said one, "how lucky Herman is at cards and how he never wins a bet on the horses."

"There's really nothing peculiar about it," replied the other. "They just won't let him shuffle the horses."

A western sheriff confiscated a bunch of slot machines on the basis of a law banning the use of steel traps for catching dumb animals.

Games

An Englishman returned to his home from a trip to America and telling his friends of the odd American games.

"And they have the queerest game in the movie houses. It is called 'Ohhell,' I think."

"Ohhell?" they asked. "How do they play it?"

"Well, when you go in they give you a card with a lot of numbers and during the intermission a man yells out the numbers. Then someone yells 'Bingo!' and everyone else yells, 'Ohhell!' "

Generosity

WEALTHY FATHER: "I hope you appreciate that in marrying my daughter you are getting a very big-hearted and generous girl."

HER FIANCE: "I do, sir, and I hope she has acquired those fine qualities from her father."

Genius

Genius: a man who shoots at something no one else can see and hits it.

Every family should have three children. If one turns out to be a genius the other two can support him.

Ghosts

Three matronly ghosts at a business convention in the spirit world were muttering angrily among themselves. The object of their wrath was a curvaceous young spook surrounded by a cluster of spectral husbands who were leaning ever closer to the young ghost's obvious charms. Finally one of the old gals could no longer contain herself.

"Hah," she sniffed. "Her and her contour sheet!"

Gifts

"I am looking for a gift for a girl," the earnest young man confided to a clerk. "I want something that will make her face light up, something that will make her eyes sparkle, something that will rekindle the fire of love."

"Well," said the clerk judicially, "if you're trying to burn her up, don't give her anything."

Son: "Dad, instead of buying me an expensive graduation gift, why not give me something you've made yourself?"

Dad: "What's that?"

Son: "Money!"

"Here's a tie for your birthday, dear. I wonder what would go best with it?"

"How about grandpa?"

Sign in gift shop: "For the man who has everything—a calendar to remind him when the payments are due."

Golf

The minister met one of his lady parishioners on the street one day. After exchanging pleasantries, the woman asked: "Reverend, isn't it sinful the way my husband plays golf every Sunday morning?"

With a twinkle, the good minister replied: "The kind of golf your husband plays is sinful on any day."

Golfer: "I don't seem to be playing my usual game today."

Caddy: "What game do you usually play, sir?"

Golf is no longer a rich man's game. There are millions of poor players.

Irate golfer: "You must be the world's worst caddie!"

Caddie: "Oh, no sir—that would be too much of a coincidence."

Golfer: "Well, caddy, how do you like my game?"

Caddie: "I guess it's all right. But I still prefer golf."

I'm not saying Uncle Buckle is cheap, you understand. But yesterday he lost his first golf ball in ten years. The string broke."

"Just give me my golf, the great outdoors, and a beautiful girl, and you can keep my golf and the great outdoors."

A golfer was having a bad day on the links. Finally on the 13th hole, he flubbed a two foot putt. That did it. He picked up the ball and threw it as far as he could, broke two clubs, and sat down on the grass, a picture of total frustration.

"I've got to give it up! I've got to give it up!" he said to his caddy.

"Give up golf?" asked the caddy.

"No," answered the golfer, "the ministry."

A golfer's daughter
        Was Mary Anna Pound;
    That's why she liked
        To play around.

Several times I've almost made a hole-in-one. The last time I was close. I only missed it by three strokes.

Some men play golf religiously every Sunday.

The sweet young thing asked me if I could tell her how to play golf.
"Sure, it's easy enough," I told her. "All you do is smack the pill and then walk."
"How interesting," she replied. "Just like some auto rides I've been on."

A funeral procession filed by and it was seen that there was a bag of golf clubs reposing atop the coffin in the hearse.
"Isn't that odd," someone remarked. "That man must be a golf maniac."
"Oh, it isn't the deceased," a friend remarked. "The husband is the golfer. His wife died and he's got an important match this afternoon."

A golfer is a guy who can walk several miles toting a hundred pound bag but who has junior bring him an ashtray.

"Golf is like a love affair. If you don't take it seriously, it's no fun. If you do, it breaks your heart."—Arnold Daly

"Well, you said I had to choose, didn't you?" demanded the husband in bed with his golf clubs.

GOLF PRO: "Now just go through the motions without driving the ball."
DUB: "That's precisely what I'm trying to overcome."

JUDGE: "How did the trouble start?"
DEFENDANT: "Well, she asked me to play a round and I didn't know she was a golfer."

WIFE: "Well, what excuse do you have for coming home at this hour of the night?"
HUSBAND: "Well, my dear, I was playing golf with some of the office staff."

WIFE: "What, at 2 A.M.?"
HUSBAND: "We were using night clubs."

Golf is like children. It takes time and patience to master them.

GOLFER (*to member ahead*): Would you mind if I played through? I just heard my wife has been taken seriously ill."

An ardent golfer is Roland Rhoda;
His favorite shot is scotch and soda.

The real test in golf and in life is not in keeping out of the rough, but in getting out after we are in.

Ever notice that there seems to be a limit to almost everything except the number of wrong ways a golf ball can be hit?

"Golf! Golf! Golf!" she wailed. "I believe I'd drop dead if you spent one Sunday at home!"
"Now, now," he replied, "you know you can't bribe me."

Then there was the golfer who had hit 12 balls into the water on a short water hole. Suddenly, something snapped. He pulled his clubs out of the bag, broke each one and threw them one by one into the water. Then he threw the bag into the water and then the golf cart. He turned and ran all the way to the clubhouse, pulled open his locker, ripped up his golf clothes and set fire to them. Grabbing a razor, he slashed his wrists. An ambulance came and as he was being carried to it on a stretcher, he noticed in the crowd of shocked spectators one of the members of his foursome.
"Sol," he whispered, "what time do we tee off tomorrow?"

Cheer up! The average golfer will eventually break 100, but it will take a lot of digging.

A preacher one day decided to take up golfing. On his first swing at the ball, it sailed into a clump of trees. A moment later, a big bird flew out of the trees, circled the ground and dropped the ball neatly into the cup.
Looking up the preacher cried, "But Father, please, I'd rather do it myself."

By the time a man can afford to lose a golf ball, he can't hit it that far.

One of the quickest ways to meet new people is to pick up the wrong ball on the golf course.

Do you know some fellows play golf on week-ends to forget their business troubles while others work all week trying to forget their lousy week-end golf scores?

"I'm anxious to make this shot. That's my mother-in-law up there on the clubhouse porch."
"Don't be a fool. You can't hit her at 200 yards."

I wonder if more gals would be interested in golf if the men could drive with one arm?

We heard about the gal who was going to take up golf because she heard someone had found a diamond in the rough.

We keep hearing that a main rule of golf is to keep your eye on the ball, and then girls start going around the course in shorts.

I understand more golf games have been won with pencils than were ever won with putters or drivers.

Never judge a man's religion by what he says and does when he misses a six-inch putt.

Two men, strangers, met on the golf links and agreed to play around the course together. After a couple of holes they got behind two very slow women. One man offered to ask the women if they might go ahead. When he returned he said he hadn't asked because just as he neared them he recognized his wife and girl friend. Understanding the situation the other gentleman offered to ask the ladies. In a few seconds, he returned, only to comment,
"Small world, isn't it?"

In the uncivilized countries, native tribes sometimes beat the ground with clubs and utter blood-curdling yells. Anthropologists call this "primitive self-expression." Over here we call it golf.

A man returned from a round of golf and his young son wanted to know, "Well, did you win, Dad?"
"Let me put it this way," was the reply, "Your father got to hit the ball more times than anyone else."

Two Spanish detectives were standing over the body of Juan Gonzales. "How was he shot?" inquired the first.

"I theenk eet was a golf gun," said the other.

"But what ees a golf gun?"

"I don't know, but eet sure made a hole in Juan."

An avid golfer married a gal whose favorite hobby was attending auctions. Both talked in their sleep. From his side of the bed would come the mumbled warning: "Fore." And from her side the sleepy response: "Four twenty-five."

"That's quite a slice you had on that golf ball," the angry cop said to the sheepish duffer. "It curved clear off the course and broke the windshield in my squad car. What do you intend to do about it?"

"Well," replied the golfer. "I was thinking that probably the best thing to do would be to try moving my thumb a little farther up on the club."

I see by the papers where a sports writer says golf balls will last longer if kept in the refrigerator. COMMENT: Sure they will! Taking them out on the course and smacking them around is what wears them out.

DEWEY: "It says here in the paper that a man beat his wife to death with a golf club."

ROD: "In how many strokes?"

The duffer was playing golf when his ball rolled over among a bunch of anthills. After fidgeting to his stance for several minutes he swung wildly at the ball but hit the ground about six inches ahead of the ball. Disgusted, he went through the same procedure again, this time hitting the ground about six inches behind the ball. Two ants came up out of the ground, and one said to the other: "We better get on the ball or he'll knock hell out of us."

ROBERTS: "What are you looking so glum for, Frank?"

HILL: "My doctor tells me I can't play golf."

ROBERTS: "So, he's played with you, too."

Playing a water hole at a local golf club, an avid golfer, the guest of a club member, promptly drove the ball into the pond. Then he asked his host to supply him with another as he had no spares. The guest unerringly drove the new ball into the pond, too, and did the same with a third, fourth and fifth.

"Ralph," the host protested, "those are my brand new $1.25 golf balls you're losing."

"Look here, Cary," replied Ralph, the dunker, "if you can't afford this game, you shouldn't be playing it."

When you're playing golf nothing counts like your opponent.

Good Sport

The trouble with being a good sport is that you have to lose to prove it.

A wealthy sportsman received a telephone call from a girl. "Bill, this is Janie, remember me?" Bill thought for a minute, then said, "No, I can't recall who you are."

"Oh, now, Bill," replied Janie, "you must remember. I'm the pretty blonde who went on your yacht with you a few months ago. We had such a nice time. We fished, and we dined, and we danced, and I did everything you asked me to do. You told me what a good sport I was, remember?"

"Oh sure, Janie! Now I remember. How are you?" enthused Bill.

"Well I'm going to have a baby, and I'm going to commit suicide," sobbed Janie.

"Gad," replied Bill, "you *are* a good sport!"

Gossip

SHE: "I know nothing but good of Alice."
OTHER SHE: "Then let's talk of someone else."

Gourmet

Gourmet: A glutton who owns a tux.

Guests

BOSS: "Are you sure your wife knows you're bringing me home to dinner?"

LUKE: "Does she know! We argued about it for half an hour this morning!"

Our society's two biggest liars: The guest who keeps saying he must be going and the host who asks, "What's your hurry?"

Hair

Stepping into a drug store, a man overheard a couple of clerks chatting about a new hair tonic. "Is this stuff really any good?" asked one.

"Is it good? Why, I spilled some of it on my comb last week and now it's a brush."

"Why do men have hair on their chests?"
"Well, they can't have everything!"

The reason a man's hair turns gray quicker than his whiskers is because it has a 20-year start.

Happiness (see Unhappiness, Satisfaction)

It is a great blunder in the pursuit of happiness not to know when we have got it.

Money doesn't always bring happiness. A guy with ten million is no happier than a guy with nine million.

"For twenty long and wonderful years my wife and I were deliriously happy."
"Then what happened?"
"We met."

A smile is a curve that sets many things straight.

Happiness sneaks in through a door you didn't know you left open.

A smile goes a long way, but it usually comes back home.

Harem

Harem: a floor show with a husband.

Health

"Doc, I'm worried," said the man. "About a week ago I came home to find my wife in the arms of another man. Before I could say a word in protest, this fellow talks me into going down to the corner drug store and talking things out over a cup of coffee."

"The following night the same thing. Down to the corner we go to 'talk things out over a cup of coffee.' "

"And last night, there he was again. Again he talks me into going down to the corner for a cup of coffee and a man-to-man talk."

"Listen, mister," said the doc, "you don't want a doctor. You want a lawyer!"

"No," said the husband, "I need a doctor. I want to know if I'm drinking too much coffee."

A drug concern is toying with the idea of combining aspirin and chlorophyll to get rid of those stinkin' headaches.

DOCTOR: "You've got to have more diversion and relaxation."
PATIENT: "But I'm too busy."
DOCTOR: "Nonsense. The ants are hardworking creatures but they have time to attend all the picnics."

The condition of a man can best be judged by what he takes two-at-a-time—stairs or pills.

SADIE: "I like this resort. All the men are so full of passion."
LULU: "Passion, hell! This is a health resort for asthma victims."

Getting up in the morning is simple—just a question of mind over mattress.

Home (see Real Estate)

Sign in front yard: "Anyone is welcome to use our lawn mower, providing they don't take it out of the yard."

"Well," said the architect, "just what kind of home do you want?"
"We want a house," said the homebuilder, "to go with an antique door-knocker my wife picked up in Mexico."

"Found a new house yet?"
"We've stopped looking. After reading the appraiser's description of the one we have, it seemed to be just the place we were looking for."

A couple whose new home was completed very recently had hardly moved in before the neighbors came over to inspect it. Naturally, the conversation was on the subject of the house.

"It's very nice," commented one of the neighbors, "but I don't see why you call this type of house a bungalow."

"Well," explained the owner, "we just don't know what else to call it. The job was a bungle, and we still owe for it."

An up-to-date house has wall-to-wall carpeting, wall-to-wall windows, and back-to-back financing.

Home: where part of the family waits until the rest of them bring back the family car.

The newly married youngster mentioned to a fellow worker that he had seen quite a few moths flying around in his clothes closet. The worker suggested that he immediately obtain some mothballs.

A few days later, the subject came up again: "Those mothballs you suggested sure do the trick. I've used up about 10 boxes of them, and in another couple of days I should have the problem licked."

"Ten boxes! What in the world did you do with that many mothballs?"

"Well, them little things fly around so fast that I just can't him 'em every time."

A man recently had a new house built. Inspecting it with his architect, he mentioned that the house didn't look very strong.

"Well, after all," the architect replied, "you've got to consider that that we haven't got the wallpaper on yet."

An Eskimo won a trip to New York as a prize for catching the most seals in a season. When he returned home, he brought with him a length of pipe, which he set up in his igloo so it protruded through the roof.

His wife asked what it was for, and he replied: "That's a trick I learned in New York. When you want more heat you bang on this pipe."

SWEET YOUNG WIFE: "Now over in this corner, we'll have a loveseat, over there we'll have a loveseat, and here by the fireplace we'll have another loveseat."

DECORATOR: "My word, do you call this a living room?"

YOUNG WIFE: "Why of course. If that isn't living, I don't know what is!"

Honesty

Honesty may be the best policy—but there are some people who don't seem to think they can afford the best.

The captain wrote in the ship's log:

"Mate was drunk today." After sobering up, the mate went to the captain and pleaded with him to strike out the record. "It's the first time in my life I've been drunk," he pleaded, "and I promise never to do it again."

"In this log we write only the truth," said the captain.

The next day it was the mate's turn to keep the log, and in it he wrote: "Captain was sober today."

One look at the brassiere ads is enough to convince one that honesty is no longer the bust policy.

Horses

Stevens fell off his horse and broke his leg. The horse picked him up by the seat of his pants, threw him into the saddle, took him home, put him to bed and called a doctor.

"Smart horse," one of his friends said.

"Not so smart," replied Stevens. "The darn fool called a horse doctor."

When you're going for a ride, advises a friend of ours just returned from a dude ranch, never choose a horse that is too polite. That just happened to me. Before he jumped a fence he stopped so I could go first.

The staid old gentleman was acting as honorary judge at a fancy horse show. As he looked over the scene he was puzzled by the attire of many contestants in the show. He turned to the person sitting next to him and said: "Just look at that young person with a poodle cut, the cigarette and blue jeans. Is it a boy or a girl?"

"It's a girl," was the reply. "She's my daughter."

"Oh, forgive me, sir," apologized the old fellow. "I never dreamed you were her father."

"I'm not," snapped the other. "I'm her mother!"

JOE: "My horse wanted to go one way; I wanted to go the other."
MOE: "What happened?"
JOE: "He tossed me for it!"

Horse Racing

Father looked up from his racing news and noticed the baby in the buggy. Turning to his wife he said: "Baby's nose is running."

His wife snorted and snapped: "Don't you ever think of anything except horseracing?"

The sweet old lady, always eager to help the needy, pressed a dollar into the hand of the old man near the alleyway.

"Chin up!" she said brightly, and was delighted to see him walk away briskly.

The next day, passing the same alleyway, at the same time, she was surprised when approached by the same sad-looking old man, who slipped a sheaf of bills into her hand.

"Nice picking!" he whispered. "He paid nine to one."

Some horse-racing fans were arguing with a contingent of baseball fans about the relative attractions of those two sports as seen on TV. "One thing we got over you," a horseplayer said, "at least we don't have to watch a horse shaving."

A race horse owner from the West showed up at Churchill Downs in Louisville with an eight-year-old horse that had never been in a race before.

Since an eight-year-old non-started is hardly a betting attraction he was a 100-to-1 and galloped home first by ten lengths.

The stewards suspected dirty work at the crossroads and demanded of the owner, "Is this horse unsound?"

"No, sir," asserted the owner. "Soundest horse you ever saw."

"Well," persisted a steward, "why haven't you raced him before?"

"To tell the truth," said the Westerner sheepishly, "we couldn't ketch him till he was seven."

Jack Lynn, an avid baseball fan and player, once was persuaded to attend the races, where he put a $2 bet on a 50-to-1 shot. As his horse came down the stretch neck-and-neck with the favorite, Jack hollered:

"Slide, yuh bum! Slide!"

The horse trainer confessed that just before the big race he had given his nag a big shot of whiskey. "Did he win?" asked a friend. "Nope," said the trainer, "but he was the happiest horse in the race!"

A colt trotted up to the bookmaker at the race track and neighed, "I want to bet $2 on myself to win in the third."

"What!" screamed the gambler.

"Surprised to learn I can talk?" asked the horse.

"No," said the bookmaker, "I just don't think you can win!"

"Now, don't tell stories, Jimmy. You know your father never took you to the zoo in his whole life."

"Yes he did, Mommy, and one of the animals paid twenty-seven dollars!"

Hospitals

It was a good two hours after the scheduled time before the orderly arrived to take the patient to the operating room.

Said the patient: "They must be awfully busy this morning. You're so late."

Said the orderly: "Oh, it's been murder up there!"

Hotels and Motels

HE: "May I have some stationery?"

CLERK (*haughtily*): "Are you a guest of the house?"

HE: "Heck, no, I'm paying twenty dollars a day."

BELLHOP (*after guest has rung for ten minutes*): "Did you ring, sir?"

GUEST: "No, I was only tolling. I thought you were dead."

It was his first visit to the big city and the small-town country boy didn't like everything that he saw. "I ain't going to pay my good money for this little pigsty without even a window. Just because I'm from the country, don't think . . ."

"Get in, sir," said the bellboy, "get in. This isn't your room—this is just the elevator."

A salesman bought some Limburger cheese to eat in his hotel room. When he got ready to leave he still had about half of the cheese left. He didn't want to pack it, and he didn't want to leave it lying in the room.

Finally he removed a plant from its pot, buried the cheese, and replaced the plant. A few days later he received this telegram from the management of the hotel: "We give up; where did you put it?"

You can have those thick, luxurious hotel towels if you want them, but I prefer those old fashioned dinky things. They are easier to pack in your luggage.

It was a small hotel on upper Miami Beach and the young lady was on the roof taking a sun bath, clad only in a skimpy bathing suit. In looking around she discovered there were no tall buildings nearby where inquiring eyes could see her so she decided to take a real sun bath. Taking off her bathing suit and lying on her stomach she was enjoying herself when she heard footsteps approaching. She quickly grabbed a towel and looked up to see the hotel manager coming near.

"Young Lady," he said, "we don't mind you sun bathing up here but we do not allow nude bathing!"

"But," she protested, "there are no high buildings close enough to see me."

"I know," he said. "But you're lying on the skylight over the dining room."

Some years ago a hotel in Louisville adopted the custom of naming a room in the hotel for each winner of the Kentucky Derby. There is a Zev Room, a Gallant Fox Room, a Whirlaway Room, and so forth.

But after the 1946 Derby the management decided to abandon the practice. The winner that year was Assault.

When the businessman, after a particularly trying day, arrived at a hotel, the room clerk informed him there were no more rooms available.

"Look, son," said the businessman, "I've had a hard day and to-morrow will be even worse. Will $50 help you find a room for me?"

"I'm sorry, Sir. All our rooms are taken."

"Well," said the businessman, "if the President of the United States were coming here, would you have a room for him?"

"Oh, yes, sir," answered the clerk.

"I've got news for you. He isn't coming, so you can give me his room!"

Hunting

The member of a hunting party had been specifically requested to bring only male hounds. One indignant member, however, owned only a female, and out of courtesy was finally permitted to include her. The pack was off in a flash. In a matter of seconds they were completely out of sight. The confused hunters stopped to question a farmer in a nearby field.

"Did you see some hounds go by here?"

"Yep," said the farmer.

"See where they went?"

"Nope," was the reply, "but it was the first time I ever seen a fox runnin' fifth!"

"I ain't impressed," announced the old hunter, "with any of the stories about people hittin' game from a triflin' 300 or 400 yards. Why, one day I was a-slouchin' along the trail when these old telescope eyes spots a nice buck. I rammed a charge down the gun barrel, then some wadding and a couple of ounces of salt. Then I let 'er fly—BANG—and that old buck dropped."

"That's very interesting," an old crony remarked, "but why the salt?"

"Shucks, bud, that deer was so far off I had to do somethin' to keep the meat from spoilin' before I could get there."

A big game hunter was captured by jungle headhunters whose chief interest in life seemed to be shrinking heads. He was thought lost forever but two years later he managed to escape. His first action after reaching civilization was to phone his wife:

"I need some clothes," he told her. "The headhunters fed me, but my clothing is in tatters. Send me some shirts, size 16 and a suit, size 38 and some socks, size 11½."

"Anything else?" asked the wife.

"Oh, yes," said the husband. "I need a hat, size one!"

The mighty hunter was not as good a shot as he pictured himself when relating his adventures. But what he lacked in ability, he made up in confidence.

Duck hunting with some friends, he sighted his game within easy shooting distance. As his shotgun blasted the morning stillness, the duck flew squawking away.

"Fly on, you fool bird," shouted the hunter. "Fly on with your stubborn heart shot out."

As the purchasing agent walked in the front door of his house, he was confronted by his angry wife: "Jim, one of those pheasants you were hunting last fall called up today and left her telephone number."

You've no doubt heard about the disgusted deer hunter who went out on his first deer hunt. He found a good spot where several trails crossed and sat down for a little action. He waited hour after hour. And just about sunset he spotted a deer within rifle range coming along one of the trails.

He took two quick shots. By the time he got the cork back in the bottle, the deer was gone.

Two men, one a teetotaler, the other an alcoholic, went duck hunting. The teetotaler took along a thermos jug of tea. The alcoholic, of course, took his "fifth."

All day they sat in the cold wet duck blind without a chance at a shot. The teetotaler's tea was almost gone. His friend was enjoying a drunken doze with the empty fifth at his side.

Suddenly a lone duck appeared above. The tea drinker raised his gun and fired. A complete miss! This aroused the drunk who grabbed his gun and dropped the duck with one shot.

"That's something," said the sober one. "You, likkered up, outshoot me."

"Aw, I don't think I wash so damn good," said the soak "Usually when I shoot into a flock like that I get three or four."

A father was telling his son what a good shot he was and probably exaggerated the truth somewhat. However, to prove his point, he took the boy out duck hunting with him one day. Ducks were scarce but finally a lone duck flew overhead and the father took careful aim and fired. The duck kept right on going. Turning to the boy he said: "Son, you've just witnessed a miracle. There flies a dead duck."

"Is it true that wild beasts of the jungle will not harm you if you carry a torch?"

"It all depends," answered the practical explorer, "on how fast you carry it."

Husband (see Wives, Marriage, Family)

"City Hall," said the switchboard operator, answering a call. There was no sound on the other end of the line. "City Hall," the operator repeated. Still no reply.

Finally, after the third time, a rather nervous female voice said: "Is this really City Hall?"

"That's right, madam," said the operator. "With whom do you wish to speak?"

There was silence. Then the female voice said softly, "I guess nobody. I just found this number in my husband's pocket."

The foreman's wife firmly believed that every man should have one night out alone each week, and she decreed that Thursday was the day. So every Thursday, rain or shine, he went out. One Thursday he went out as usual, but didn't show up for exactly five years. That Thursday he walked in just as if nothing had happened. His wife was so overjoyed to see him that she immediately began telephoning all her friends.

"What do you think you're doing," asked the foreman suspiciously.

"I'm calling all our friends to arrange a welcome home party for you," answered his wife.

"No you're not," he growled. "Not on my night out!"

Wonder if anybody reads the ads on paper match books except wives who are curious about their husbands' meanderings?

Two spinsters spent an afternoon together, sewing. "Last week," one of them confided, "I advertised in the paper for a husband."

"You don't mean it!" exclaimed the other, excitedly. "Did you have any replies?"

"Hundreds of them," was the answer. "And they were all the same. They all said, 'You can have mine.'"

"Mrs. Smith seems to have gotten over the death of her first husband."

"Yes, but her second husband hasn't."

WOMAN (*to floorwalker*): "I was to meet my husband here two hours ago. Have you seen him?"

FLOORWALKER: "Anything distinctive about him?"

WOMAN: "Well, by this time, he's probably purple."

FIRST SHOPPER: "Hello, you seem to be busy."

SECOND SHOPPER: "Yes, I'm trying to get something for my husband."

FIRST SHOPPER: "Have you had any offers yet?"

"You say this woman shot her husband with this pistol, and at close range?" asked the coroner of the eye-witness to the tragedy.

"Yes, sir."

"Were there powder marks on his face?"

"Yes, sir; that's why she shot him!"

A husband is a man who wishes he had as much fun when he is out as his wife thinks he does.

A wife and husband were asleep. About 2 A.M. the wife dreamed she was in another man's arms. Then she dreamed she saw her husband coming toward her. In her sleep she shrieked out loud, "My husband!"

Her husband beside her was awakened by her cry and leaped out the window.

"I understand you want to see me about your husband. Just what is the matter with him?" asked the psychiatrist.

"He's always washing the car," the woman pathetically replied.

"There's nothing wrong with that," said the doctor. "Lots of husbands like to wash their cars."

"In the bathtub?" queried the woman.

The average husband is 42 around the chest, 42 around the waist, 96 around the course—and a nuisance around the house.

"What does your husband like for breakfast?" asked the neighbor. "Oh, anything I don't happen to have in the house."

"My husband runs around at night. Can you suggest a way to keep him at home?" asked the pretty wife.

"Some use flatirons, others hammers. Personally, I think you would do best with a black negligee."

A henpecked husband was being examined during a court trial. "Do you mean to tell me that you've always treated your wife with respect?" asked the examiner.

"Always," replied the husband.

"And you've never spoken harshly to her?"

The man paused a moment and the attorney, quick to seize his opportunity, said, "Be careful how you answer."

"Well," said the husband. "I do recall I yelled once to 'Put down that poker.'"

"I heard your husband is in the hospital. What's the trouble?"

"It's his knee. I found a strange woman on it."

"Where's that pretty blonde who was passing out cocktails a minute ago?"

"Oh, you looking for a drink, lady?"

"No, I'm looking for my husband."

"Doctor, I wish you would see my husband. He blows smoke rings from his nose, and I'm terribly frightened."

PSYCHIATRIST: "Well, that's a bit unusual that he blows them from his nose, but it's nothing to be alarmed about; many smokers blow smoke rings by the hour."

"I know, doctor, but my husband doesn't smoke."

SON: "Father, why was Adam made first?"

FATHER: "To give him a chance to say a few words."

A henpecked husband was terribly disappointed when his wife gave birth to a baby daughter.

He confided to a friend: "I was hoping for a boy to help me with the housework."

FATHER: "Now, kids, tell me which one of the family was the most obedient during the past month and did everything mother asked?"

CHILDREN: "You, Daddy."

MRS. BLACK: "Emily's husband must smoke a great deal—I heard him say he always smokes three cigars after a good dinner."

MRS. WHITE: "My dear, I don't believe he smokes more than three cigars a month."

A mother hopes that her daughter will get a better man than she did, but she knows that her son will never get as good a wife as his father did.

What's wrong with women buying their husbands Mother's Day gifts? If it weren't for husbands, they wouldn't be mothers.

"What shall I do?" wailed the bride-to-be. "I'm engaged to a man who just cannot bear children."

"Well," remarked the kindly old lady. "You mustn't expect too much of a husband."

"I want a birthday present for my husband."

"How long have you been married?"

"Twelve years."

"Bargain basement is one floor below."

Maybe you'll never be as big a hero as your son thinks you are, but you'll never be as big a fool as your wife thinks you are either.

"Do you know I caught my husband flirting?"

"Well of all things! That's the way I caught mine, too."

"What," said the visitor, "do you have in that lovely vase on the mantel?"

"My husband's ashes," she replied.

"Oh, I'm so sorry," was the embarrassed rejoinder. "I didn't know that he had died."

"Dead? Who's dead? The bum's just too lazy to look for an ashtray."

GINGER: "Isn't your husband wearing a new suit?"

PEACHY: "No."

GINGER: "He looks different."

PEACHY: "He's a new husband."

A husband returning home unusually late was tiptoeing into his bedroom when his wife woke up. "Is that you, John?" she asked.

"Well," he answered, "it better be."

JUDGE: "What do you wish to charge against your husband?"

WIFE: "Free love, Your Honor. He ain't supported me for six years."

A husband, complaining about the food he was getting at home, was met with a strong argument by his wife.

"What's the matter with you?" she demanded. "Monday you like veal cutlets, Tuesday you like veal cutlets, Wednesday you like veal cutlets, now Thursday, all of a sudden, you don't like veal cutlets."

The occasion was an amateur musicale. The kind-hearted hostess spied a lonely-looking little man huddled in a corner of the room and paused to make conversation.

"Tell me," she asked, "do you play any musical instrument?"

"Not away from home," he replied.

"What instrument do you play at home?"

"Second fiddle," he husband replied.

Visitor, noting array of books: "Is your husband a book worm?"

"No," replied the wife, "he is just the ordinary kind."

Hypocrite

A hypocrite is a fellow who isn't himself on Sundays.

Income—Salary

He had a good job, but his wife complained because his average income was around midnight.

The progress civilization has made so far has been due largely to man's insistence on living beyond his income.

"Honey," said the husband, "I'd be the happiest man in the world if you could bake bread like my mother used to bake."

"I know," his wife agreed thoughtfully. "But you know, dear, you would make me the happiest woman alive if you could just make dough like my dad used to."

The conductor never let his wife know what he earned, but one day he was ill she picked up his check.

"John, I never realized that you made all that money!" she exclaimed.

He was equal to the occasion.

"There's really not much left for me," he explained, "after I finish paying for the engineer, the fireman and the brakeman."

JONES: "How do you spend your income?"

JOHNSON: "About 30 per cent for shelter, 30 per cent for clothing, 40 per cent for food, and 20 per cent for recreation and fun."

JONES: "But that adds up to 120 per cent!"

JOHNSON: "Don't I know it!"

SECRETARY *(to boss):* "The rat race being what it is, I could use more cheese each week."

"I'll have to have a raise, sir," said the bookkeeper. "There are three companies after me."

"What three?" demanded his boss.

"Light, telephone and water," was the reply.

Infidelity

The traveling husband had been suspecting his wife for some time. One week he slipped into town on Thursday night instead of Friday.

He crept silently up to the bedroom. Sure enough, there was a strange man with his wife. Both were blissfully asleep.

The husband silently retraced his steps down stairs and out of the house, returning shortly with a huge flat rock. Again he climbs the stairs, and with great care, placed the huge flat rock squarely on the stomach of the strange man, and quietly left.

Presently the intruding man awoke. Feeling the weight on his stomach, he looked and was startled and mystified. Climbing laboriously out of bed, he held the big rock to him and carried it to the open window.

Just as he heaved it out, with a mighty effort, he noticed a large penciled note attached to the underside of the huge flat rock, which read: "You have 2 seconds to cut this string."

The jealous husband returned home from a business trip a day early and, discovering a strange coat in the front closet, stormed into the living room with the accusation that there was another man in the apartment.

"Where is he?" the husband demanded, as he stalked from room to room, searching.

"You're mistaken, dear," the wife insisted. "That coat must have been left by one of your friends the last time you threw a poker party. Since you've been gone, I haven't seen or looked at another man."

The husband searched through the entire apartment and, finding no one, decided his wife must be telling the truth. Apologizing for his unwarranted display of temper, he then went to the bathroom to wash up. He was running water in the basin, when he noticed that the shower curtain was pulled closed. Rather peculiar, he thought. He ripped the curtain open and

—sure enough—there was a strange man. But before the astounded husband could utter a word, the man jerked the curtain closed again, saying, "Please! I haven't finished voting yet."

"I feel I ought to warn you that my husband will be home in less than an hour."
"But I've done nothing I shouldn't do."
"Well, I just wanted to warn you."

A woman believed her husband was having an affair with his secretary, but was unable to prove it, so hired a detective. She said, "My husband loves golf, and I don't play, so I have agreed that he could play a round every Tuesday with his secretary. I want you to follow them and see if they stick to golf."
A few weeks later the detective came back and said, "You were right. I followed them for two rounds, and every time your husband sliced into some woods on the third hole. His secretary went into the woods to help him find the ball, and they stayed quite a while."
"Did you follow them into the woods?"
"Certainly. I watched every move they made, and have definite proof."
"Can you give me an idea of how long this has been going on?"
"Not exactly, but from the number of freckles on his back, it must have been going on all season."

Inflation

Inflation is being broke with a lot of money in your pocket.

1942: You went broke, so you ate hamburgers for a week.
1965: You ate hamburgers for a week, so you went broke.

Insane—Insanity

It is now rather clear that insanity IS hereditary—parents get it from their children.

VISITOR AT ASYLUM: "Do you have to keep the women inmates separated from the men?"
ATTENDANT: "Sure. The people here ain't as crazy as you think!"

A poker player went crazy and was sent to an asylum. For years he was served toast for breakfast. He always looked at the toast, sneered "I pass!" and pushed it aside.

One morning they served him raisin toast—just one raisin in the middle of the slice. Looking at the toast excitedly, he yelled, "I open with aces!"

MEDIC: "Is there any insanity in your family?"
BILL: "Yes, I'm afraid there is. They keep writing me for money."

PASSENGER: "Conductor, that fellow opposite is a lunatic and is scaring my wife and children. He claims he is George Washington."
CONDUCTOR: "I'll take care of it. *(Shouting)* Next station, Mount Vernon!"

An attendant in a mental home was making his evening rounds when he came upon one of the patients industriously fishing in a wash basin with a rod and line.

Wishing to humor the man, the attendant asked him if he had caught anything.

"What!" said the patient. "In a wash basin? Are you crazy?"

In a mental institution one patient suffered under a compulsion to tear off his clothes. The doctor offered him a reward of 10 cents for each day he refrained from doing so.

The man kept his clothes on through Monday, Tuesday, Wednesday, Thursday, Friday and Saturday, but on Sunday he tore them off again. The doctor chided him for his relapse.

"Well," retorted the astonished patient, "you didn't think I was going to work on Sunday, did you?"

During a tour of a mental institution the visitor stopped to chat with one of the inmates. He noticed that the patient spoke quite intelligently and this caused him to ask why the man was there.

"It's because I prefer shoes to boots," was the reply.

The visitor was amazed. "But thousands of people prefer shoes to boots," he said. "As a matter of fact I do myself."

"Yes, I know that," replied the inmate, "but how do you like them—fried or boiled?"

An inmate of an asylum stood inside a high wire fence watching a neighboring farmer cultivate his strawberry patch.

"What's that you're putting on your strawberries?" he finally asked.

"That's manure," replied the farmer.

"Manure!" exclaimed the nut. "We put cream and sugar on ours and they think we're crazy!"

Insects—Insecticide

"Oh, I feel so stupid," said one glow-worm to another. "I've been talking to a cigarette butt for the last five minutes."

There's a new insecticide for flies—half DDT and half Spanish Fly. It doesn't exactly kill the flies, but you get two with every swat!

Insurance

JANE: "Alice, where did you get that fur coat?"
ALICE: "Just a piece of good luck; George fell and broke his leg and the insurance company sent us the money."

The insurance salesman had the sale wrapped up and was just completing the application. "Now, let's see," he said, "this is to be monthly payments on a straight life. That's what you wanted, isn't it?"
"Well," replied the customer somewhat wistfully, "I would like to fool around a little on Saturday nights."

Some weeks after receiving $800 compensation for the loss of her jewelry, an elderly woman informed her insurance representative that the missing property had turned up in a cupboard.
"I didn't think it would be fair to keep both the jewels and the money, so I thought you would be pleased to know that I have sent the $800 to the Red Cross," she wrote.

A farmer's barn burned down and the agent for the insurance company, explaining the policy that covered the structure, told him that his firm would build another barn of similar size instead of paying the claim in cash. The farmer was furious. "If that's the way your company does business," he exploded, "you can cancel the insurance policy on my wife."

A wealthy client insured her wardrobe while traveling in Europe. Upon reaching London she found an article missing and immediately cabled her agent in New York. "Gown Lifted in London."
The agent replied, after deliberation, "What do you think our policy covers?"

An applicant for an insurance policy turned in his completed form. The agent looked it over. "This seems in order, Mr. Jones," he said, "except for one thing. When it asks for the relationship of Mrs. Jones to you, you should have said 'wife' not 'strained.'"

Two vacationing businessmen were comparing notes on the beach in Hawaii. One said: "I got $100,000 for flood damage."

There was a long, thoughtful pause. Then the other man said, "Tell me, how do you start a flood?"

The life insurance salesman thought he was on to a good prospect. He explained the policy to the man, drew out his fountain pen and pointed to the dotted line on the application. The man signed.

"Now, who would you like to be your beneficiary?" asked the salesman.

"Myself," replied the man. "I believe in reincarnation."

JUDGE: "What proof have you that your client is insane?"

ATTORNEY: "Your honor, he thinks he knows just what his insurance policies cover."

It seems that a persuasive insurance salesman had sold a policy to the father of an uneducated mountaineer. The payments came through the mail for seven years, then they suddenly stopped.

The insurance company sent several formal notices, then received this explanation.

"Dere Sirs: Pleze excuse the stoppage of payments on Ben. We can't pay his insurance because he died last September."

An insurance salesman was about to write up a policy. The prospect said he recognized the need, meant to buy, but was inclined to wait awhile. "Later," he said. "Come back in June."

The insurance man's hand was on the doorknob, and as he was leaving he asked: "Whom shall I ask for if you're not here in June?"

Jokes

FATHER: "Junior, would you like to hear a little story?"

FIVE-YEAR-OLD JUNIOR: "Sure, Pop, but keep it clean. Mom might be listening."

When telling an allegedly funny story, always make it as short as possible. If you build it up and stretch it out, you give your listener time to think of a worse one to tell you.

Two practical jokers shared a hotel room at a big convention in Chicago. One sneaked in early the second night, filled the bathtub and deposited therein two live ducks he had procured after a long search. His companion was properly flabbergasted when he saw the ducks paddling about in the tub.

"They must have flown in through the window while we were out," surmised the jokester.

"Sure, sure," agreed his friend, "but what bugs me is, how the dickens did they turn on the water?"

Judgment

Two men were hotly discussing the merits of a book. Finally one of them, himself an author, said to the other:

"No, John, you can't appreciate it. You never wrote a book yourself."

"No," retorted John, "and I never laid an egg, but I'm a better judge of an omelet than any hen in the state."

Don't forget that people judge you by your actions, not your intentions. You may have a heart of gold, but so does a hard-boiled egg.

Landlord

A housewife answered her doorbell to find a man collecting money for a poor woman in the block. He said the old woman owed for coal and groceries and was about to be evicted because she owed four months' rent.

"Sir," the housewife said, "it's nice of you to take it on yourself to get money for the poor woman. Who are you?"

"I'm the landlord," the man answered.

Language

HELEN: "Has your boy friend's English improved any?"
MARY: "No, he still ends every sentence with a proposition."

YOUNGSTER: "Why do they call it the 'mother tongue'?"
DAD (cryptically): "Who uses it most?"

Laundries

A lady who had been having trouble with commercial laundries shrinking her wash found a huge railroad spike and tied a tag on it bearing the words, "Try and shrink this!"

When her laundry returned she opened it and found a small carpet tack in it. There was a tag attached to it. It read,
"We did!"

Leader

The trouble with being leader today is that you can't be sure whether people are following you or chasing you.

Life–Living

The ladder of life is full of splinters, but you never realize it until you begin to slide down.

Life must be worth living. The cost has doubled and we still hang on.

Life is cruel to men. When they're born, their mothers get compliments and flowers; when they get married, the bride gets presents and publicity; and when they die, their wives get the insurance and the sympathy.

You can preach a better sermon with your life than your voice.

We should live and learn; but by the time we've learned, it's usually too late to live.

If you think the world owes you a living, hustle out and collect it.

Doubtfully the young mother examined the toy. "Isn't this rather complicated for a small child?" she asked.
"It's an educational toy, madam," replied the clerk. "It's designed to adjust a child to live in the world of today. Any way he puts it together, it's wrong."

The modern idea of roughing it is to sleep without an electric blanket.

Living in the past has one thing in its favor—it's cheaper.

Lifeguard

A man six feet eight inches tall applied for a job as a lifeguard.
"Can you swim?" asked the pool manager.
"No," he replied, "but I sure can wade."

Loan

If you have tried lately to borrow a couple of bucks 'til Saturday, you've found that all the untouchables don't live in India.

The owner of a financially tottering business had approached the president of his local bank for a $100,000 loan. "That's a lot of money," said the president. "Can you give me a statement?"

"Yes," said the businessman. "I'm optimistic."

The small businessman asked his brother for a loan. The brother was happy to accommodate—for 9% interest. "Well," said the businessman, "I ain't kicking, but what will our poor dead father say when he sees his own flesh and blood gouging 9% interest from his brother?"

"I wouldn't worry," replied the brother. "From where Pa is it will look like 6%."

An Indian came into a bank and asked about a loan for $200.

"And what security have you?"

"Got 200 horses."

This seemed sufficient security and the loan was made. Later, the Indian came back with $2,200 in cash, paid off the note and started to leave.

"Why not let me take care of that $2,000 for you?"

Looking the banker straight in the eye, the Indian asked,

"How many horses you got?"

The tycoon and his friend had stopped off for a bit of "cold remedy" before going home. As they leaned against the bar, a gunman rushed in and commanded everyone to empty their pockets. In a flash, the tycoon pulled a bill out of his pocket and handed it to his friend.

"Joe," he said, "here's that $100 you lent me last week."

Love

The American girl, while visiting in Paris, met a charming French girl and their conversation turned to the ever interesting subject of love. "The Frenchman is very subtle in his love-making," explained the little Parisian. "First he kisses your fingertips, then your shoulders, then your ear, then the back of your neck . . ." Her American companion interrupted: "Gosh, by that time an American is back from his honeymoon."

Platonic love is like being invited down to the cellar for a bottle of ginger ale.

When Lem was a strapping young fella in his twenties he married a beautiful gal, but as the years went by she became pretty messy, not only in her looks but with her household chores as well. Lem was sick of it, but he didn't have enough grounds for divorce, so he decided to kill her. He talked to his neighbor Otis about it.

"Love her to death," advised Otis. "First thing in the morning, make love to her. When you come home to lunch, make love to her. When you come home to dinner, make love to her. If you get the chance, run home during the afternoon and make love to her. Follow my advice and she'll be dead in six months."

Five months went by and Otis hadn't seen Lem. He decided to go over and investigate. He found Lem hunched over in his rocker, pale and wan, looking twenty years older and seventy pounds lighter.

"Are you sick?" Otis asked anxiously.

"Naw," said Lem. "Naw, but just listen to my old woman out there in the kitchen singing and slinging the pots and pans around. The damn fool don't know she's only gonna live another month!"

Mail

The owner of a small crossroad store in South Carolina was appointed postmaster. For six months not a single piece of mail left the town. Deeply concerned, postal authorities in Washington wrote to inquire why.

They received this terse explanation:

"The bag ain't full yet."

Manners

A vivacious young Texan shocked her Boston-reared beau by drawing on her gloves as they started down the street on their first date.

"Where I come from," chided the young man, "people would as soon see a woman put on her stockings in public as her gloves."

"Where I come from," retorted the young lady, " they'd rather."

Etiquette is knowing which finger to put in your mouth when you whistle for the waiter.

French explorers pushing through dense African jungles came upon a party of cannibals about to have a feast on a late enemy. The cannibal chief greeted them in perfect French. When they showed surprise, he explained that he had studied in France, including two years of literature at the Sorbonne.

"You've been educated in France," exclaimed the explorers, "and you return to feed on human flesh?"

The chief replied, "Now I use a fork."

Marriage (see Husbands, Wives, Old Maids, Courtship, Divorce)

She married him for life and later discovered he didn't have any.

"My husband has no idea what I go through when he snores."
"Mine never misses his small change either."

HUSBAND: "Darling, if I had it to do over again, do you know whom I'd marry?"
WIFE: "No, I don't. Who?"
HUSBAND: "You, dear."
WIFE: "Oh, no, you wouldn't."

"There's a mutual feeling between my wife and I."
"That's nice."
"No, it isn't. We hate each other!"

The man who says marriage is a 50-50 proposition doesn't understand women . . . or fractions . . . or both.

Sad thought: By the time a man finally understands women, his wife won't let him out of the house at night and he's too old to care anyway.

A man with a little black bag knocked at a dilapidated home.
"Come in, come in," said the father of fourteen children, "and I sure hope you're the piano tuner."

All marriages are happy. It's the living together afterwards that causes all the trouble.

BILL: "Do you still act toward your wife the same as you did before you were married?"
BOB: "Just the same. I remember when I first fell in love with her. I would lean over the fence in front of her house and gaze at her shadow on the curtain, afraid to go in. And I act exactly the same way now."

"You promised me before we were married that you would never look at another woman," said his wife.
"Oh," he replied, "I thought you understood it was only a campaign promise."

A man and his wife were in the midst of a heated argument, when she suddenly broke in and said: "There's no use discussing things with you any more. We can't agree on a single thing."

"You're wrong there," he said. "For instance, if we walked into a room with two beds in it, a woman in one and a man in the other, in which would you choose to sleep?"

"Why, with the lady, of course," she replied.

"You see? We agree."

Marriage entitles women to the protection of strong men who steady the stepladder for them while they wash the kitchen walls.

"Do you believe marriage is a lottery?"

"No. In a lottery a man is supposed to have a chance."

Any man who thinks he's more intelligent than his wife is married to a smart woman.

Call marriage a union if you choose
But why must the man pay all the dues?

Bachelors have no idea what married bliss is. And that's true of a lot of married men, too.

"Dad," asked the small boy. "Why is a man not allowed to have more than one wife?"

"My son," replied the father, "when you are older you will realize that the law protects those who are incapable of protecting themselves."

WIFE: "Every time you see a pretty girl, you forget you're married."

HUSBAND: "No, you're wrong, my dear. Nothing brings home the fact so forcibly."

"For managers and overseers," proclaimed a geat Chinese land-owner, "always give me married men."

"For what reason?" a visitor asked.

"Because," said the Chinese, "I abhor the muddled, unclear reports that have been sent in to me by bachelors. They have never had to explain anything to a wife."

Ever notice that before marriage the girl gets into her boy friend's wallet on a picture, but after marriage she gets into his wallet . . . period.

"What did your wife say when you came in intoxicated last night?"

"Nothing. And I was going to have those front teeth pulled anyway."

MAIZIE: "When George and I get married, we're going to Bali Bali to see what it's like."

DAIZIE: "Silly! It's the same wherever you go!"

Matrimony is one state that permits a woman to work 18 hours a day.

She married him for better or for worse—but not for good.

Happiness in marriage may depend upon whether the parties consider a wedding ring a symbol of love and affection or a place for staging fights.

When John and his wife have a few words, they send the kids out to play. Man! Are those kids ever sunburned!

There's one advantage to being married; you can't make a fool out of yourself without knowing it.

Marriage is something that reduces bushels of kisses to a few little pecks.

A farmer's wife had lost all semblance of sanity and it was necessary to remove her from her home to a nearby institution.

In trying to explain her sudden loss of sanity, her husband said he just couldn't understand it. "Why, nobody ever bothered her," he said. "She hasn't been out of the kitchen in nearly 20 years."

"Not really, Jack! But how did you get that heiress to marry you?"

"Simple. I gave her 25 roses on her 33rd birthday."

SUZY: "You deceived me before we were married. You told me you were well off."

JIMMY: "I was, but I didn't know it."

A woman rushed into a marriage license bureau waving a sheet of paper. "Did you, or did you not, issue me this license to marry Jim Macomber?"

"I sure did," replied the registrar.

"Well," snapped the woman, "what are you going to do about it? He's escaped!"

A young up-and-coming starlet was revealing her views on marriage to an interviewer.

"Love is more important to me than money," she said solemnly. "I intend to wait until the right millionaire comes along."

He's always troubled with five o'clock shadow. Every time he goes out after five o'clock, his wife shadows him.

Bub: "But, Dad, don't you believe two can live as cheaply as one?"
Dad: "Sure, your mother and I are living as cheaply as you."

A very sick man said to his wife: "After I die, I wish you'd marry Deacon Brown."
Wife: "Why so, Hiram?"
Hubby: "Well, the deacon trimmed me on a horse trade once."

"Joe, you look all-in today. What's the trouble?"
"Well, I didn't get home until after daylight, and I was just undressing when my wife woke up and said: 'Aren't you getting up pretty early?' Rather than start an argument I just put on my clothes and came down to the office."

All the lights in the house suddenly went out, so Mad and Pa went down to the cellar to investigate. "Put your hand on this wire, Ma," ordered Pa, "and tell me if you feel anythin'."
"Good," said Pa. "Now just don't touch the other one, or you'll most likely drop dead."

"I can't marry you," said the justice of the peace. "This girl is only 17 and you'll have to get her father's consent."
"Consent!" yelled the groom-to-be. "Say, who do you think this old guy with the rifle is, Daniel Boone?"

He: "My wife worships me."
Him: "Is that so?"
He: "Yeah, she places burnt offerings before me every evening."

A fellow finally quits horsing around when some dreamy-eyed filly makes a groom out of him.

It isn't tying himself to one woman that a man dreads when he thinks of marriage, it's separating himself from all the others.

Grandma was giving the recent bride a heart to heart talk.
"Child, I hope your lot's goin' t' be easier than mine," she said. "All my wedded days I've carried two burdens—Pa and the fire. Every time I've turned to look at one, the other has gone out."

A widow married her late husband's brother very soon after his death. Her neighbors considered this quite indecent. But she did have the kindness to hang a picture of her departed mate in the parlor. One day a stranger asked her: "Tell me, who is the distinguished-looking gentleman?" nodding toward the picture.

"Oh," said the recently remarried lady, "that's my poor brother-in-law. He passed away recently."

A husband and wife were in sharp disagreement over what suit he should purchase. Finally, the wife relented and said:

"Well, go ahead and please yourself. After all, you're the one who will wear it."

In a meek voice the man replied, "Well, dear, I did figure that I'd probably be wearing the coat and vest anyway."

Psychiatrists say girls tend to marry men like their fathers. Now we know why mothers cry at weddings.

Said a small boy: "My maw and paw had an awful time getting married. Maw wouldn't marry paw when he was drunk, and paw wouldn't marry maw when he was sober."

A young girl, talking to her grandfather, asked, "Grandfather, how old does a girl have to be to get married?"

GRANDFATHER: "She must be old enough, yet young enough, big enough, yet little enough, wise enough, yet dumb enough, weak enough, yet strong enough, to chase a man until he catches her."

A fellow ran into the fire engine house and very excitedly shouted: "I'm sorry to bother you, but my wife has disappeared again."

"That's too bad," sympathized the captain of the station, "but why tell us? Why not notify the police?"

"Well, I'll tell you," explained the bothered man. "I told the police the last time she disappeared, and they went out and found her."

"How are you getting on at home since your wife went away?"

"Fine, I've reached the highest point of efficiency. I can put my socks on from either end."

When Joe learned of the birth of his first grandchild, a friend asked how it felt to be a grandfather. "It's good news, of course," Joe replied, "but I'll have to get used to the idea of being married to a grandmother."

FIRST MAN: "The greatest person who ever lived was Huggins—brilliant, broadminded, tolerant, generous, temperate; yet he died with his talents unsuspected."

SECOND MAN: "How did you manage to find out about him?"

FIRST MAN: "I married his widow."

Marriage is just another union that defies management.

The husband was trying to get himself out of trouble with his wife. "I did not say you were built like a truck. I merely said people were afraid to pass you on the right."

Yesterday I cleaned my shotgun on the front porch and today my daughter had eight proposals.

After the hillbilly wedding, one of the local citizens approached the bride's father and said: "Hey, Zeke, your son-in-law marched up to the altar as though he had lead in his pants!"

Zeke shifted his chaw of tobacco, spat out of the side of his mouth and replied: "He did."

Marriage License

In a rural courthouse, the clerk puts this sign over the marriage license window at lunch time: "Back at 1 o'clock—think it over!"

Martian

A Martian landed in Las Vegas and watched people playing slot machines. The Martian finally went up to a machine and said, "I don't know what office you're running for but try to smile a little more when you shake hands."

The space ship from Mars landed in Las Vegas about the time a slot machine addict hit the jackpot.

As the shower of half dollars rolled out of the machine a Maritan stepped up to it, patted it tenderly and remarked:

"Buddy, you'd better do something about that cold."

The Britisher, who was having tea on his lawn, calmly watched the space ship as it came to earth a few yards away.

He watched intently as a weird-looking creature stepped from the craft and slowly approached him. The thing had two heads, with one eye in the center of each head. It had only one arm that protruded from the middle of its chest, and instead of legs, it walked on a pair of short flippers.

"Earthman," the apparition squeaked, "I want to see your leader."

The Englishman stirred his tea, and gazed with cool distaste at his strange visitor.

"Nonsense, old man," he said, "what you want to see is a plastic surgeon."

Masquerade

The masquerade was in full swing. There was some confusion regarding the character one of the guests represented. He was attired in a Roman toga, with appropriate etceteras. "Pardon me," ventured an inquisitive dancer, "you're Titus Andronicus, aren't you?"

"What!" roared the Roman indignantly, "the very idea! Why, man alive, I haven't even discovered where the bar is yet!"

The nudists planned a masquerade and the ladies worried over what they should wear. "Well" said one, "with my varicose veins I think I'll go as a road map."

> I knew a cute girl from St. Paul
> Who wore a newspaper dress to a ball,
> Someone set it afire, and burned her entire
> Front page, sport section and all.

Memory

WIFE: "Do you have a good memory for faces, dear?"
HUSBAND: "Of course I have."
WIFE: "That's good, I just dropped your shaving mirror."

Memory is what tells a man his wedding anniversary was yesterday.

Men

It seems that when the Creator was making the world, he called Man aside and bestowed upon him 20 years of normal sex life. Man was horrified. "Only 20 years?" But the Creator didn't budge. That was all he would give him.

The he called the Monkey and gave him 20 years. "But I don't need 20 years," the monkey protested. "Ten is plenty." Man spoke up and said, "Can I have the other 10 years?" The monkey graciously agreed.

Then he called the Lion and gave him 20 years. The Lion too, only needed 10 years. Again Man asked, "Can I have the other 10 years?" The Lion roared, "Of course."

Then came the Donkey. He was given 20 years, but like the others, 10 years was enough. Man asked for the spare 10 and got them.

This explains why Man has 20 years of normal sex life, 10 years of monkeying around, 10 years of Lion about it, and 10 years of making an Ass of himself.

Adam . . . the one man in the world who couldn't say, "Pardon me, but haven't I seen you before?"

In a genteel and fashionable tea room in Boston, two youngish spinsters were overheard discussing a matrimonial prospect over cinnamon toast.

"I know he is rich," said the first, "but isn't he too old to be considered eligible?"

"My dear," replied her friend with a sigh, "he's too eligible to be considered old."

There are three kinds of men in this country—the intellectual, the handsome and the majority.

"Miss Jones," said the exasperated professor, "the quotation is, 'All men are created equal,' and not, 'All men are made the same way.'"

Sugar Daddy: A form of crystalized sap.

Old Wolves? They never die . . . their eyesight fades away!

Middle Age (see Old Age, Youth, Age)

Middle age is that age when your friends get so stout and bald they can't recognize you.

You're middle-aged when the telephone rings and you hope it's not for you.

By the time in life when you can afford champagne, you're so tired you wish you were home—alone.

There was the middle-aged man who married a girl half his age. He didn't know whether to take her on a honeymoon or send her to camp.

It's a sign of middle age when a man looks back and thinks how reckless he used to be and how narrow his escapes were.

Middle age is when a night out is followed by a day in.

When we were young we used to think money was the most important thing in life. Now that we're middle-aged, we're sure of it.

You've reached middle age when your wife tells you to pull in your stomach—and you already have.

Growing old is a bad habit. A busy man never gets it.

> It's sad for a girl to reach the age
> Where men consider her charmless;
> But it's worse for a man to attain the age
> When girls consider him harmless.

Forty-five is said to be the prettiest age for women. But whoever heard of a woman that old!

Every young man starts out in life expecting to find a pot of gold at the end of the rainbow. By the time they are middle-aged, most of them at least have found the pot.

At the age of twenty, we don't care what the world thinks of us; at thirty we worry about what it is thinking of us; at forty we discover that it wasn't thinking of us at all.

We call it middle age because that's where it shows first.

Middle age is the period of life when you'd do anything to feel better, except give up what's hurting you.

> Men are like wine,
> Aged in wood;
> Age sours the bad,
> Betters the good.

We're as old as we feel, sad to say.

You've reached middle age when a doctor tells you to slow down instead of a policeman.

The trouble with life is that by the time a fellow gets to be an old hand at the game, he starts to lose his grip.

About the time you learn to make the most of life, the most of it is gone.

As we grow older, we find the best time for a cold shower is some other time.

A fly was walking with her daughter on the head of a middle-aged man who was very bald.

"How things have changed, my dear," she said. "When I was your age, this was only a footpath."

You've reached middle age when your spending money goes for health remedies rather than drinks for a girl at the bar.

Middle age is when you don't care where you go, just so you're home by 9 P.M.

Most women will overlook a man's middle age bulge if he's got one in his hip pocket.

If you can't grow old gracefully, do it any way you can.

Middle age is when you've given up everything you can and still don't feel good.

Middle age is the period of life when children leave you one by one, only to return two by two.

Military

If you think old soldiers just fade away, try getting into your old army uniform.

A sailor was escorting a group of visitors through the battleship and as they passed a raised bronze plaque near the bridge, he lowered his voice in reverence and said: "This is where our brave captain fell."

"He should have," said one of the visitors. "I almost tripped over the darn thing myself."

Assigned guard duty, a Navy recruit had strict orders to admit no car unless it bore a special tag. He stopped a car carrying a high-ranking officer, who instructed his chauffeur: "Drive right through."

"Sorry, sir," said the recruit respectfully, "but I'm new at this. Do I shoot you or the driver?"

A milkman inducted into the Army wrote back home from camp:
"Bessie, I sure do like this Army life. It's nice to lie abed every morning until five thirty."

As he was drilling a batch of recruits the sergeant saw that one of them was marching out of step. Going to the man as they marched, he said sarcastically:
"Do you know they are all out of step except you?"
"What?" asked the recruit innocently.
"I said they are all out of step except you," repeated the sergeant.
"Well," was the retort, "you tell 'em. You're in charge."

"So you were brave and stepped forward when the Captain asked for a volunteer?"
"Well, not exactly. The rest of the company stepped back."

Colonel Blimp, all of 75, startled the community by marrying a girl of 18. A year later, when she presented him with a fine nine-pound son, the proud colonel assembled the entire regiment, mounted the band stand, cleared his throat, and announced. "I have called you all together to tell you that my wife gave birth this morning to a strapping baby boy. Gentlemen, I thank you."

The Russian soldier had been assigned to patrol duty in East Germany. Whenever he became lonely, he would stop a German and engage him in conversation, usually trying to stress the importance of his family's background.
"You know," he said to a German one night, "I come from a fighting family. My great-great-grandfather, great grandfather, grandfather and father were all fighting men. They fought in wars down through history."
The unimpressed German merely shrugged and asked: "What's the matter with your family? Don't they ever get along with other people?"

Lt. Colonel: "What are your objections to overseas duty?"
GI: "My wife is not pregnant, sir, and I don't want to leave her in that condition."

A commercial airline pilot was engaged in conversation at the airport by a man who identified himself as a former World War II pilot with the Japanese air force.
"What's your name?" inquired the commercial pilot.
"My name is Chow Mein," said the former warrior.
"And you said you were a Kamikaze pilot? How could that be? You were supposed to have gone on a suicide mission."
"My name is Chicken Chow Mein."

A very military major at an overseas post was discussing the evening's program with a troupe of show girls sent out to entertain his detachment.

". . . and," said the major, "at 1600 hours, if you like, you girls can mess with the enlisted men."

"Sure," answered a blonde, "but first we'll have to get something to eat."

"Tell me what you know about George Washington—was he a soldier or a sailor?"

"I think he was a soldier."

"Why do you think he was a soldier?"

"I saw a picture of him crossing the Delaware—and anybody who'd stand up in a rowboat ain't no sailor."

CHIEF: "I thought you said your locker contained nothing except clothes. What's that whiskey doing in it?"

SEAMAN: "Oh, that's my nightcap."

The old Army sergeant's voice was unusually calm and consoling as he spoke to the rookie. "You know, Jones, you and General Eisenhower have one achievement in common."

"We have?" The browbeaten recruit brightened.

"Yes. You've both reached the highest rank you'll ever get in the Army."

The squad of new recruits had just been taken onto the rifle range for practice, and one soldier in particular seemed to be hitting the bull's-eye quite often. After watching him for ten minutes or so, the Captain in charge called the Sergeant. "Better check up on that man, Sergeant," he said. "Every time he fires a shot he wipes off his fingerprints."

The janitor reported 10 minutes late for work and the manager asked: "What did they do in the Army when you were 10 minutes late in the morning?"

"Everytime I came in late," the janitor said, "they all stood up, saluted and said: 'Good morning, Colonel!' "

ARMY DOCTOR: "Any physical defects?"

RECRUIT: "Yes; no guts."

QUARTERMASTER SERGEANT TO ROOKIE: "Well, speak up there! How do you want your uniform—too big or too small?"

An icy voice cut into an uninhibited telephone conversation, "Do you know whom you are addressing?"

"No," said the sergeant.

"Well, this is Major Throckmorton."

"Major," said the sergeant, "do you know whom you are addressing?"

"NO!" thundered the major.

"Thank God!" said the sergeant and hung up.

The raw recruits were worse than ever that morning, much to the annoyance of the petty officer. He decided to make an example of the recruit named Black.

"Black!" he roared, "take two paces to the rear!"

Two men stepped out of the ranks. The petty officer glowered at the second man.

"Hey, you," he shouted. "Is your name Black, too?"

"No, Brown, sir," came the reply.

"Then are you deaf, mixed up or what?"

"No, color blind, sir."

A hard-fighting Marine outfit returned to the rear lines after several months of combat during which supply lines sometimes took a beating. Wandering among the men as they sat in the bivouac area eating chow was a war correspondent. He noticed a particularly hungry looking young leatherneck eating out of a mess kit with his fingers and walked up to him.

"What's the matter, fella, didn't they issue you a knife and fork?"

"Yeah," said the Marine, "and they were delicious."

A bright young farmer in the Army overseas received a letter from his wife. She wanted to know how she was going to plant the potatoes in the east 40 without help.

The soldier wrote back, "Whatever you do, don't dig up the east 40. That's where the guns are buried."

As is customary in wartime, his letter was read by the censor. Not long afterward he received a reply from his upset young wife saying, "A company of soldiers over-ran the east 40 and dug it all up. What shall I do now?"

"Plant the potatoes!" came his reply.

COLONEL *(after receiving troops):* "What's the idea of parading all the big men in front of the little men?"

LIEUTENANT: "It's the sergeant's fault, sir. He used to run a fruit store."

He appeared before the company officer, charged with using insulting language to his sergeant.

"Please, sir," he protested, "I was only answering a question."

"What question?" snapped the officer.

"Well, sir, the sergeant said 'who do you think I am?' and I told him."

CORPORAL: "Now, Private, if you stood with your back to the north and your face to the south, what would be on your left hand?"

PRIVATE: "Fingers."

Miser

He throws away money like it was an anchor.

Misfortune

I'm a hard-luck fellow. Four days after buying my first two-pants suit, I burned a hole in the coat.

Mistakes

"Okay, Okay, Mr. Looney, so my mistake cost the company $275,000. For goodness sake, I said I was sorry."

To err is human. But when the eraser wears out before the lead in the pencil—beware!

A mistake is evidence that someone has tried to do something.

An irate employee went to the paymaster and carefully counted the money in his pay envelope. "It's one dollar short. What's the meaning of this?" The paymaster checked a record sheet and smiled broadly, "Last week we overpaid you a dollar. You didn't complain about that mistake then, did you?"

"An occasional mistake I can overlook, but not two in a row," replied the angry man.

Models—Modelling

A model asked her booking agent to get a friend of hers a job.

"What's her measurements?" he asked.

"26—32—85," says the girl.

"Holy Smoke," says the agent, "what does this female do?"

"She poses," says the girl, "for pyramids."

A girl was entertaining her girlfriend and was pouring the tea when her friend spied a full-length nude painting hung on the wall. "Why, Mabel, that is a painting of you! Did you pose like that?"

And Mabel's reply: "Why, yes, it's me, but of course I did not pose for it. The artist painted it from memory."

Modesty

Modesty: The feeling that others will discover how wonderful you are.

Money

Money doesn't talk these days—it goes without saying.

One comforting thought: There are more than 182 million people in the United States who are not millionaires!

The dime isn't completely worthless. It still makes a fairly good screwdriver.

Money: The principal export of the United States.

A badly needed invention in America today is some kind of dough that really sticks to your fingers.

Lots of things are more important than money. The trouble is that you need money to buy them.

Appearances are deceiving. A dollar looks the same as it did ten years ago.

Mixed greens are good for you . . . especially the fives, tens, and twenties.

Most people's financial problems are simple. They're short of money.

"Tight money" isn't something you save up to get drunk on.

Money isn't everything. There are stocks and bonds, too.

No matter how low the dollar may fall, it will never fall as low as some people stoop to get it:

The package arrived fresh from the counterfeiter. But when the crook opened it, he found he had spent his good money for a batch of $18 bills instead of the $20 bills for which he had contracted.

Since complaints were frowned upon by his supplier, he decided to try passing them off on some unsuspecting hill folk deep in the heart of the Ozarks.

At a likely looking cross-roads general store, he presented one of the bills and asked for change. "Sure thing, Sonny," said the storekeeper. "Howdya want it—two nines or three sixes?"

A man was walking along the street one afternoon when he saw a friend approaching with a gloomy look on his face. "What's the matter with you?" asked the first man.

"I'm in trouble," said his friend, "and I need five dollars right away. I've only got four dollars, and I don't know what to do."

"I'm broke myself," said the first man, "but I can tell you how to get the other dollar."

"How?"

"It's simple," was the reply. "Go to a pawnshop and pawn your four dollars for three dollars. Then find somebody and sell the pawn ticket for two dollars. Then you've got your five!"

Mother-in-Law

They solicited Luke for something for the Old Ladies Home, so he sent his mother-in-law.

"Where have you been, Buckle?"
"I've been on a pleasure trip."
"Where'd you go?"
"Took my mother-in-law home."

Having been married 25 years, a couple decided to celebrate their anniversary by taking a little trip. While talking over their plans one evening, the husband now and then glanced into the next room where a little old lady sat knitting. "The only thing is," he said in a whisper, "that for once I'd like to be by ourselves. I'd like to take this trip without your mother."

"My mother!" exclaimed the wife. "I thought she was *your* mother!"

It was an accident that shocked the mountainside; a mule had kicked the farmer's mother-in-law to death. Long before time for the service the minister marveled at the crowd of men and observed: "She must have been a wonderful woman. So many men have left their work to attend her funeral."

"They ain't all here for her funeral," the farmer explained. "Most of 'em want to buy the mule."

The hardest time to disguise your feelings is when you're putting your mother-in-law on the train.

A man brought a cocker spaniel to a veterinarian and ordered him to cut off the dog's tail. "I want it all off," he said, "so that not even a hair of the tail remains."

"Sorry," the vet replied, "I couldn't do that to a dog. Why should you want to cut the tail from an innocent little dog?"

"My mother-in-law is visiting us next month," the man replied, "and I want to eliminate any possible sign or indication of welcome."

Motion Pictures—Drive-in Movies

The movie producer was planning a war picture. "This will be the production to end all productions," he commented. "I'm going to use full armies—3,000 men on one side and 4,000 men on the other."

"We're going to have 7,000 men in one movie?" exclaimed the director. "How can we afford to produce such an extravaganza?"

"It'll be easy," answered the producer. "We'll just use real bullets."

A modern miracle would be a diamond wedding anniversary in Hollywood.

A theater owner tried an experiment. He ran the same picture for 30 days straight under nine different titles. Only four customers complained. There might have been more but it was a drive-in movie.

If he wipes off the windshield in a drive-in movie, he's a married man with his own wife.

Music

The real music lover is the woman who applauds when her husband comes home singing at 3 o'clock in the morning.

MUSICIAN (*in N.Y. City for first time*): "Hey, buddy, how can I get to Carnegie Hall?"

NEW YORKER: "Practice, man! Practice!"

"If you don't stop playing that drum," yelled a neighbor over the telephone to a young musician, "I'll go crazy!"

"It's too late," said the boy. "I stopped a half hour ago."

"Your son is making good progress with his violin," remarked a musician friend of the family. "He is beginning to play quite well."

"Do you really think so?" beamed the father. "We were afraid that we merely had become used to it."

A henpecked-looking little man was escorting his wife to a concert. They arrived late. "What are they playing," he whispered to his neighbor.

"The Fifth Symphony," was the reply.

"Well, thank goodness. I've missed four of them anyway."

One of the women had just finished singing "My Old Kentucky Home" at a woman's club musicale when a man in the audience was seen in tears.

"Are you from Kentucky?" a club member asked.

"No," he replied. "I'm a musician."

Name

TRAFFIC COP: "What's your name?"

TRUCK DRIVER: "It's on the side of the truck."

COP: "It's obliterated."

DRIVER: "You're crazy. It's O'Brien."

"Paging Mr. Sleidopavrikanwoskytotovitch. Is that you, sir?"

"Might be. What initials?"

A woman who was living in a San Francisco apartment house hired a Chinese boy. "What's your name?" she said.

"Wong Fu Tsin Mei," he replied.

"Your name is too long. I'll call you John."

"What's your name?" asked the boy.

"Mrs. Jonathan Percy Whitenhouse."

"Your name too long. I'll call you Charlie!"

SIDEWALK TV QUIZMASTER: "Now, sir, if you found an expensive billfold on the street containing a lot of money, would you return it to its owner?"

PEDESTRIAN: "Yes, if my name wasn't stamped on it."
QUIZMASTER: "Naturally! What is your name, by the way?"
PEDESTRIAN: "Genuine Alligator!"

A woman, describing her holiday, said she had visited San Jose.
"It's San Hosay!" said her friend. "In California, you pronounce all the j's as h's. When were you there?"
"In Hune and Huly," she replied.

Nepotism

Nepotism—Putting on Heirs.

Nerve

Nerve: That which enables a man seated on a bus to flirt with a woman who is standing.

Newlyweds (see Marriage, Wives, Husbands, Weddings, Divorce, Courtship)

The bride-to-be was advised by the marriage counselor to never completely disrobe in front of her husband when retiring.
One night, six weeks after the wedding, the husband said to his bride, "Is there any insanity in your family?"
"Why, no," she said. "Why do you ask?"
"I was merely wondering," said he, "why you haven't taken your hat off since we've been married."

The bride, showing her uncle over her new home, said: "This is our room. We have twin beds. That is Harvey's, this is mine."
Then the uncle noticed a fine clock and mentioned it.
"It's a wedding present from Grandma," said the bride.
A few weeks later the uncle received a note from the bride saying the clock had disappeared. Could he throw any light on the subject?
The uncle answered by return mail: "Look in Harvey's bed."

GIRL FRIEND TO NEW BRIDE: "Well, Doris, how are you getting along with your cooking?"
DORIS: "My husband does all the cooking—he doesn't want me to lean over the stove and endanger my career."

"I am sorry, my dear, that the dinner was a little burned tonight," apologized the new bride. "Before I could decide what to have, there was a fire in the delicatessen."

A college professor had checked out of his hotel and realized that he had left his umbrella. Returning he learned that a newlywedded couple had taken the room.

They were in that baby talking stage, and as the professor peeked through the keyhole, he saw the groom pointing to the bride's mouth and heard him say: "Who's 'ittle mouth is that?"

"Yours," she cooed.

"And whose 'ittle nose?" he continued.

"Yours, darling," she assured him.

"And those 'ittle hands?" he asked, kissing them.

"Yours, of course, dearest," she replied.

"Listen here, young fellow," called the impatient professor through the transom, "when you come to an umbrella, it's mine."

Two pairs of honeymooners struck up a close acquaintance on the train and chose adjoining suites in the same hotel upon arrival at Niagara Falls.

The very first evening they had supper together. After dining, they decided that they should all go to bed, since they were all so tired from the frantic activities of the day. Just as they approached the elevator, the house generator kicked off, throwing the entire hotel in darkness.

Groping their way to the stairs and up to their rooms as best they could, they quietly undressed in the dark. George, who was a very devout man, knelt at the bed for the regular evening prayer. And just as he ended his prayer, the lights came on again.

Much to his surprise, there in bed dressed in the sheerest of night-gowns was June, the other man's wife, instead of his own bride, Ann.

In a panic, he started to rush to the other room. Then he heard June saying coyly: "It's too late to hurry now. My John never prays."

FIRST BRIDE: "Does your husband snore in his sleep?"

SECOND BRIDE: "I don't know. We've only been married three days."

GROOM: "Now perhaps I'll be permitted to point out a few of your defects.

BRIDE: "It won't be necessary, darling. I know them. They kept me from getting a better man than you."

A marriage is a success when it lasts until they get to Niagara Falls.

FOREMAN: "How long do you want to be away on your honeymoon?"

EMPLOYEE: "Well, how long would you suggest?"

FOREMAN: "How do I know, I haven't seen the bride."

A bride and groom came down to breakfast in the hotel where they had spent the first night of their honeymoon.

"Now be casual and they won't know we're newlyweds," cautioned the groom.

While he studied the menu, his bride gave her order to the waiter. "Tea and toast without butter, please," she said.

Whereupon the husband exclaimed in a voice that could be heard all over the room: "Good heavens, is that all you eat for breakfast?"

As the newlyweds were about to slip into their limousine for the honeymoon trip, an urgent call for the groom came from India. The oil deal with fifty million dollars at stake was ready to be closed.

"It's business, you understand," the bridegroom explained to his bride. "I'll have to make at least five phone calls immediately, and that will take hours of negotiation."

"But darling, this is our honeymoon," wailed the bride.

"Business is business," insisted the groom. "But you go ahead, I'll catch a plane later and join you tonight."

"But you said it might take hours," sobbed the bride. "What if it takes longer? What if you can't make it tonight?"

"In that case," snapped the groom, reaching for the telephone, "you go ahead and start without me."

NEW GROOM: "I can tell when my wife's mad at me. When I come home she refuses to kiss me."

OLD MARRIED MAN: "I can tell when my wife is mad at me when she serves me frozen dinners without defrosting them!"

BRIDE: "John, dear, let's try to make people think we've been married a long time."

GROOM: "Okay, honey, you carry the suitcase."

New York

A New York businessman visiting Salt Lake City strolled about the city and made the acquaintance of a little Mormon girl.

NEW YORKER: "I'm from New York. I suppose you do not know where New York is?"

GIRL: "Oh, yes I do. Our Sunday-school has a missionary there."

Nudist Colony

SHE: "Is it difficult to become a member of this nudist colony?"

HE: "No. All you have to do is leave your name and a dress."

Nurse

Then there is a nurse who is so conceited that when she takes her patient's pulse, she subtracts ten beats for the effect of her personality.

Old Age

The oldest inhabitant—a man of great importance—had just celebrated his 90th birthday, and all the local newspapers interviewed him.

"Tell us, sir," said one reporter, "if you had your life to live over again, is there anything you would change?"

The nonagenarian appeared lost in thought for a few seconds, then nodded his head. "Yes," he said gravely. "I believe I'd part my hair on the side."

"I'll be 90 tomorrow and haven't an enemy in the world."

"A wonderful thing," said the interviewer.

"Yes, sir," went on the old man. "I've outlived them all."

The old man noticed the young fellow with a bottle in one hand and his arm around a pretty girl.

"The dern fool is wasting a lot of time," he mused. "He can drink when he gets old like I am."

The old man came home, bringing with him a new wife, some forty years his junior. He introduced her to his servants, and afterwards he asked the oldest of his employees what he thought of his new mistress.

The man thought a minute, then he said: "She's a beautiful lady, sir. But I hate to see a man start out on a day's work so late in the afternoon."

The old man was asked what hereditary diseases had afflicted his ancestors.

"Longevity," was the reply.

The man was being interviewed on his 100th birthday.

"You must have seen a lot of changes in your time," commented the reporter.

"Dang right I have," remarked the old timer. "And I've been agin every one of them."

Susan Smith brought a friend home from her college for a visit—an extremely attractive blonde—and introduced her to her family which included her great-grandfather. "And just think, Marilyn," she said. "He's in his nineties."

"My *early* nineties," the old gent amended with a gleam in his eye.

Be thrifty when you're young and when you're old you'll be able to afford the things only the young can enjoy.

The doctor gave his 80-year-old patient a very curious look.

"I've been practicing for two decades," said the doctor, "but I'm darned if I ever heard of a complaint such as yours. What do you mean your virility is too high?"

"It's all in my head," sighed the old man.

"That pain in your leg is caused by old age," commented the doctor.

"Don't be silly," said Grandpa. "My other leg is the same age and it doesn't hurt at all."

For every man 85 years of age, there are seven women. But it's too late for them.

Old age is a period when a man pays more attention to his food than he does to the waitress.

Uncle Alf had gone to the funeral of a friend and, after the ceremony, sat in the chapel of the undertaking parlor until the crowd had thinned out. The mortician sat beside him and began passing the time of day.

"How old are you, sir?" he asked Uncle Alf.

"Eighty-nine," chirped the old man.

"Eighty-nine, eh?" mused the undertaker. "Hardly worth going home, is it?"

The best thing to save for old age is yourself.

An old-timer is one who remembers when a baby sitter was called "Mother."

"Grandpa, what are you crying for?" asked his daughter.

"It's the book I'm reading, *Forever Amber*."

"But that's not a sad book."

"It is at *my* age."

"To what do you attribute your longevity?" asked the reporter on the man's 90th birthday.

"I never wasted energy resisting temptation."

Do not resent growing old—many are denied the privilege.

Nothing will age a man faster than furiously saving money for his old age.

When men get too old to set a bad example, they start dishing out advice.

There's a prominent citizen who is far past the age when most successful men are content to retire and reap the rewards of past industry. We met him the other day and complimented him on his apparent youthfulness, energy and professional acumen. "Yes," he said, "I feel just as full of energy and ideas as a man of forty." Then he added, "—for about half an hour each day."

"So you are 100 years old," said the young reporter to the centenarian. "How have you managed to live so long?"

"Well, son," answered the aged man, "I got married when I was 21 and the missus and I made an agreement. We decided that, if we had arguments, the loser would take a long walk to get over being mad. And I suppose I have been benefited most by 79 years of fresh air."

My boss wouldn't chase after women. He's too fine, too decent, and too old!

A sign of old age is when you feel your corns more than your oats.

Seven Ages of Man: At 5 months, all lungs; at 5 years, all ears; at 15 years, all hands and feet; at 25 years, all muscle; at 35 years, all bustle; at 45 years, all tummy; and at 95 years, all in.

Young men see Paris with a wild yell; old men with a deep sigh.

A man could retire nicely in his old age if he could dispose of his experience for what it cost him.

A special course of treatment was recommended for an old man. "A few weeks of that," said the doctor, "and you'll think you're ten years younger."

"Wow!" said the elderly patient, and then added, "It won't affect my pension, will it?"

A reporter, interviewing a man who had reached his 99th birthday, said: "I certainly hope I can come back next year and see you reach 100."

"Can't see why not, young feller," the old-timer replied. "You look healthy enough to me."

I am almost 72, and I find growing old isn't so bad, when you consider the alternative.

Three decrepit, gray-haired gentlemen were seated together in the park discussing their personal philosophies for achieving ripe old age.

"I'm eighty-six," said the first, "and I wouldn't be here today if I hadn't scorned tobacco and alcohol in every form, avoided late hours and the sinful enticements of the opposite sex."

"I owe my ninety-three years to a strict diet of blackstrap molasses, wheat germ bread and mother's milk," the second old man said.

"When I was eighteen," the third man said, "my father told me that if I wanted to enjoy life as much as he had, I should smoke black cigars, drink nothing but hard liquor, and carouse with a different woman every night. And that's exactly what I've done."

"Incredible," said the first old man.

"Amazing," said the second, looking at the third old man who had reported on his life of dissipation. "And how old are you?"

"Twenty-two," he replied.

Old-timers are people who remember when a sensational novel contained asterisks.

Old Maid (see Courtship, Marriage, Wives, Bachelor, Husband)

FIRST OLD MAID: "Oh, Agatha, I'm going out with a used car salesman!"

SECOND OLD MAID: "What's the difference if he's used, as long as he's healthy."

Old Maid: One who knows the answers and keeps praying she'll be asked the questions.

Take your choice—be an old maid and look for a husband every day or marry and look for him every night.

Old maids are girls who talk of boy-gone days.

An old maid after years and years and years was invited out to spend the evening with a man. The next day a friend asked how she enjoyed the evening. "Fine—it was the first time I ever knew you could have fun without laughing."

"You mustn't be discouraged," the psychiatrist was telling the troubled young spinster. "In this world there's a man for every woman and a woman for every man. You can't improve on an arrangement like that."

SPINSTER: "I don't want to improve on it. I just want to get in on it."

And then there was the old maid who wrote a new song, "Praise the Lord, I've Got a Proposition."

An old maid appeared before the Pearly Gates: St. Peter looked her over, then asked, "Yes, what is it you want?"

"I want to get in."

"And why should we let you in?"

"Because," said the old maid, "I've been pure and chaste all my life. I never drank or smoked, petted, or went to wild parties. But why should I tell you all this? You have all this information in your records."

"I'm sorry, but we don't keep any records," said St. Peter, "But step inside and sit down on the bench, and your case will be considered."

The old maid entered, sat down and looked around. Nearby she saw a big circle of women, their hands joined. She watched as one of the women walked outside the circle. Then she stopped, kicked one of the women on the seat, and took her place in the circle where the kicked woman dropped out. The woman who had dropped out repeated the performance. This went on for some time. Finally, the old maid called to St. Peter: "What is that game those women are playing?"

"I don't know," shrugged St. Peter. "All I know is they've been playing it ever since they learned that we don't keep records!"

Opportunity

If the door to opportunity does not open to polite knocks, kick it in.

Opportunity knocks on the door but once. Trouble is more persistent.

Opportunity doesn't knock so very often but temptation seems to pound away every day.

There's plenty of opportunity in a land where even a horse can make a million dollars.

Somebody said that opportunity knocks but once, while temptation hangs around all year. However, it's a fact that you have to get the opportunity first before you can do much with temptation.

Even when opportunity knocks, you still have to get up and open the door.

Optimist

The biggest optimist of them all is the guy who wolf-whistles through false teeth.

An optimist is a man who marries his secretary and thinks he can go on dictating to her.

A pessimist is a guy who thinks all the women are wild.
An optimist is a guy who hopes they are.

If you see good in everyone, you may be an optimist. Then again you may be nuts.

An optimist is a man who goes downstairs with a fish pole when he finds his basement flooded.

Optimist: A guy who believes everything he reads on a book jacket.

A Hollywood producer called a staff conference to discuss a story called, "The Optimist."
"Gentlemen," he said, "we'll have to change this title to something simpler. We all know what an optimist is, but how many of the public will know that the hero is an eye doctor?"

An optimist and a pessimist were shipwrecked and in time their raft came within sight of a tropic isle. The pessimist expected the worse, saying: "I'll bet it is inhabited with a bunch of wild men."
But the optimist was more cheerful, saying, "Cheer up, pal. Where there are wild men, there are wild women."

Organization

Organization is the art of getting men to respond like thoroughbreds. When you call on a thoroughbred, he gives you all the speed, heart and sinew in him. When you call on a jackass, he kicks.

Painters–Decorating

The home-owner was delighted with the way the painter had decorated his house. "You did a fine job," he said, "and I'm going to give you a little something extra. Here's $10. Take the missus to a show."

That night, the doorbell rang and the painter stood at the door all dressed up. "What is it?" the home-owner asked. "Did you forget something?"

"Nope," said the painter, "I just came to take the missus to a show."

A lady who was going out of town for a few weeks called in a painter and told him to paint her bedroom while she was away. She handed him a small mauve enameled ash tray and said firmly that she wanted the bedroom done in exactly the same shade.

For nearly three days the painter mixed valiantly, and by the time the lady returned she gazed happily upon the perfect match the painter had obtained.

"Funny thing about it," the painter explained to a friend several days later, "she still doesn't know I repainted that blasted ash tray with the same paint I put on the bedroom!"

Mrs. Jones, having her living room walls repainted, was explaining to the unsympathetic painter just what she wanted. "I want a light green blue, which will be sort of a cross between a darker blue and a light bluey blue," she explained.

The painter gave her a stony stare and replied, "There ain't no such color, lady. What you're describing is nothin' but a pigment of your imagination."

Panhandlers

"My poor fellow," said the kind old lady, "it must be dreadful to be lame. But just the same, think how much worse it would be if you were blind."

"You're right, lady," agreed the beggar. "When I was blind, I was always gettin' counterfeit money."

A panhandler stopped a wealthy man on the street. "Can you give me six cents for a cup of coffee?"

"Why, coffee is a dime."

"So who buys retail?" said the panhandler.

A voice in the dark, on a lonely street: "Would the gentleman be so kind as to assist a poor hungry fellow who is out of work? Besides this revolver, I haven't a thing in the world."

A panhandler collapsed on the street and immediately a large crowd gathered.

"Give the poor man a drink of whiskey," said a little old lady.

"Call an ambulance," someone suggested.

"Give him a drink of whiskey," repeated the little old lady.

"Give him some air," said several men.

The babble continued until suddenly the victim sat bolt upright and demanded: "Will you all shut up and listen to the little old lady?"

Parties

"Well," said the guest, "this is a surprise party! Only 38 candles on your birthday cake."

They were holding an all-night poker party in a hotel room. As the party progressed, so did the sound of revelry. Finally, at 3 A.M., a weary guest in the adjoining room started to pound on the wall.

"Well," shouted one of the merrymakers indignantly, "this is a hell of a time to be hanging pictures!"

It was two days after a big party when two friends met on the street.

"Well, old man," said one of them, "how did you get along after I left you the other night? Did you get home all right?"

"No," was the reply. "A policeman saw me and he took me to the station and I had to spend the night in jail."

"You sure were lucky," said the first. "I got home!"

Partnership

A partnership of Brown and Wilson threatened to go on the rocks when Wilson fell madly in love with Brown's wife. Brown was very understanding about the whole thing, but finally told his partner, "This thing cannot go on any longer. What do you think of playing one game of canasta to see who gets the girl?" Wilson thought his proposition over for a few minutes, then agreed. "Let's play for a penny a point on the side," he replied, "just to make it interesting."

Paternity

Paternity is a career that is imposed upon a man one fine morning without any inquiry as to his fitness for it. That is why there are so many fathers who have children, but few children who have fathers.

"Bonjour, Monsieur," said the little girl to the priest.
"Just call me Father," was the reply.
"Oh, will Mother ever be glad to see you!" cried the child. "She's been looking for you ever since I was born!"

Pedestrian

Pedestrian: A man who has two cars, a wife and a son.

According to the dopesters, by the year 1970 there will be more than 200 million automobiles in use. So, all you pedestrians who want to cross the street, you'd better do it now!

Pedestrian· A husband who didn't think the family had any need for two cars.

Pedestrians: To stay in the pink, watch the red and green.

Perjury

Two old friends, who hadn't seen each other for quite a spell, met at the club.
"Hiya, Bill, you old coot, it's good to see you again. Where the heck you been keeping yourself?"
"Wal, I'll tell you, Jonathan. Been out of circulation for 90 days."
"Been sick?"
"Nope, been in jail!"
"Jail! What for?"
"Wal, you remember that young widder woman I used to occasionally squire around to the movies and Joe's hamburger stand—durned if she didn't charge me with rape! At my age I felt she was paying me a real compliment, so I pleaded guilty and the durn old judge sentenced me to 90 days."
"Ninety days is a pretty light sentence for rape."
"He didn't sentence me for rape. The ninety days was for perjury!"

Personality

Some persons think they have a dynamic personality if they occasionally explode.

Pharmacy

CUSTOMER: "You made a mistake in that prescription for my mother-in-law; instead of quinine, you used strychnine."

DRUGGIST: "You don't say! Then you owe me 20 cents more."

Plumber

PLUMBER: "Is this where you wrote for a plumber to come, lady?"

LADY: "Plumber, indeed! Why, I wrote last August."

PLUMBER: "Come on, Joe, wrong house. Party we're looking for wrote last May."

The plumber worked and the helper stood helplessly looking on. He was learning the business and this was his first day.

"Say," he inquired timidly, "do you charge for my time?"

"Of course," said the plumber. "Somebody's got to pay for your learning your trade."

"But I haven't done anything," said the helper.

The plumber, to fill in the hour, had been looking at the finished job with a lighted candle. Handing the two inches that were still unburned to the helper he said:

"Here, if you gotta be so darned honest, blow that out."

Plutocrat

A plutocrat is a fellow who can get his hair cut the day before pay-day.

Police—Detectives

The old lady had lost her purse. She rushed into the police inspector's office and tearfully told her story. The inspector was very kind and calmed her fears as best he could. Laying his hand on her arm, he said, "We will leave no stone unturned to find your purse, Madam."

Leaving his office she noticed a group of city workers busy tearing up the street for a new sewer line, and she remarked to herself, "Well, they didn't lose much time, I'll say that for them."

A floorwalker, tired of his job, gave it up and joined the police force. Several months later a friend asked him how he liked being a policeman.

"Well," he replied, "the pay and the hours are good, but what I like best is that the customer is always wrong."

When Doyle joined the police force, the sergeant told him: "You are on the night beat: it's from here to that red light and back."

They didn't hear from Doyle for two days. Finally he showed up at the station house.

"Where have you been?" thundered the sergeant. "I told you your beat was from here to that red light."

"Yeah," said Doyle ruefully, "but that red light was on the back of a truck."

Politics

The trouble with political jokes is that sometimes they get elected.

Uncle Grover was pretty unpopular, I'm sorry to say. One year he ran for public office unopposed—and still lost.

A successful politician is a man who can rock the boat himself and then persuade everybody else that there is a terrible storm at sea.

"I've been elected," the successful candidate excitedly telephoned his wife.

"Honestly?" replied the wife.

"Now, why go into that?"

Elections are influenced not so much by what the candidate stands for as by what the voter falls for.

No woman is likely ever to be elected President—they never reach the required legal age.

A politician was being interviewed by the press. One reporter asked, "Do you feel you have influenced public opinion sir?"

"No," he answered. "Public opinion is something like a mule I once owned. In order to keep up the appearance of being driver, I had to watch the way he was going and follow closely."

A cinch to win is Senator Munn,
He just kisses babies over twenty-one.

Some candidates don't put enough fire into their speeches. Others don't put enough of their speeches into the fire.

The political speaker was orating fervently before a civic group. "We need a man who will drive straight to his goal, looking neither to right nor left; one who presses forward, and neither friend nor foe can delay nor turn him from his course. All who cross his path do so at their own risk. Now where will we find such a man?"

"Driving any bus," shouted someone in the rear.

"Vote for me," boomed the youthful politician in the village hall, "and I'll give you better roads. What's more, I'll give you one-way streets."

"That's no good here," interrupted a villager with a grin. "We've only got *one* street."

A politician is a guy who works his gums before election and gums up the works afterwards.

"There were some things in your speech that I didn't quite understand," said a listener following a political rally.

"Probably," replied the Senator. "Those were the topics I referred to in a confident, off-hand way, so as to avoid disclosing that I don't understand 'em either."

Two men were working on the White House lawn, picking up papers with a long spear. Just as one started to spear a piece of tissue a gust of wind blew the paper through an open window and into the White House.

The frantic man rushed into the building, but soon returned, saying, "I was too late. He had already signed it."

A sidewalk interviewer asked one of our old timers what he thought of the two candidates for election. "When I look at them," he said sorrowfully, "I'm thankful only one of them can get elected."

Two congressional secretaries were conversing on Capitol hill.

"Do you like conceited politicians as much as the other kind?" asked one.

"What other kind?" said the other.

A doctor, an engineer, and a politician were arguing which of their professions was the oldest.

The doctor said: "Of course, medicine was the oldest. Mankind has always had physicians, and they are even mentioned in the Bible."

"That's nothing," said the engineer. "The Bible tells how the world was created out of chaos, and how could there be any order brought out of chaos without an engineer?"

"Wait a minute," said the politician. "Who do you think created the chaos?"

The strongest objection socialists and communists have against capital is that they don't have any.

A politician is a man who approaches every problem with an open mouth.

The polls are places where you stand in line for a chance to decide who will spend your money.

During his speech a politician noticed an old woman sitting down front who appeared particularly interested in what he said. Afterwards, he took occasion to meet her and ask for her vote.

"Well, sir," the old lady said, looking him in the eye, "you're my second choice."

The politician thanked her and asked cheerfully, "And who is your first choice?"

"Oh," she replied, "just anybody."

"You say you've always been a Democrat, yet I remember when you voted for Hoover."

"That I did. I figured that anybody smart enough to invent a vacuum sweeper was smart enough to be president!"

A taxpayer is a guy who works very hard and saves his money. A politician is another guy who, were it not for the first, would have to do the same.

Politics is the most promising of all careers—promises, promises, promises . . .

Politics is the art of looking for trouble, finding it everywhere, diagnosing it wrong, and applying unsuitable remedies.

"A good politician must also be an acrobat."

"How do you figure that?"

"Ever try straddling a fence, keeping your finger on the pulse of the nation, pointing with pride, and looking to the future while keeping both ears to the ground?"

A truck driver was taking a civil examination and was asked:

"Did you ever belong to an organization that is trying to overthrow the government in Washington?"

To the surprise of the examiner, the applicant replied, "Yes."

"You did! What is that organization?" asked the examiner.

"The Republican party."

The time many a politician really stumps his state is after it has elected him.

A well-known political leader in the Middle West completed a full course of study in veterinary surgery, but never practiced. He branched out into politics. During a campaign, his political enemies referred to him with mingled sarcasm and scorn as "the Vet," and one day at a heated debate one of them asked, "Are you really a veterinary surgeon?"

"Why do you ask?" queried the quick-witted politician. "Are you ill?"

Politicians who try to please everybody often look like a small puppy trying to follow four boys home at the same time.

A politician who had changed his views rather radically was congratulated by a colleague. "I'm glad you've seen the light," he said.

"I didn't see the light," came the terse reply. "I felt the heat."

TEACHER: "Harold, what are the three great American parties?"

HAROLD: "Republican, Democratic and cocktail."

A Matador is a man who throws the bull. In this country, we call them Senators.

At a political gathering in Washington, D. C., an elderly matron was seated next to a senator at the banquet table. During a pause in the conversation, she turned to him and asked, "Why is it, Senator, that the Committee on Foreign Relations is in the Senate and the Committee on Foreign Affairs is in the House?"

The senator turned to her and said, "There's a good reason for that, ma'am. It's because we senators just have relations. We're too old to have affairs."

A popular candidate for public office in a rather tolerant community sometimes embarrassed his supporters by appearing in public in a slightly befuddled condition.

Hoping to take advantage of this, the editor of the opposition paper instructed his reporter to write down the politician's speeches exactly as they were delivered. Sure enough, at a men's club rally, the candidate imbibed too freely and delivered an incoherent talk to the members.

When the reporter typed up the speech, he did not have the heart to turn it in. He took his papers over to the old gentleman to let him edit the speech. Still a bit unsteady from the night before, the candidate slowly and laboriously scratched out and interpolated until he made sense out of the manuscript.

As he handed it back to the reporter he said: "Young man, let me give you some sound advice. Never again attempt to take down a speech in such a deplorable condition as you were in last night."

The reason some congressmen want to get home to mend their political fences is to have a safe place to sit until after the elections.

It seems one of those sales ladies who won a trip to Miami had a real experience. During her visit she reported to the police that she had been assaulted and it is reported that the interrogation went like this:

POLICE: "Was he white?"

GIRL: "I don't know."

POLICE: "Was he short—tall?"

GIRL: "I don't know."

POLICE: "Well, what can you tell us about the man that will assist in catching him?"

GIRL: "Well, I know he was a Democrat."

POLICE: "How in the world did you know that?"

GIRL: "I never had it so good before!"

Prayers

A little girl was moving with her family from Virginia to New York, and she was more than a trifle unhappy about it. The night before the family's departure she said her prayers, finishing off with the usual, "God bless Mommy and Daddy, little brother Tommy, and everybody else." Then with emphasis she added, "This is goodbye, God—we're moving to New York."

And here's one about a little girl. Attending church with her mother for the first time, the child was awed by everything. When the congregation knelt, she asked what the people were doing. "Saying their prayers," her mother whispered.

The child looked around in amazement, then turned again to her mother to ask: "Saying their prayers with all their clothes on?"

The twins, five years old, had knelt for bedtime prayers. Little Clara prayed first, concluding: "Amen. Goodnight God. And now stay tuned for Clarence."

A little boy was saying his go-to-bed prayers in a very low voice. "I can't hear you, dear," his mother said.

"Wasn't talking to you," said the boy.

Preachers (see Church, Prayers)

A minister who was very fond of pure, hot horseradish, offered some to a dinner guest who took a big bite. When the guest was finally able to talk, he turned reproachfully to the minister.

"I've heard many preach Hellfire," he choked, "but you're the first one I've met who serves it!"

The pastor was rejoicing with a little old lady over one of her elderly relatives, who had finally seen the light and joined the church after a lifetime of riotous living.

When she wondered if all the oldster's carrying on would be forgiven, the pastor assured her, "Yes, indeed, the greater the sinner the greater the saint."

"Preacher," she mused wistfully, "I wish I had learned this forty years ago.

PREACHER: "Do you say your prayers at night, little boy?"
JIMMY: "Yes, sir!"
PREACHER: "And do you say them in the morning, too?"
JIMMY: "No, sir, I ain't scared in the daytime."

A minister whose parakeet said nothing but "Let's pray," loaned his bird to a young couple whose parakeet said nothing but "Let's neck," hoping to educate the latter.

On the first encounter, the delinquent said, "Let's neck," and the minister's bird replied, "My prayers have been answered."

The pastor of a small rural church in southern Italy ended his sermon with the following observations: "At the door, as usual, there will be someone to accept your gifts. I should like to remind you, my dear brethren, that the anatomical construction of the angels precludes their use of your pants-button contributions."

A minister looked at one of his parishioners coldly. "I hear you went to the ball game Sunday instead of church," he said.

"That's a lie," he said. "I've got a fish to prove it."

The preacher hoping to get acquainted with one of the new members of the congregation, knocked on the front door of her home one evening.

"Is that you, Angel?" came the woman's voice from within.

"No," replied the preacher. "But I'm from the same department."

"And when I get through with my sermon, I'll ask those of the congregation who want to contribute toward the mortgage on the church to stand up," said the preacher to the organist. "In the meantime, play the appropriate music."

"What do you mean, appropriate music?" asked the organist.

"Play the Star Spangled Banner," replied the preacher.

A minister thought he could offset his careless memory of a member of the congregation and, after the amenities, confided that he always had trouble with her name. Was it spelled with an "e" or with an "i"?

"With an 'i'," she said. "The name is "Hill."

At a banquet, a clumsy waiter dropped a plate of hot soup in the lap of the bishop. The clergyman glanced around with a look of agony and exclaimed, "Will some layman please say something appropriate?"

The two American ministers traveling in Germany decided to go to church. Knowing no German, they figured to play safe by picking out a dignified-looking gentleman sitting in front of them and doing whatever he did.

During the service the pastor made a special announcement, and the man in front of them rose. The two Americans rose quickly only to be met by roars of laughter.

When the service was over, they discovered the pastor spoke English and asked what the cause of the merriment had been.

"Oh," said the pastor, "I was announcing a baptism and asked the father of the child to stand."

TEARFUL PARISHIONER *(saying farewell to a departing minister):* "I don't know what we will do when you are gone."

DEPARTING MINISTER: "Oh, the church will soon get a better man than I am."

TEARFUL PARISHIONER: "That's what they all say, but they keep getting worse and worse."

A pastor was being entertained at dinner. He was suffering with a boil on the back of his neck, so he wore a soft shirt with the collar unbuttoned. In response to his hostess' expression of sympathy, he said:

"We must endure such misfortunes with patience. I assume that suffering is inflicted on us at times to try us."

The six-year-old daughter of the hostess listened to his remarks and then asked earnestly: "Well, if you're supposed to suffer, why don't you button your collar?"

A minister from the hill country went to the big city, and for the first time in his life he stayed in a large hotel.

The bellboy was very solicitous, carrying the bags for him, pressing his suits, and doing all manner of errands to make his visit easy and pleasant. However, the minister never gave him a tip.

Finally, the bellboy explained, "Reverend, in a hotel, it is the custom that when somebody does something for you, you're supposed to do something for him in return."

The minister said, "Son, I'm sorry but I didn't understand that. So, tell me, son, do you drink?"

"You bet," replied the bellboy.

"Then get down on your knees and I'll give you the pledge," said the minister.

A group of ministers and a salesmen's organization were holding conventions in the same hotel. The catering department had to work at top speed serving dinners to both.

The salesmen were having "Spiked Watermelon" for dessert. But the harassed chef discovered this alcoholic tidbit was being served to the ministers by mistake.

"Quick!" he commanded a waiter. "If they haven't eaten the watermelon, bring it back and we'll give it to the salesmen."

The waiter returned in a minute and reported that it was too late— the ministers were eating the liquor-spiced dessert.

"Well," demanded the excited chef. "What did they say? How did they like it?"

"Don't know how they liked it," replied the waiter, "but they're putting the seeds in their pockets."

A layman once took two priests on a fishing trip. It was the first time either of them had ever fished, and upon rowing out into the middle of the lake one discovered that he had left his pole ashore. Unperturbed, he stepped out of the boat and walked across the water to get it. Shortly after he had come back the second one discovered that they had no bait, and he also walked across the water to get some. Well, upon his return the layman quite confidently announced that he could walk on the water if they could. But upon stepping out of the boat, he immediately sank. The one priest looked at the other and asked, "Shouldn't we have told him where the rocks are?"

Pride

Temper gets you into trouble; pride keeps you there.

Prisoner

"I feel sure, my poor man," said the sympathetic old lady, visiting a state prison, "it was poverty that brought you to this."

"No, ma'am, quite the contrary," returned the prisoner. "I happened to be coining money."

The social worker, visiting the inmates of the local jail, asked a variety of questions as she went from cell to cell. Finally, of one prisoner who was enjoying a long stay in the workhouse, she asked:

"Was it your love of liquor that brought you here?"

"Hell, no, lady," he replied. "You can't get nothin' in here."

CHAPLAIN: "My man, I will allow you five minutes of grace before your electrocution."

CONDEMNED MAN: "That's not very long, but bring her in."

A newspaper was running a competition to discover the most high-principled, sober, well-behaved local citizen. Among the entries came one which read:

"I don't smoke, touch intoxicants, or gamble. I am faithful to my wife and never look at another woman. I am hard-working, quiet, and obedient. I never go to the movies or the theater, and I go to bed early every night and rise with the dawn. I attend chapel regularly every Sunday without fail.

"I've been like this for the past three years. But just wait until next spring, when they let me out of here!"

Profanity

The chairman of the board was known for his mild-mannered conduct. But one day, while hurrying to an important business meeting, he was involved in a traffic accident with a taxicab. The cab driver spared no profanity in telling the dignified gent what he thought of him and his driving. Then it was the chairman's turn:

"My good man," he said, "I certainly do not condone your choice of expressions. Neither would I stoop to answer you in kind. I will say this, however: It is my wish that when you arrive home tonight, your mother will run out from under the porch and bite you!"

"I nearly ran over a pedestrian a few minutes ago and I think he was from Miami."

"How do you know he was from Miami?"

"Well, when he reached the sidewalk I heard him say something about the sun and the beach."

Profits

Two grads met at the 20th reunion. One had been on top of the class, the other had a tough time getting his diploma, having had particular trouble with math. The latter seemed to have prospered.

"Joe," said the top man, "you seem to have done exceptionally well. How did you do it?"

"Well," said Joe, "after graduation I realized I was pretty dumb, and I had better get into some line where I didn't need to be smart like you and some of the others. So I found a product I could make for one dollar and sell to the public for five dollars and believe me that steady four percent really mounts up over the years.

ONE MAN TO ANOTHER: "We're a non-profit organization. We don't mean to be, but we are."

Nero was talking finances with one of the officers in the amphitheater in Rome. "We aren't making much money from this building," Nero said. "Any idea why?"

"Yes," replied the officer, "the lions are eating up all the prophets."

Psychiatry—Psychiatrists

MOTHER OF A SMALL BOY TO CHILD PSYCHIATRIST: "Well, I don't know whether or not he feels insecure, but everybody else in the neighborhood certainly does!"

A psychiatrist received a postcard from a vacationing patient. "Dear Doctor," it said. "Having a wonderful time. Wish you were here to tell me why."

A confirmed drunkard had at long last been cured of the bottle and his psychiatrist was about to test him to see if he was cured completely.

"Now, then," he asked, "what does the name Gordon convey to you?"

The patient thought. "Wasn't that the name of a famous general?"

"Very good," said the psychiatrist. "And what does the name Haig mean?"

"He was a noted Earl," was the reply.

"Excellent," said the psychiatrist. "What does Vat 69 mean to you?"

The man thought deeply. "Isn't that the Pope's telephone number?"

A psychiatrist was walking along the street when a man leaned out of an upper window and called, "Would you mind coming up here and helping me with this elephant?"

No psychiatrist worth his salt could withstand such a request, so, anxious to oblige, he hurriedly ascended the stairs. At the apartment door he was met by the man and escorted into the room. The place looked normal, except that in one corner stood an elephant, medium size, lustily waving his trunk at the visitor.

The doctor didn't try to conceal his surprise. "I thought you were just imagining this elephant," he gasped.

"What elephant?" asked the other. "There's no elephant here. I did it for a bet."

"Doctor, I need help," said the man to his psychiatrist. "You see, my wife has developed an inferiority complex."

"I see," said the doctor, "and you want to help her overcome this."

"Oh, no," said the man. "My problem is, how can I keep her that way?"

A woman visited a psychiatrist to see what could be done about her husband, who imagined himself to be a refrigerator.

"Well," said the psychiatrist. "This must bother you a great deal."

"It certainly does," she replied. "He sleeps with his mouth open and the light inside keeps me awake."

The patient complained to his psychiatrist that every night he dreamed that there was a ravishing blond with a million dollars that continued to beg him to marry her.

"That's very interesting," said the psychiatrist. "But what's so bad about it?"

"Waking up," he replied.

"Doctor, I'm worried about my husband. He thinks he's a washing machine. Keeps rolling his head 'round and 'round. And soap and hot water come out of his ears!"

"Now, now, Mrs. Tyson—a harmless delusion. I wouldn't worry about it if I were you."

"But Doctor, he isn't getting the sheets clean!"

PSYCHIATRIST: "Now tell me about this dream."

LADY PATIENT: "Well, I dreamed I was walking down the street with nothing on but a hat."

PSYCHIATRIST: "And weren't you embarrassed?"

LADY PATIENT: "I certainly was! It was last year's hat."

PSYCHIATRIST TO PATIENT: "When did you first discover you enjoyed paying your income tax?"

There was a fire in the middle of the night in a New York apartment house. The tenants ran into the street carrying their prize possessions.

One of the women noticed that the man who lived directly above her was carrying a covered cage.

"What have you there?" she asked out of curiosity.

"That's my pet rooster," he replied.

The woman gasped and fainted.

When she was finally revived, she explained: "I've never fainted before. But, you see, for the past year I've been under treatment by a psychiatrist because I keep hearing a rooster crowing."

A disheveled man stumbled into a psychiatrist's office, tore open a cigarette and stuffed his nose with the tobacco.

"I can see that you need me," the psychiatrist said. "How can I help?"

"Got a light?" the man asked.

Then there was the kangaroo who went to see his psychiatrist because he wasn't feeling jumpy.

A little man came into the office of a psychiatrist.

"I was wondering," the little man said timidly, "if you couldn't split my personality."

The doctor looked puzzled. "Split your personality? Why in the world do you want that done?"

Tears tumbled down the little man's face and he said "Oh, Doctor, I'm so lonesome!"

The psychiatrist turned to his patient and said: "You are now cured."

"Some cure," said the patient. "When I came here I was Napoleon. Now I am just another nobody."

A psychiatrist has been defined by H. E. Martz as a guy who specializes in trying to find out what's kooking.

Frowning psychiatrist to office nurse on the phone: "Just say we're terribly busy—not, it's a madhouse!"

"When I go to bed nights I always see yellow lights and green spots before my eyes," the girl told her friend.

"Have you ever seen a psychiatrist?"

"Oh, no. Just yellow lights and green dots."

A woman visited her psychiatrist and said: "You've got to help my husband. He has delusions and thinks he's an elevator."

"You send him in to see me," replied the psychiatrist, "and I'll try to straighten him out."

"Oh, I can't do that," answered the wife. "He's an express and doesn't stop at your floor."

PSYCHIATRIST: "So you think you're a dog?"
MAN: "Arf-Arf!"
PSYCHIATRIST: "How long have you been thinking you're a dog?"
MAN: "Ever since I was a puppy."

PSYCHIATRIST: "Do you have trouble making up your mind?"
PATIENT: "Well, yes and no."

"Come, come," the smiling psychiatrist said to his sobbing patient. "You mustn't carry on like this. Cheer up! Be happy!"

"Be happy!" echoed the tearful woman. "How can I be happy? Sixteen children I've had by that husband of mine, and he doesn't even love me. What is there for me to be happy about?"

"Well," suggested the doctor, "imagine what it would have been like if he did love you."

Since Ed couldn't stop snapping his fingers, he went to see a psychiatrist.

"Why do you do this?" asked the doctor.

"It keeps the tigers away, Doc."

"My good man," replied the psychiatrist, "there are no tigers within 6,000 miles."

"Effective, isn't it?" he asked.

A Park Avenue psychiatrist told a story about a patient he felt was making good progress in the cure of a split personality. "I was optimistic," confessed the psychiatrist, "until this patient called and demanded to know why he'd received only one bill."

The purchasing agent had been tormented for weeks by the same nightmare: He dreamed that grotesque animals and reptiles were rushing in and out under his bed. His psychiatrist tried all sorts of things to help him, but nothing seemed to work, until one day the man came in with a big grin and related how his brother-in-law had solved his problem.

"Is your brother-in-law also a psychiatrist?" asked the doctor.

"Nope, he's a carpenter. He just sawed the legs off the bed."

The first time she came into my office—I'm a psychiatrist—a new patient seemed to have great difficulty in expressing herself. She didn't know what to say, or she was reluctant to say it. I wasn't concerned because this often happens at the beginning and I felt that this problem would work itself out in further sessions.

At the second session, after a long and fidgety silence, she looked at me hesitantly and said, "I don't mean to tell you how to run your business, Doctor, but I talk much more freely after four old fashioneds."

After a long hard struggle the man finally gave in and went to a psychiatrist. The head doctor began his testing by drawing a straight line. "What does that make you think of?" he asked his patient.

"Two people making love," was the answer.

The doctor then drew two straight lines and asked the same question.

"Four people making love," came the reply.

Now the doctor drew three straight lines and asked the question the third time, only to be answered, "six people making love."

The psychiatrist put the pencil down, shook his head and said, "You really are obsessed with sex."

"Look who's talking; there is nothing wrong with me. You're the guy who sits there drawing dirty pictures."

A psychiatrist saw another psychiatrist plodding down the street carrying a couch on his head. "Why the couch?" he called after his colleague.

Came the reply from the burdened one, "House call."

A psychiatrist's couch is where you land when you go off your rocker.

Ad placed by a psychiatrist: "Satisfaction guaranteed or your MANIA back."

WORRIED MAN TO PSYCHIATRIST: "All day long I eat grapes."
PSYCHIATRIST: "So what? Lots of people eat grapes."
WORRIED MAN: "Off the wallpaper?"

Simile: As helpless as a psychiatrist without a couch.

"I'm worried," said the wife to the psychiatrist. "My husband thinks he's a horse."

"I believe I can cure him," said the psychiatrist, "but it'll take quite a lot of money."

"Oh, money is no object," said the wife, "he just won the Kentucky Derby."

PSYCHIATRIST: "Now, Mr. Smith, I want you to fix your gaze on the small black square on the card until I say 'stop.'"

SMITH *(when doc stops him):* "Okay, now what?"

PSYCHIATRIST: "Tell me, my boy, while you were staring at the black square, what were you thinking about?"

SMITH: "I was thinking of necking with a beautiful woman."

PSYCHIATRIST: "Mr. Smith! I've been in this profession for 35 years, and I've always used this test with success, but your reaction is the strangest and the first of its kind I've ever experienced!"

SMITH: "Hell, Doc! What's so odd about it? That's what I'm always thinking about."

Railroads

"Now, sir. You've applied for a job as a switchman. What would you do if you saw two trains approaching on the same track?"

"I'd throw the lever and switch one onto another track."

"And if the lever was jammed?"

"I'd grab a red flag and run out on the track."

"And if the engineer didn't see you?"

"I'd call my sister."

"Your sister? What could she do?"

"Nothing, but she just loves to see train wrecks."

A reporter was first at the scene of a railroad wreck. Rushing up to a battered man, he asked: "How many were hurt?"

"Haven't heard of anyone being hurt," said the battered man.

"What was the cause of the wreck?" asked the reporter.

"Wreck? I haven't heard of any wreck."

"You haven't? Who are you anyway?" inquired the reporter.

"I'm the claim agent of this railroad," replied the battered man.

Eagle Eye, the Indian detective, ran low along the railroad ties. His partner, Half Squint, ran up and asked, "What you look-um for, Eagle?"

"Me look-um for Big Chief who own railroad."

"Think maybe you find him?"

"Sure. Me on his track."

Reading Matter

Asked the old question, "If you were marooned on a desert island, what would you like to have for reading matter?" a chorus-girl unhesitatingly replied, "A tattooed sailor."

Real Estate (see Homes)

The real estate salesman spent all day Sunday showing a couple through model homes.

"And here," he wearily said at the tenth home he had shown, "is the hobby room. Do you folks have any hobbies?"

"Yes," replied the woman, "looking through model homes on Sundays."

The salesman was showing his prospect through a house. Everything was fine until the prospect glanced up at the ceiling and found unmistakably obvious signs of water damage. "It's a bit damp, isn't it?" he asked.

"Damp!" the salesman enthused. "Of course it's damp! Just think what an advantage that would be in case of fire!"

PROSPECT: "Ye gads! What a tumbled-down looking shack. What's holding it together?"

AGENT: "The termites are holding hands."

A contractor took a friend to see some inexpensive houses he had just built. The friend stood in one room, the contractor in the next and the latter asked, "Can you hear me," in a very low voice.

"Sure."

"Can you see me?"

"No."

"Them's some walls for you, ain't they?"

Relatives (see Ancestors)

A close relative is one you see occasionally between funerals.

HE: "Do you have a fairy god-father?"

SHE: "No, but we've got an uncle we're not sure of."

"Sir, I'll have you understand that I'm related to the Boones."

"Oh, yes, now I remember. Your grandmother's first name was Bab."

Religion (see Preachers, Church)

"What is the person who brings you into contact with the spirit world called?"

"A bartender, my boy."

A minister walked through the lobby of a hotel one morning and noticed a ballplayer he knew by sight. So he sauntered over to the player and introduced himself and said: "One thing I've always wondered . . . why must you play ball on Sunday?"

"Well, Reverend," smiled the player, "Sunday is our biggest day . . . we get the best crowds . . . take in more money . . . and, after all, Sunday is your biggest day, too, isn't it?"

There was a nod of understanding, but the minister explained: "Yes, but there's a little difference. You see, I'm in the right field."

The player brightened and responded eagerly: "So am I . . . and ain't that sun hell out there?"

"You shouldn't play such flippant tunes on Sunday," her pastor told a young girl. "Don't you know the Ten Commandments?"

"I'm not sure, but if you'll whistle a bit of it, maybe it will come to me."

The young minister sitting down to dinner was asked by his equally young wife to say grace. He opened the casserole dish she had prepared from a new French recipe book and encountered a number of refrigerator left-overs. "Well, I don't know," he said dubiously, not being a casserole man himself, "it seems to me I've blessed all this stuff before."

SHOUTED THE EVANGELIST: "Adultery is as bad as murder! Isn't that so, Sister Johnson?"

SISTER JOHNSON: "I don't rightly know. I ain't never killed nobody."

A man entered the post office with a package containing a Bible. The postal attendant looked over the tightly wrapped parcel, shook it, and asked, "Is there anything breakable in this?"

"Nothing but the Ten Commandments," was the reply.

The priest met Mary O'Brien and asked what she was concealing under her cape. She said it was holy water. The priest reached for the bottle, uncorked it and sniffed. "Why, Mary," he exclaimed, "this isn't holy water; this is gin!" Whereupon Mary crossed herself and said: "Glory be to God, another miracle!"

"Miss Helen," said the parson impressively, as he led her into the brook for baptism, "I'se gwine lead you out inter dis heah stream, an' wash out ever' spot o' sin you's got."

"Lawsy, Pahson," giggled the erstwhile frolicsome damsel, "in that li'l ole shallow creek?"

A Scottish minister, asked if he thought it wrong to take a walk in the country on Sunday, said, "Well, as I see it, there's no harm in takin' a walk on the Sawbath, sae long as ye dinna enjoy yourself."

LADY *(engaging new maid)*: "And what denomination are you?"
MAID: "Well, mum, mother goes to the Baptist Church and father goes to the Methodist, but speaking for myself, I'm radio."

ST. PETER: "Welcome, friend. Here's your golden harp."
NEWCOMER: "Thanks. When is the first payment due?"

Reputation

A prim little old lady was telling her friend about her awful shock upon finding two empty whiskey bottles in her garbage can.

"You can imagine my embarrassment," she said. "I got them out fast, because I didn't want the garbage man to think I drink."

"What did you do with them?" asked her friend.

"Well, the preacher lives next door," was the reply, "so I put them in his can. Everybody knows he doesn't drink."

SHE: "Do you know what they are saying about me?"
HE: "Sure do. Why do you think I'm here?"

The pretty young thing had convinced the ardent young man of her purity, and that way kept him somewhat in check. However, as they parted that night, he begged for "just one good night kiss."

"But I can't kiss you here in the hall," she replied. "Someone might see us and what would they think?"

"Then let's step into your room."

"My roommate would resent that," she assured him.

"Oh, now," he cajoled, "I'm sure your roommate wouldn't mind me taking just one sweet kiss from your chaste lips."

"You're wrong there," she told him. "He's extremely jealous of me."

Resolution

A New Year's resolution is something that goes in one year and out the other.

Restaurant

Sign in Restaurant: "The silver is not medicine. Please do not take it after meals."

IMPATIENT CUSTOMER: "I only get an hour for lunch, Miss."
WAITRESS *(as she hurries by):* "I can't discuss labor troubles with you now."

CUSTOMER: "My word, waiter, what kind of soup is this?"
WAITER: "It's bean soup, sir."
CUSTOMER: "I don't care what it's been, what is it now?"

DINER: "Waiter, where's the ham in this sandwich?"
WAITER: "Take another bite, sir."
DINER *(taking huge mouthful):* "Hmmm. Not yet."
WAITER: "Darn it, you must have gone right past it."

DINER: "Waiter, this soup is cold. Bring me some that's hot."
WAITER: "What do you want me to do? Burn my thumb?"

A gentleman was dining at an exclusive restaurant. It seems his veal chops were rather tough, so he called the waiter over to complain.
DINER: "These chops are much too tough to be veal."
WAITER: "I can assure you, sir, that they are veal. I was a butcher once and I can tell you that not more than three months ago that meat was on the hoof, following the cow around."
DINER: "Probably so, but not for milk!"

Don't censure a man for flirting with the waitress. He may be playing for big steaks.

There's the restaurant that served bread sprinkled with sand to keep the butter from slipping.

"I'm sorry," said the diner, "but I haven't any money to pay for that meal."
"That's all right," said the cashier. "We'll write your name on the wall and you can pay the next time you come in."
"Don't do that. Everybody who comes in will see it."
"Oh, no they won't," said the cashier. "Your overcoat will be hanging over it."

The pretty waitress complained that everything she did seemed wrong.
"How about a date tonight?" asked the diner.

Said the diner to the waitress: "Is your ice cream pure?"
WAITRESS: "As pure as the girl of your dreams."
DINER: "Give me the apple pie."

SCOTSMAN: "I see there's a rule against tipping here."
WAITRESS: "Well bless your little heart, apples were forbidden in the Garden of Eden, too!"

"Waiter, bring me some of this Spumoni Vermicelli on the menu."
"I'm sorry, sir. That's the proprietor and he's out right now."

A man walked into a restaurant and left the door open.
A rough character called out: "Shut the door! Were you brought up in a barn?"
The man closed the door, went to a vacant table, sat down, and began to cry.
The shouter looked most uncomfortable so he went over to the man, patting him on the shoulder and said: "I'm sorry. I didn't mean to hurt your feelings. I only wanted you to close the door."
"I'm not crying because you hurt my feelings," was the reply. "But the fact is, every time I hear a donkey bray, it makes me feel homesick."

Waiters usually size you up—from tip to tip.

In bringing the change from a $5 for a $1.45 check the waiter gave the patron three dollars, a half dollar, and a nickel.
The patron fumbled for a moment, and then picked up the half dollar, the dollar bills and left the nickel.
"You should use better judgment," said the patron. "You should have brought me two quarters instead of the half dollar."
"Well," said the waiter. "Let us say I gambled and lost."

"I'll take the dollar dinner."
"On white or rye bread?"

FATHER (to waitress): "Wrap up the rest of the steak for the dog."
SMALL SON: "Oh, goody! We're going to get a dog."

FUSSY DINER: "Waiter, bring me one large chop, with French-fried potatoes, and I'll have the chop lean."
WAITER: "Yes, sir. Lean which way, sir?"

WATIER: "And how did you find your steak, sir?"
DINER: "Why, I just moved this little piece of fried potato, and there it was."

A long-suffering diner noted that his coffee was served without a spoon. "This coffee," he remarked proudly, "is going to be pretty hot to stir with my finger."

Soon the waiter returned with another cup of coffee.

"Maybe this isn't so hot, sir," he said.

Luke had been drinking beer all afternoon and finally wandered into a restaurant to eat a bite.

"Bring me an order of sardines," he said.

"Do you wish them served in the can, sir?" the waitress asked.

"No, but you better hurry."

MAC: "Gimme two eggs."

NICK: "How d'you want 'em cooked?"

MAC: "Is there any difference in price?"

NICK: "Nope, same price any way you take 'em."

MAC: "Good! I'd like 'em cooked with a slice of ham."

There's a Chinese restaurant in Chicago that serves you all the food you can eat for 50 cents. Trouble is, they only give you one chopstick.

"Waiter, I ordered chicken pot pie but there isn't a piece of chicken in it!"

"That's no surprise," the waiter answered. "Don't expect too much in our cottage cheese, either."

CY YOUNG: "How long have you been working here?"

WAITER: "Just started a week ago, sir."

CY: "Then you can't be the one who took my order."

A waiter in a chic restaurant stumbled accidently, pouring a drink, ice cubes and all, down the back of a lady customer.

The woman gasped, giggled, wriggled and writhed as she tried to get the ice cubes out. With all eyes on her she leaped to her feet, overturning the table and knocking her escort to the floor. Then the two hurried out in wild confusion.

"Waiter," called an onlooker on the other side of the room, "we'll have two of whatever they had."

A diner rushed over to the manager of the restaurant.

"I turned my head and someone stole my topcoat," he screamed.

"What kind of topcoat did you have?" asked the manager.

"It was a brown tweed coat with raglan sleeves," replied the customer.

"Mmmmmm!" mused the manager. "Come to think of it, I saw a man walking out of here with that very coat on."

"Quick!" demanded the customer. "What did the guy look like?"

The manager shook his head. "Terrible," he sighed, "the sleeves were too short for him."

"Miss, this coffee looks like mud."

"I don't doubt it at all, sir; it was ground this morning."

A man who was a dog trainer suddenly found himself nearly bankrupt and was forced to go to work until he could recoup his losses so that he could start out in the dog raising business again. He found a job as a waiter in a small restaurant in a nearby town and after working for a few days, he said brightly to the owner of the place:

"I'm turning out to be a pretty good waiter, don't you think?"

"Well," said the owner, "if you don't mind, I'm going to make a couple of suggestions about your work."

"Such as?" asked the waiter.

"Well," said the owner, "when the customer refuses to eat his food, we don't rub his nose in it!"

The sign in the restaurant window read: "$500 reward to anybody who orders something we can't furnish."

A fellow read the sign and decided to pick up what he thought would be an easy $500. Entering, he sat down at a table and said to the waitress, "Bring me an elephant ear sandwich." The gal's face fell. Hurrying to the kitchen, she said to the chef: "Better get ready to fork over 5 C's. There's a guy out front who wants an elephant ear sandwich."

"What!" bellowed the chef. "You mean to tell me we're out of elephant ears?"

"No, we're not out of elephant ears," replied the waitress, "but we ain't got no more of them big buns."

Retailing—Shopping

"How do you like being in business for yourself?" the salesman asked of his newly established customer.

"I'm not sure yet," was the reply. "The police won't let me park in front of my store, the tax agents tell me how to keep my books, my banker tells me how much I have to keep in my account, the building inspector tells me how my building must be maintained, my customers tell me what kind of goods I have to carry, and the post office tells me how big my mailings have to be. To top it all off, I just got married."

The executive stopped in a grocery store on his way home and selected six medium-sized apples. "That will be $1.80," said the clerk. The executive handed him two dollars and started to leave. "You forgot your change, sir," called the clerk.

"That's all right," replied the exec. "I stepped on a grape on the way in."

CUSTOMER: "Why is it I never get what I ask for here?"
SALESGIRL: "Perhaps, madam, we are too polite."

WOMAN CUSTOMER TO FURRIER: "Could you have the coat delivered with the price tag still on it to my neighbor Mr. Flegenheimer by mistake?"

NICE SALESLADY (*showing lingerie to much frustrated gentleman customer*): "This is the only place you can touch these for anything near the price."

After looking at the thermometers for a few minutes, a woman finally picked one out. "I'll take this Fahrenheit one," she said to the clerk. "I know it's a good brand."

A dignified-looking middle-aged gentleman decided to take advantage of a special sale and buy his wife a pair of nylons. After waiting about an hour on the fringe of a screaming, pushing mob of women, he plunged towards the counter with both arms flying. Suddenly a shrill voice hollered out, "Can't you act like a gentleman?"

"I've been acting like a gentleman for over an hour and it got me nowhere," he replied, still plowing toward the counter. "Now I'm going to act like a lady!"

Retirement

A farmer retired and moved to the city. On the first morning in their new home his wife said: "Pa, it's time you got up and started the fire."

"Not me!" he exclaimed, nestling deeper in bed. "We might as well start now getting used to all the city conveniences. Call the fire department!"

One woman's definition of retirement: Twice as much husband and half as much income.

Russia

Russia—a place where nobody sits up all night to see how the election came out.

In Russia, it doesn't take a fellow long to talk his head off.

Everyone is proving himself physically fit by walking 50 miles against the clock. Even the Russians have joined the marathon. And they claim a new record.

A Red Army general has gone 100 miles by foot in a little under 12 hours—on the back of an enlisted man.

"Oh, boy!" cried the Russian genius who had gotten hold of an American mail-order catalog. "Look at all these wonderful new things to invent!"

Three cellmates in a Red prison were talking things over. The first factory hand said he was accused of absenteeism for being late to work. The second told how he was five minutes early for work and was charged with spying. The third one said: "I came to work on time, and they accused me of buying a Western watch."

The manager of a Russian factory was boasting to a foreigner.
"Would you believe it, our production increased 640 per cent last month!"
"What do you make?" asked the visitor.
"We manufacture signs that read 'Out of Order.'"

A bull may be only a bull but he declared war on the Red flag long before any of the rest of us knew what it stood for.

The Russian big shot, making a tour of his country's grade schools, was impressed by the answers he was getting from one bright sixth grade boy.
"What can you tell me about the United States?" asked the man from the Kremlin.
The lad answered: "The United States is a country where a few rich men dominate millions of poor people, most of them downtrodden, illiterate, starving and stupid."
"Ah," beamed the Russian leader, "very good. Now tell me, what is the aim of Russia?"
"To catch up with the United States," said the lad.

Safety

A taxi driver was darting in and out of heavy traffic with complete abandon. After a few harrowing blocks, the passenger leaned forward and said, "Would you be more careful, please? I have eight children at home."

The driver glanced over his shoulder at her and replied, "Lady! You're telling *me* to be careful?"

The best insurance against auto accidents is a Sunday afternoon nap.

Satisfaction

"Wonder who is more satisfied—a man with a million dollars or a man with six kids?"

"A man with six kids."

"Can you prove it?"

"Well, a man with a million dollars always wants more."

There is no greater satisfaction than parking on what's left of the other fellow's nickel.

Savings—Thrift

Savings: About the only thing you can save out of your pay these days—is the envelope.

Thrift is a wonderful thing—and who hasn't wished his ancestors had practiced it more!

Here's a fool-proof method on "How to become a millionaire." You merely go to the bank every week and deposit $20,000. At the end of the year, you are a millionaire.

School (see Education, College)

A principal, proud of a newly painted wall in his school, had the following sign put up: "This is a partition, not a petition. No signatures are required."

"Dad, I put a stick of dynamite under the teacher's chair today."

"What! Well, you go right back to school and apologize this minute!"

"What school?"

Scotsmen

An Irishman, after paying his respects in the cemetery, walked about looking over some of the old tombstones. He stopped before one on which was engraved: "Here lies Sandy MacGregor—A Generous Father and a Pious Man."

"Huh!" exclaimed the Irishman. "Just like the Scots—three men in one grave!"

A young Scot went into the telegraph office early one morning and wired a proposal of marriage to his sweetheart. After spending the entire day and part of the night waiting, he was finally rewarded by an affirmative reply.

"If I were you," suggested the operator who delivered the message, "I'd think twice before I'd marry a girl who kept me waiting all day for my answer."

"Na, na," replied the young Scot. "The lass who waits for the night rate is the lass for me."

The Scot said to his neighbor, "So your fifth daughter's getting married, Jock. You must be very pleased."

"Aye," returned Jock, "but the rice is gettin' awful dirty."

Did you hear about the Scot who was building a home, and called up the Masonic Hall to send him two free masons?

Having noticed that his Scottish guide usually went bare-headed in all sorts of weather, the London sportsman made him a gift of a fur cap with heavy ear flaps. On his next visit to the shooting box, he asked the old Scot how he liked the cap.

"I hae not wore it since the accident," was the gloomy reply.

"What accident?" asked the sportsman.

"Jock MacLeod offered to buy me a drink and I didna hear him."

"Won't you give a shilling to the Lord?" asked the Salvation Army lassie.

"How auld are ye?" inquired the Scotsman.

"Nineteen, sir."

"Ah well, I'm past seventy-five. I'll be seein' Him afore ye, so I'll hand it to Him myself."

A Scotsman and a dozen friends had just finished eating when the waiter arrived with the check.

"Give it to me; I'll pay it," came in loud tones from the Scotsman.

The following day headlines appeared in the newspapers stating, "Scotsman kills ventriloquist."

The day after MacTavish's wife presented him with offspring, the proud father was seen buying a baby bottle.

"Hoot, mon, what an extravagance," said a friend.

"No," sighed MacTavish, "this time 'tis not—the woman's gone and had triplets."

A canny Scot was engaged in an argument with a conductor as to whether the fare was to be five or ten cents. Finally the disgusted conductor picked up the Scot's suitcase and tossed it off the train just as they were crossing a bridge. It landed with a mighty splash.

"Hoot, mon," screamed the Scot. "First ye try to rob me and now you've drowned me boy."

Secretary

"What previous experience have you had and what type of work did you do?" asked the manager.

"I was a secretary. All I had to do was look like a girl, think like a man, act like a lady, and work like a dog."

If you want a job done fast, give it to a busy executive. He'll have his secretary do it.

"When I applied for a job the manager had the nerve to ask if my punctuation was good," said the secretary.

"What did you tell him?"

"I said I'd never been late for work in my life."

Boss to his voluptuous secretary: "Take the afternoon off, Miss May —I want to think."

One stenographer to another: "You'll like it here—lots of opportunity for advances."

EMPLOYER: "Who told you that you could neglect your office duties just because I kissed you once in a while?"

SECRETARY: "My lawyer."

"I'm Mr. Brown's wife," said a brunette, introducing herself to an attractive blonde at a party.

"I'm his secretary," said the blonde.

"Oh," said the brunette, arching her eyebrows slightly, "were you?"

HOSTESS: "I have a lonesome bachelor I'd like you girls to meet."

ATHLETIC GIRL: "What can he do?"

CHORUS GIRL: "How much money does he have?"

SOCIETY GIRL: "Who is his family?"

RELIGIOUS GIRL: "What church does he belong to?"

SECRETARY: "Where is he?"

SECRETARY *(to busy executive over the intercom): "*Your little girl wants to kiss you over the phone."

BUSY EXECUTIVE: "Take the message. I'll get it from you later."

"Well, my dear," said the businessman who had married his secretary. "I must get someone to replace you at the office."

"I've been thinking of that," replied the bride. "My cousin is just leaving school."

"What's her name?"

"John Smith," said the bride.

Two hard-working secretaries were heard singing the blues while riding home from work on the bus. "Isn't it fierce the way we have to work these days?"

"Fierce is not the word," replied the other. "Why, I typed so many letters yesterday that last night I finished my prayers with 'Yours truly.'"

Oil and water mix better than wives and secretaries.

It was Friday at 5 P.M. and the office staff was about to leave for the week-end when the boss rushed out and asked his secretary, "What are you going to do this Sunday night, Miss Jones?"

"Why nothing, nothing at all," she replied.

"Wonderful!" he exclaimed. "Then maybe you'll be on time next Monday morning."

BOSS TO STENOGRAPHER: "Congratulations, Miss Hopkins. This is the earliest you've been late."

"If I'd ask you to become my secretary at $150 a week would you say yes?"

"Sure. A dozen times a day, if necessary."

BOSS: "You are twenty minutes late again. Don't you know what time we start work?"

STENO: "No sir, They're always at it when I get here."

"I'm really not late, boss," said the tardy secretary, hanging up her hat. "I just took my coffee break before coming in."

The tycoon's secretary was just comfortably settled on his lap when the great man looked up and saw his wife entering his office. With remarkable presence of mind he immediately started dictating:

"Jones Furniture Company. Gentlemen. Strikes or no strikes, how long do you think I can run an office with only one office chair? We must have delivery immediately!"

On bulletin board in big office building: "Owing to the shortage of heating fuel, employers are asked to take advantage of their typists between the hours of 12 and 2."

"My wife engaged a new secretary for me."
"Well, there's nothing wrong about that. Is she blonde or brunette?"
"He's bald."

BOSS TO NEW SECRETARY: "You're improving, Miss Talbot. Several of these one- and two-letter words are spelled correctly."

BOSS: "Why are you late this morning?"
"STENO: "On my way to work a man followed me all the way."
BOSS: "And you think that's sufficient excuse for being so late?"
STENO: "Well, you see . . . the man walked so slowly!"

SEXY OFFICE STENO: "Can you tattoo a cat on my right knee?"
TATTOO ARTIST: "Sure—but there's a special discount on giraffes this week!"

HUSBAND: "Why shouldn't I be friendly with my secretary? We work together every day—it's only logical."
WIFE: "Wouldn't 'biological' be a better word, dear?"

"There goes the only woman I ever loved."
"Why don't you marry her?"
"I can't afford to—she's the best stenographer I've got."

The boss was exasperated with his new secretary. She ignored the telephone when it rang. Finally he said, irritably: "You must answer the phone."

"Okay," she replied, "but it seems so silly. Nine times out of ten it's for you."

Hard times note: The girl received a pay cut. She said: "There go my dollar lunches." She got another pay cut. She said: "There goes my extra hose." Later she got still another cut. Wailed she: "There goes my amateur standing!"

A business school teacher was quizzing her class of stenographers. "What is the first thing you do when your employer buzzes?"

A hand shot up quickly: "You pick up your notebook and pencil and answer that buzzard promptly."

Two executives were in the woods hunting for moose. "I'll sound my new moose-call horn," one said confidently, and did so. "There! That'll bring 'em."

But no moose appeared—instead, dozens of mice came running. The executive who had sounded the horn stared, then uttered an imprecation. "That secretary of mine!" he fumed. "I ordered a moose-call by mail—and she had to make a typographical error!"

The head of a firm was frowning over a letter. Calling his chief clerk he said, "That new stenographer—you surely did not hire her on account of her grammar!"

"Grammar!" echoed the clerk. "Gosh, Boss, I thought you told me to pick one out for *glamour*."

The stenographer seemed a terrible grouch. Nobody could ask her anything without getting his head snapped off. She growled at this and grumbled at that, and made herself generally unpleasant the whole day long. But being a good worker she was kept on.

The very next morning she came in all smiles. She hummed to herself as she rattled the keys. When the boss gave her a mess of correspondence she did it in jig time, dropped it on his desk, and asked for more.

"Well, I'll be damned!" exclaimed the boss. "Are you sick, by any chance?"

"Am I sick?" she grinned back at him. "I'll tell the world I'm sick!"

'Tis said that if wives knew what secretaries think of their husbands, they wouldn't worry.

The secretary said she'd do anything for a fur coat. When she finally got it, she couldn't button it.

STENOGRAPHER: "Did you know that this 'To Be Done Today' memo on your desk calendar is two months old?"
Boss: "Sure, that's all right. I haven't done it yet."

WIFE: "I got you this bottle of hair tonic, darling."
HUSBAND: "But my hair isn't falling out."
WIFE: "I know, but I want you to give it to your typist at the office; her hair is coming out rather badly."

There's the gal who handed her boss the morning mail, and pointed to the top letter: "This one was marked 'personal' and 'confidential'—but it really isn't."

JANET: "How is your typing coming along?"
JUNE: "Fine, I can type 20 mistakes a minute."

Selling—Salesmanship

"How are you getting along?" asked the old timer of the new salesman.
"Not so good," came the disgusted reply. "I've been insulted in every place I made a call."
"That's funny," said the old man. "I've been on the road 40 years, I've had my samples flung in the street, been tossed downstairs, manhandled by janitors, and rolled in the gutter, but insulted—never!"

SALES MANAGER: "Gather around me, you so-called salesmen, while I tell you about a sales contest I'm gonna conduct, a contest by which the winning salesman gets to keep his job!"

The weary door-to-door salesman was stopped late one afternoon by a police officer who demanded to see his solicitor's license. "I don't have anything like that," replied the salesman.
"Don't you know you can't sell anything without a license?" the officer asked.
"Thank you for telling me," said the salesman. "I knew I wasn't selling anything but I couldn't figure out why."

LADY OF THE HOUSE: "I don't need none!"
SALESMAN: "How do you know? I might be selling grammars."

"In order to be a top-notch salesman, you must be a real psychologist," bragged a hot-shot salesman. "You must not only outguess the other fellow, you also have to be able to read his mind. For example, right this minute I know exactly what you are thinking."

"Gee, that's swell," said the purchasing agent, with a touch of sarcasm, "Then, why don't you go there?"

The cub salesman was about to go off on his first field trip. As he was making up his schedule, he realized he didn't know the flying time to his destination, so he telephoned the airline and asked: "How long does it take to fly to Los Angeles?"

"Just a minute," replied the switchboard operator.

"Thank you," said the young man and hung up.

"I can't get back to the office this afternoon," reported the salesman to his sales manager on the phone. "A bunch of thieves stripped my car while I was at lunch. They've stolen the steering wheel, the brake pedal, the accelerator and the entire dashboard."

The sales manager expressed his regrets, suggested a call to the police, and said he'd see the salesman in the morning. A few minutes later the phone rang again.

"I'll be in after all," said the salesman, with a slight hiccup. "I got in the back seat by mistake."

A supersalesman is a husband who can convince his wife she's too fat for a mink coat.

"But how can you sell hair tonic when you have no hair?"

"What's wrong with that? I know a guy who sells brassieres."

REPORTER TO CITY EDITOR: "Here's the perfect news story."

CITY EDITOR: "Man bites dog?"

REPORTER: "No, this is even better . . . the bull threw the salesman."

The boss and his sales manager looked gloomily at the sales chart on the wall. In one corner was a graph showing the company's descending profits. The rest of the chart contained a map of the territory with pins stuck in it, showing the location of each salesman.

"Frankly," the sales manager sighed. "The only hope is to take the pins out of the map and stick them in the salesmen."

The receptionist was pretty, and the visiting salesman lost no time in trying to impress her with his many charms. He bragged on and on about his exploits in selling, his former life as a football hero, his success with the fair sex, and everything else he could think of.

The young lady tried to get on with her work, but that didn't dissuade the story-teller. Finally, she looked up innocently and asked, "Tell me, have you ever had a group photograph taken of yourself?"

A good salesman is one who sells goods that don't come back to customers who do. The ultimate salesman is the guy who can make his wife feel sorry for the girl who lost her compact in his car.

"Are you a salesman, bill collector, or friend of the boss?" asked the receptionist.

"All three," said the salesman.

"Well, then, he's at a conference, out of town, and step into the office and see him."

"Well," said the farmer, "that fellow was sure some salesman. He sold me two milking machines for one cow and then took the cow as a down payment."

A persistent salesman refused to leave when the secretary told him the boss was out. An hour passed, then two. Finally, weary of being a prisoner in his own office, the boss admitted the salesman.

"My secretary told you I was out," exclaimed the puzzled boss. "How'd you know I was in?"

"Easy," explained the salesman. "Your secretary was working."

Mr. Ego, the hot-shot salesman, was dictating his sales report to a public stenographer. After addressing it to his boss, and detailing his successes, he went on with:

"I feel you should know, sir, that in order to obtain the above mentioned contract, I found it necessary to employ every ounce of my personal charm and magnetism, my diplomacy was the most deft, and flawless tact was imperative. With these fine efforts, I am pleased to inform you, I was able to crown my approach with success."

The steno smiled wryly and asked, "Crowtation marks on that last paragraph?"

WIFE: "What's all the excitement about—why are you throwing things out of drawers? What have you lost?"

SALESMAN HUSBAND: "I got an order today, and I've mislaid the address of my firm."

The sales manager believed in pressuring his men constantly. Nothing they could do was ever right, and he was forever haranguing at them. One day he called one of his men on the carpet and started his usual needling:

"Jones," he shouted, "you'd better shape up around here! This is the fourth month in a row that you've been only 20% over your quota. And one of your customers told me you sometimes fib a little."

"Yes, but I mean well," replied the salesman meekly. "I think it's a man's duty to speak well of his boss once in a while."

A supersalesman was hunting one Sunday morning out in the woods and went down to a nearby spring with his gun and a water pail to get water with which to make his coffee. Upon straightening up from the spring he found himself face to face with a very vicious looking bear. Dropping the pail but still hanging on to his rifle, he cleared a nearby fence in one bound to find himself confronted by an enraged bull. Being a super-salesman, however, he turned and fired his one cartridge through the fence, killing the bear. He knew that he could shoot the bull any time.

"I want to see your boss," snapped the ill-mannered salesman to the secretary.

"I'm sorry, sir," she replied, "he isn't in this morning. May I help you?"

"No! I never deal with underlings! I'll wait!"

At 5 o'clock the obviously annoyed visitor demanded, "When will your boss be in?"

"In about two weeks, sir," the secretary replied sweetly. "He left yesterday on his vacation."

A salesman rapped on the screen door at a house where, just inside and plainly visible, an eight-year-old was painfully practicing his piano lesson. "Sonny," he inquired pleasantly, "is your mother home?"

The boy gave the salesman a murderous look over his shoulder, then growled, "What do you think, mister?"

"George is so forgetful," the sales manager complained to his secretary, "it's a wonder he can sell anything. I asked him to pick up some cigarettes on his way back from lunch, and I'm not sure he'll even remember to come back."

Just then the door flew open and in bounced George. "You'll never guess what happened," he shouted. "While I was at lunch, I met old man Brown, who hasn't bought anything from us for five years. Well, we got to talking and by the time we reached dessert he gave me this half-million dollar order!"

"See," sighed the manager, "he forgot the cigarettes."

The sales manager took one of his men off to the side for a friendly bit of advice. "If I were you, Jones, I wouldn't let your wife go around this year's sales convention like she did last year saying she's made a man of you. You don't hear my wife saying that."

"No," Jones agreed, "but I've heard your wife telling my wife that she'd done her best."

The ambitious young salesman set out to conquer the world, but after his very first sales call, he returned dejectedly to his office. "What happened?" asked his sales manager.

"I guess I just didn't hit it off with my prospect," said the salesman sadly.

"Didn't he even invite you to come back some other time?"

"Ask me!" replied the youngster, with tears in his eyes. "Ask me? He dared me!"

Item in a country newspaper: "Miss C____ H____ reported to the police the loss of $20 today. She said the money was concealed in her stocking, and the loss was discovered soon after the departure of the vacuum cleaner salesman who had been demonstrating his line."

"No, I'm afraid you can't interest me in a vacuum cleaner. Try the lady next door. I always use hers and it's absolutely terrible."

"When is the best time to see Mr. Brown?"

"It's hard to say," replied the receptionist. "Before lunch he's grouchy, and after lunch he has indigestion."

Trying to sell a housewife a home freezer, a salesman pointed out, "You can save enough on your food bills to pay for the freezer."

"Yes, I know," the woman replied, "but you see we're paying for our washing machine on the laundry bills we save, and we're paying for the house on the rent we save. We just can't afford to save any more right now."

Two salesmen were verbally raking their sales manager over the coals. "To me," said one, "he's a pain in the neck!"

"That's funny," said the other. "I have a much lower opinion of him."

Servants—Help—Maids

MISTRESS *(to maid who had just given notice):* "Haven't we always treated you like one of the family, Mary?"

MAID: "Yes, ma'am, you have, and I can't stand it any longer."

MISTRESS: "When you were hired you told me one reason you were such a good maid was that you never got tired. This is the third afternoon I've come into the kitchen and found you asleep."

MAID: "Yes, ma'am. That's how I never get tired."

A haughty dowager visited the hospital to see her chauffeur, badly injured in an auto accident. The head nurse hesitated:

"He's very sick and should see no one but his family. Are you his wife?"

Highly indignant, the dowager blurted out: "I certainly am not—I'm his mistress."

MRS. SMYTHE: "There is no honesty anywhere! My maid has run away and taken three of my best dresses."

MRS. BROWNE: "Which ones, dear?"

MRS. SMYTHE: "Those I smuggled through the customs when I returned from Paris!"

Hilda the servant girl approached the mistress in tears, to announce that she must leave. The shocked housewife demanded the reason since she appeared to be perfectly happy. The maid explained that she had met a handsome soldier who had talked fast and acted faster, and now she was waiting for a little stranger. The wife consulted her husband and soon returned with the comforting assurance that the couple would adopt the coming baby. Some months later, a son was born, adopted legally, and all was well again until the maid again announced she was leaving, this time because a sailor talked fast and acted faster. The couple consulted again and decided to adopt the second child, which proved to be a darling baby girl. All was well again, until the blow fell. The maid resigned. "Don't tell me," gasped the wife, "that this time it was a marine!"

"It's not that at all," said the maid with quiet dignity. "I am resigning because I can't work for such a large family."

"I have a new maid coming Monday," said one Park Avenue matron to another.

"How thrilling," said the other. "What are you going to wear?"

The maid had been surreptitiously using the bathtub of her employer, an elderly bishop. He was a bachelor, very fastidious about his toilet, and desired the exclusive use of his tub.

He reprimanded the maid with much indignation.

"What distresses me most, Mary, is that you have done this behind my back."

Mrs. Jones: "Now, Mary, when you are serving my husband tonight, be sure not to spill anything."

New Maid: "Don't worry, Ma'am. I won't tell a thing!"

"Can you serve company?" asked the housewife when she was hiring a new maid.

"Yes, mum, both ways."

"What do you mean, both ways?"

"So's they'll come again or stay away."

Mrs. Smith *(interviewing a new maid)*: "I forgot to ask you if you had any religious views."

New Maid: "No, mum, but I've got some dandy snapshots of Niagara Falls and the Smoky Mountains."

Sexes

Teacher: "How many sexes are there?"

Little Boy: "Three."

Teacher: "What are they?"

Little Boy: "The male sex, the female sex and insects."

The weaker sex is the stronger sex because of the weakness of the stronger sex for the weaker sex.

Sex Life

The pompous, overbearing businessman was attending a business luncheon. When dessert was being served he refused it, saying, "I've tried it before and didn't like it."

When offered a cigar, he refused and said, "I tried smoking once and didn't like it."

Brandy was also refused with the remark, "I once tried an alcoholic beverage and didn't like it. I've never touched a drop since."

The diner sitting across the table had observed the goings on. After the last remark, he leaned over and commented, "Sir, I understand that you have only one child."

Ship Launching

At a recent shipyard launching, the young woman who was to christen the boat was so nervous that the shipyard manager asked her:

"Do you have any questions, lady?"

"Yes," she replied. "How hard do I have to hit to knock it into the water?"

Shipwreck

A castaway on a desert island, following another shipwreck, pulled ashore a girl clinging to a barrel.

"How long have you been here?" asked the girl. "Thirteen years," replied the castaway.

"All alone? Then you're going to get something you haven't had for thirteen years," said the girl.

"You don't mean to tell me there's beer in that barrel," said the castaway.

A ship was torpedoed and several life boats were searching for survivors. A completely bald-headed sailor surfaced by the side of one of the boats, and an Irishman at the oars spotted him. He brought his oar down smack on the man's bald skull. "Sure, 'tis no time for fooling," said he. "Go down and come up straight."

Slander

"Pardner," said the western rancher, "where'd you move from?"

"Illinois."

"Illinois, heh? How come you leave a settled country like that and come to these lonesome hills?"

"Well, sir, my neighbors got to sayin' mean things about me."

"Why didn't you challenge them to prove their slanderous statements?"

"I did. And they did."

The slander action had been bitterly fought through the courts for several wearying days. At last the Judge got down to the essentials, and asked the defendant what he had said.

"M'lud, I merely observed that he was a sculptor who ought to wash more often."

"That seems innocuous enough," said the Judge, "but what were your exact words?"

"I said he was a dirty chiseller."

Sleep

During a conversation with an old friend he hadn't seen for some time, a Florida farmer was asked how he had been sleeping.

"I sleep good nights," he said, "and I sleep pretty good mornings, but afternoons, I just seem to twist and turn."

A vice president we heard about had more than his share of troubles. His secretary quit because, after all those coffee breaks, she couldn't sleep nights.

The older generation thought nothing of going to bed at 9 P.M. The younger generation doesn't think much of it either.

The man was more than a little annoyed when a neighbor telephoned at 3 A.M. and complained, "Your dog is barking so loudly that I can't sleep." The neighbor hung up before he could protest. The following morning at 3 A.M. he called his neighbor and said, "I don't have a dog."

"Me slept with daddy last night," said the small child to the kindergarten lady who believed in correct diction, even by the very young. With emphasis the teacher said, "I slept with daddy last night."
"Well, then," said the child, "you must have come in after I went to sleep."

An auditor got out of bed one morning and complained that he had not slept a wink. "Why didn't you count sheep?" asked his wife.
"I did, and that's what got me in trouble," he answered the auditor. "I made a mistake during the first hour, and it took me until I got up this morning to correct it."

Small Town

A small town is one where the folks know all the news before the paper comes out, but merely take it to see whether or not the editors got the stories according to the way they heard them.

The woman reporter for a newspaper in a small city was asked the secret of her journalistic success. As usual, the answer was simple.
"When a woman in a small town wears a hat and gloves on any weekday," replied the reporter, "something's going on. So I just grab her and get the dope!"

A small town is usually divided by a railway, a main street, two churches and lots of opinions.

You can always tell a small town. It's where the Sunday paper can be lifted with one hand.

Smoking

There is a way to stop smoking. Simply marry a gal who objects to it.

We don't see cigar store Indians any more. Guess lung cancer finally got 'em.

A businessman was waiting in a customer's outer office that was occupied by his secretary.

While he was watching her, she reached into the drawer of her desk and brought out a fresh cigar, lighted up and began to smoke it.

The businessman, unaccustomed to seeing women smoke cigars, was quite surprised and asked her: "How did you begin smoking cigars?"

"Oh, it was quite simple," she said. "One evening my husband came home and found a lighted cigar in our living room ashtray."

CHUCK: "Have you got a cigarette, George?"
GEORGE: "I thought you had quit smoking."
CHUCK: "Well, I'm still in the first phase—I've quit buying."

A friend didn't get that hoarse voice from smoking too many cigarettes. He got it from asking for 'em.

We have read so much about the bad effects of smoking that we have decided to give up reading.

"Look, Bill," said one junior executive to another, "why don't you either give up trying not to smoke or else do it the way my late friend did?"

"How did he do it?"

"Well, first of all he tried practically everything—sucking on hard candy, chewing gum, the whole bit. Nothing helped until he tried carrying a toothpick in his mouth all the time. Day and night he kept a toothpick between his lips until finally he broke the habit."

"That's a good idea. I think I'll try it. But tell me, you speak of your 'late' friend. What did he die of?"

"Dutch Elm Disease."

Socialism

Socialism is not an equal distribution of wealth. It is equal distribution of poverty.

Son-in-Law

MOUNTAINEER: "Doc, I want you to look at my son-in-law. I shot at him yesterday and took a piece out of his ear."

DOCTOR: "Shame on you, shooting at your son-in-law!"

MOUNTAINEER: "Huh! He wasn't my son-in-law when I shot him."

"Where was your son-in-law when you first saw him?"

"Right smack in the middle of my shotgun sights!"

Complaining about his son-in-law, a man said, "He can't drink and he can't play cards."

"But that's the kind of son-in-law to have," consoled a friend.

"No," said the man, "you don't understand. He can't play cards . . . and he plays. He can't drink . . . and he drinks."

South—Southern

The man was perched on a windowsill outside the 10th floor of a hotel in a large southern city. A police officer was trying to persuade him not to jump. "Think of your mother and family," he pleaded.

"Ain't got any."

"Well, then, think of your girl friend."

"Ain't got any."

"All right," said the officer desperately, "think of Robert E. Lee."

"Who's he?"

"Jump, you derned Yankee."

The couple were visiting friends in New Orleans and one evening attended a cocktail party with them. The wife had never visited the deep South before and she had always heard that it was a romantic place, but as the party progressed, it so far exceeded her expectations that she became a little worried.

"It's just incredible," she finally confided to the hostess. "Every man who talks to me propositions me."

"My dear, don't give it another thought," assured the older woman. "At a party in New Orleans, that's just common courtesy!"

The next time a Yankee criticizes the South, just ask him if he heard of anybody retiring and going North.

The Mason-Dixon line is a division between "you-all" and "youse-guys."

In New Orleans folks enjoy telling the story of the Northern visitor who strode purposefully into a bar, demanded a shot of one of the more potent pain-killers served by that establishment—to wit, a Sazerac—and announced: "I'm disappointed in this city." Sipping a second Sazerac, he mused, "The streets are ugly, the women aren't pretty, there's no charm in the French Quarter."

He ordered three more Sazeracs, and continued his attack. After the tenth Sazerac he admitted: "Well, perhaps the women do have charm." From the dregs of the next Sazerac he bubbled, "That French Quarter is fascinating." After the dozenth dose of the same powerful potion he glowed: "Wunnaful plashe, N'Awlins!" After two more Sazeracs, he grabbed for his check, flourished a $100 bill and demanded, "Gimme my change in Confederate money."

At a party in New Orleans a New York man met a pretty blond southern belle. "Honey," he said as soon as he could get her alone, "you're the girl for me. I'm going to take you like General Grant took Richmond." Pleased by his historical comparison, he repeated, "Yes, ma'am. I'm going to take you like Grant took Richmond!"

"Do you mean," smiled the girl, "that you're going to wait a whole fo-ah yeahs for me to surrender?"

Speeches—Speaking

Nothing is opened more by mistake than the mouth.

SPEAKER *(in front of mike)*: "Can you hear me in the back?"
"No." *(from far corner)*
MAN IN FRONT ROW: "Well, you can have my seat."

Speakers who have trouble holding an audience might remember the story of the speaker who complained, "There are so many rude interruptions, Mr. Chairman, that I can hardly hear myself speaking."

"Don't let it bother you," came a voice from the rear. "You ain't missin' nothing!"

Let's give a big round of applause to Mr. Smith who left the notes for his speech at home."

"Can she talk?" said the newlywed to his best friend. "We were in Miami and when we got home her tongue was sunburned."

Two men were having lunch together and talking about their wives, as was their custom each day.

"My wife's always entering those fool contests, but she never wins anything," one of them grumbled. "It isn't that she's dumb—she just can't say anything in 25 words or less!"

Occasionally a man likes to say what he really thinks, a privilege some of us abuse.

A preacher who was popular with his congregation explained his success as the result of a silent prayer which he offered each time he took the pulpit. It ran thus:
"Lord, fill my mouth with worthwhile stuff,
And nudge me when I've said enough."

"I learned to be a public speaker by filling my mouth with pebbles and practicing enunciation."
"It's a pity you didn't try it with Portland cement."

What the world needs today is a better mouth trap.

A man was reading a prepared address to a meeting of industrialists and he swung into his speech:
"The average businessman is tired. He has worked long and diligently in difficult times and he is weary. He is physically and mentally exhausted. But he isn't nearly as tired as the girls who have to type all this hogwash."
There came a long tense pause while a delighted audience began to yelp its appreciation. The speaker stared at his script in unbelief.
"Why," he blurted at last, "I never wrote anything like that!"

Lecturers should remember that the capacity of the mind to absorb is limited to what the seat can endure.

Spendthrift

"How did George go through his rich uncle's inheritance so fast?"
"Well, he spent a good bit of it on wine, women and song. The rest he squandered."

Sports (see Football, Golf, Baseball, etc.)

Discussing his tennis technique, a stout, amiable bald man panted:
"My brain immediately barks out a command to my body. 'Run forward speedily,' it says, 'Start right away! Slam the ball gracefully over the net, then walk slowly back!'"
"And what happens?" he was asked.
"And then," replied the bald man, "my body says, 'who me?'"

A famous wrestler was visiting an old friend in the country village and the two spent their first evening in the local tap room. When they finally left, the host led the wrestler on a shortcut through a pasture, forgetting there was a mean bull on it.

The pair was half way across the pasture when the bull attacked. The wrestler grabbed the bull by the horns and rolled around the field with him until the animal managed to free himself and run off.

"Too bad I had those last three or four drinks," said the wrestler to his friend, "or I would have got that guy off his bicycle."

If you can't hear a pin drop, there's something wrong with your bowling.

An "armature" isn't a guy who boxes for nothing.

A sailor wandered into a tennis match and sat down. "Whose game?" he asked.

A shy young thing looked up hopefully. "I am."

"You taught your basketball team to be fine sportsmen," comforted a friend of a losing coach. "They are good losers."

"Good?" retorted the angry coach, "they're perfect."

BOXING INSTRUCTOR *(after first lesson):* "Now, have you any questions to ask?"

BEGINNER *(dazed):* "Yes, how much is your correspondence course?"

Students

A college student wrote to his father: "Dear father, I am broke and have no friends. What shall I do?"

His father's answer: "Make friends at once."

TEACHER *(to history student):* "You want to know why you didn't pass the history test? Well, your answer to the question 'Why did the pioneers go into the wilderness' was interesting from the standpoint of sanitation, but it was still incorrect."

Two engineering students were taking calculus for the first time and while waiting for the instructor to arrive they took a quick glance through the book. One of them came across the integral tables. "Tell me," he asked his friend, "can you read that?"

"No," replied his friend, "but if I had my flute with me I could play it."

A teen-ager complained to a friend: "My dad wants me to have all the things he never had when he was a boy—including five straight A's on my report card."

PROFESSOR: "What can you tell me about nitrates?"
STUDENT: "Well, they're a lot cheaper than day rates."

STUDENT: "I'll stand on my head or bust."
INSTRUCTOR: "No, miss, never mind, just stand on your head."

PROFESSOR *(taking up quiz paper):* "Why the quotation marks on this paper?"
STUDENT: "Courtesy to the man on my left."

A student in the English class fell asleep as the professor was reading one of the Canterbury Tales. Annoyed when he saw it, the professor let fly with the book, bouncing it off the sleeper's head.
"What hit me?" cried the victim.
"That," said the professor, "was a flying Chaucer."

A rooming house landlord received a phone call from the mother of one of her students. "Please keep an eye on Albert for me," begged the mother. "See that he gets plenty of sleep and doesn't drink or run around too much."
"You see," she added in an apprehensive tone, "this is the first time he's been away from home—except for two years in the Marines."

Success

"I had everything that a man could want . . . money, a beautiful home, the love of a beautiful redheaded woman. And then one morning my wife walks in."

A successful man is one who works hard to get rich and then spends the rest of his life sitting on the porch of a sanitarium watching the healthy poor go by.

A man owes it to himself to become successful. Once successful, he owes it to the Bureau of Internal Revenue.

Life story: He owed his success to his first wife—and his second wife to his success.

Success nowadays is making more money to pay taxes you would not be paying if you had not made so much money already.

Progress of a great man:
　　Quits shining his own shoes;
　　Quits writing his own letters;
　　Quits writing his own speeches.

I'd be quite a success if it weren't for taxes.

How to retire with $1 million: hard work, strict attention to duty, absolute honesty, economical living . . . death of a rich relative which nets you a million.

"What is the secret of your success?"
"A strong will."
"A strong will, you say?"
"Yep, a strong will that left me two hundred and fifty thousand dollars!"

Suicide

More people commit suicide with a fork than with any other weapon.

The train was about to depart when a man jumped into the compartment, to the great annoyance of the woman ensconced there, who had hoped to keep it exclusively for her daughter and herself. "I think I ought to warn you," she said, "that my daughter has German measles, whooping-cough and chicken-pox."
"Oh, that's all right," said the man. "As soon as the train gets in a tunnel, I'm going to commit suicide."

Supervisor

A good supervisor, we've heard it said, is a guy who knows how to step on your toes without messing up your shine.

Surprise

An old hillbilly took a wagonload of produce to market and received more than he had expected for it. He decided to buy some new clothes and hide them under the seat. On his way home, he came to a bridge and pulled on the reins, saying, "Whoah, Maude. Let's put on these new duds and surprise the old woman." He proceeded to discard his old clothes into the river. When he reached under the seat, the new clothes were gone too. He scratched his head and thought over his predicament for a few moments and then said, 'Giddap, Maude. We'll surprise her anyhow."

Swedish

One day two men were riding on the train discussing whether they should go to Minneapolis or Saint Paul.

"I don't want to go to Minneapolis," said one, "too many Swedes there."

"I guess Saint Paul is out, too," observed the other, "too many Swedes."

An elderly Swedish lady sitting behind them overheard their comments and she spoke up and said, "Excuse me, yentlemen, but if you are looking for a place var there ain't no Swedes—vy don't you go to hell?"

Swimming Pool

The tycoon and his wife moved into their newly built house while their daughter was away at finishing school. When she arrived home, her father escorted her on a tour of the mansion. He showed her through the house and then took her to the stables, the servants quarters, the kennels, the tennis court, and finally to the enormous swimming pool. There, diving and swimming about, were several handsome young lifeguards.

"Oh, Daddy," the young lady screamed excitedly. "It's a gorgeous pool. And to think you've stocked it just for me!"

Tact

An office boy noticed two women with the boss.

OFFICE BOY: "Who were those two girls?"

Boss: "Well, one was my wife and the other was Elizabeth Taylor."

OFFICE BOY: "Which one was Elizabeth Taylor?"

The boss took a dollar out of his pocket and gave it to the boy.

OFFICE BOY: "What's this for?"

Boss: "I just want you to remember, when you get to be president, that I once lent you money."

Tailor

CUSTOMER: "Why do you have an apple for a trademark? You're a tailor."

TAILOR: "Well, if it hadn't been for the apple, where would the clothing business be?"

Then there is the psychiatrist who told his patient he worried about money too much. "Don't worry about it so much," he advised. "Just last week I had a patient who couldn't sleep because of worry over the bills he kept getting from his tailor. I advised him to forget about them and now he feels fine."

"I know, I know," replied the patient. "I'm his tailor."

Taxes–Taxpayer

"Poor man! He was ruined by untold wealth."
"Untold wealth? How come?"
"He forgot to tell about it in his income tax return."

A dime is a dollar with all taxes taken out.

"It looks like Congress was smart when they changed the taxes. They put a big tax on liquor, then they raised all the other taxes so as to drive people to drink!"

A taxpayer is a person who doesn't have to pass a civil service exam to work for the government.

If Patrick Henry thought taxation without representation was so terrible, he should see how it is today with representation.

Now when your ship comes in, the government sees that it is docked.

The taxpayer is beginning to feel like the sick man about whom the doctor inquired, "Nurse, did the patient take the medicine religiously as I ordered?"

"No, sir," replied the nurse. "He cursed every time he took it."

It's hard to realize these days that this country was founded partly to avoid taxation.

Won't it be wonderful when income taxes get back down where we can afford to make a living?

The word "tax" comes from the Latin *taxare*, meaning "to touch sharply."
Does anyone doubt that this is what it does?

One thing in favor of death over taxes—death doesn't get worse every time Congress meets.

"How can you possibly justify a trip to Miami Beach as a legitimate business expense?" the tax investigator asked the optometrist.

"I was trying to develop contact lenses that wouldn't pop out," he replied.

Luke sent the Internal Revenue people 25 cents with a note saying he understood he could pay his income tax by the quarter.

A returning traveler was overheard describing the Eiffel Tower as "sort of like the Empire State Building after taxes."

A woman with a newly developed interest in government wrote to the editor of a big newspaper: "I want to get into politics. Do the tax-payers have a party?"

The editor answered her letter, writing: "Very seldom, lady, very seldom."

The Department of Taxation received a typed income tax return from a bachelor who listed one dependent son. The examiner returned the blank with a penciled notation: "This must be a stenographic error." Presently, the blank came back with the added pencil notation: "You're telling me!"

Politician: "Now, ladies and gentlemen, I just want to tax your memory."

Man in audience: "Good heavens! Has it come to that?"

> 365 days in the year
>   You work like the devil to make it.
> And just when you're ready to start
>   eating steady
> The government's ready to take it.

A Texan went into a bar and said, "Give me the tallest glass you've got and a lemon."

The bartender obliged.

The Texan squeezed the lemon and got almost a pint of juice. Tossing aside the lemon rind, he said, "I'd like to see anyone else get that much juice out of one lemon."

A little fellow standing nearby said, "Let me have a tall glass and the lemon rind you just threw away." He then took the lemon rind and squeezed another full glass of juice from the already used rind.

"Man!" exclaimed the Texan. "I never seen anything like that! How did you do it?"

"Well, you see," replied the man quietly, "I'm with the Internal Revenue Service."

Taxi—Taxi Driver

A certain doctor had ridden over a mile in a taxi when he suddenly discovered he had no money with him. He tapped the window and told the driver, "Stop at this cigar store a minute. I want to get matches so I can look for a $10 bill I lost in the cab somewhere." When he emerged from the cigar store there was no taxi in sight.

"You ain't got no cause to worry, lady," the driver assured the passenger as she straightened her hat while the taxi continued to swerve and skid down Main Street one wintry day. "I ain't goin' to land back in no hospital now after 18 months in one overseas."

"How dreadful," she murmured sympathetically, "you must have been seriously wounded."

"Nope," he replied cheerfully, "never got a scratch. I was a mental case!"

Teen-ager

"Do you mind if I take the car tonight?" the salesman asked his teen-age son. "I'm taking your mother to the movies and I want to impress her."

A slightly encouraging note to find your teen-ager returning from the excitement of camp still appreciative of the quiet life around home.

Telephone—Telephone Service

The sales manager was checking out of his hotel room. After he had settled up, he sought out the hotel manager and handed him a bouquet of flowers. "These are for the phone girls," he said.

"Thank you, sir," said the manager. "Thank you. I know they will appreciate the compliment."

"Compliment?" roared the guest. "I thought they all died!"

The braggart was letting everybody know that he could bend a horseshoe with his bare hands. All of a sudden one farmer had enough.

"That's nothing to brag about," he said, "my wife can tie up ten miles of telephone wire with her chin."

A telephone service girl received a call from an elderly lady:

"My telephone cord," said she, "is too long. Would you please pull it back at your end?"

If Alexander Graham Bell hadn't invented the telephone, some woman would have.

Television

At our house the TV repairman is more popular than Santa Claus and he comes more often.

Television came along to prove that some radio programs are as bad as they sound

I got to thinking yesterday—you know how you do when the television won't work.

Pay television has been with us for years. It's called the installment plan.

Children who watch TV every night will go down in history—not to mention arithmetic, geography and science.

Until television can incorporate the odor of hot dogs, a baseball telecast lacks a lot!

A fellow bought his wife the latest in TV sets—complete with 3-D knob. One day she had to get the repair man to fix it and while he was there she heard her husband's key in the lock. "Quick," she said, "hide! My husband is so jealous he'll kill you if he finds you here!"

All the cupboards were full so the repair man hid inside the back of the set. The husband settled down in his armchair and switched on the TV to watch the football game. Inside the set the repair man was cramped, getting hotter and hotter. He finally decided he'd had enough, pushed down the back of the set, marched out of the room and slammed the door. The husband stood up, looked at the set, looked at his wife and said, "I didn't see the referee send that fellow off the field, did you?"

Finally had to take my television aerial off the chimney . . . the pictures were too smoky.

Into the Electrical Showrooms one Saturday afternoon trooped Ma, Pa and the kids, and sat themselves down in front of one of those washing machines with a glass window at the front. They sat there for half-an-hour growing more and more restless, and in the end, Ma walked out snorting, "Well, if that's television, you can keep it!"

The big difference between 'em is—on radio, you wonder what the studio audience is laughing at; on TV, you wonder why!

Nowadays a husband and wife either have to have minds that run in the same channels or two television sets.

Television has made a family semi-circle out of the family circle.

Temptation

The number of times the average man says "No" to temptation is once weakly.

Three salesmen were standing on a street corner in North Africa. They were an Englishman, an Arabian and an American. Just then a beautiful dancing girl walked by.
The Englishman said, "By Jove!"
The Arabian said, "By the prophet!"
The American said, "By tomorrow night!"

"Now, madam," said the house-to-house salesman to the dazzling Venus, "this instrument I have here is made of the finest materials, painstakingly gathered at great cost from all the hemispheres, and is guaranteed without qualification or reservation to peel potatoes, pit cherries, dice carrots, trim hedges, shear the dog and slice a cake."
"My husband isn't home," said the doll sultrily, kicking off her shoes, and leaning back comfortably on the sofa.
"Is that so! Well, as I was saying, this highly polished, sturdy, lifetime instrument—"
"It's warm in here, isn't it?" commented the chick, removing her hose and garters. "My husband is rarely at home."
"Imagine that! You will note the superb chrome finish on—"
"Gosh, it's warm!" whispered the babe, slipping out of her skirt. "My husband won't be back for a month, and I'm lonesome."
The salesman put an arm around the fluff, and patted her comfortingly. "You just tell me where the rascal is, honey," he said soothingly, "and I'll go and bring him back right now!"

Texas

A motorist pulled up at a filling station in Texas and, noting an elderly man who sat sadly watching the cars go by, he remarked:

"Everything looks very dry."

"Yes."

"When did it rain last?"

" 'Bout three years ago."

"That must be very hard on the ranches around here," said the motorist sympathetically.

The man shook his head: "Don't know what's to become of us. We have sunk thousands of wells drilling for water. And what comes up? Oil."

A not-so-loyal Texan was planning a trip across the state. He was poring over his road maps when a very loyal Texan said, "Just think of it, you are going to drive 650 miles and you'll still be in Good Old Texas. Where else in the world can that be done?"

"Well," said the traveler-to-be, "there's Siberia."

A Boston salesman visited Texas and heard a Texan boasting about heroes of the Alamo who, almost alone, held off whole armies.

"I'll bet," challenged the Texan, "you never had anyone around Boston as brave as that!"

"Did you ever hear of Paul Revere?" the Bostonian asked meekly.

"Paul Revere?" queried the Texan. "Isn't he the fellow who ran for help?"

A Texan was dictating his will to his lawyer: "To my son I leave three million dollars—and he's lucky I didn't cut him off entirely."

Did you hear about the rich Texan who bought two Cadillacs and took his change in Volkswagens?

BLONDE: "Are you sure you're in love with that Texas oil man?"

BRUNETTE: "Sure? I'll say! Every time I hear his voice I get chinchillas up and down my spine."

A Texas GI was playing poker with some English soldiers. He drew four aces. "One pound," ventured the Englishman on his right.

"Ah don't know how you-all count your money," said the Texan, "but Ah'll raise you a ton."

A Texas oil man was visiting New York. His city friend showed him all the sights including the Empire State Building.

"Isn't that a magnificent structure?" asked his friend.

"Nothin'," said the Texan. "I got a outhouse bigger'n that!"

The New Yorker looked him over. "You need it!" he retorted.

We hear that a Texas oil man, unable to find a place to park his Cadillac, gave it away and bought one that was already parked.

FIRST TEXAN: "Hear you bought another Cadillac."

SECOND TEXAN: "Almost had to. I ducked into their showroom to make a phone call and didn't want to leave without buying something."

The Texas-born captain of an all-Texas company in North Africa told his men: "Our job here is to promote good neighborliness among other things. We've got to humor the natives. If they say Africa is bigger than Texas, then agree with them."

A proud young lady from Kentucky was trying to justify her state to a Texan. "In Kentucky," she said, "we have Fort Knox, where enough gold is stored to build a golden fence 3 ft. high completely around Texas."

"Go ahead and build it," drawled the man from out yonder. "If I like it, I'll buy it."

A Texan and an Oklahoman got into an argument concerning the relative importance of their respective states. "Oklahoma," drawled the Texan, "is for the birds. In fact, it's nothing but an outlying province of Texas."

"That can't be," shot back the Oklahoman, "because no one has ever heard of a state that can outlie Texas."

The mosquitoes that inhabit the swamps of the Texas coast are famous for their size and ferocity. Travel, except in a closed car, is forbidden in those parts after nightfall.

A foolish horseman ventured into the coastal area a while back, and before he knew it, had been jerked from his saddle by two mosquitoes.

The first mosquito said, "Let's carry him in the swamp."

"No," said the second mosquito, "let's eat him here. If we carry him in the swamp, the big mosquitoes will take him away from us."

A Texan struck oil and built a mansion and three swimming pools. One pool he keeps filled with cool water and the other with warm water; the third he keeps empty. He explains: "A lot of my friends can't swim."

There had been a death and the funeral services were being held. As the minister finished his prayer, he said, "Would anyone like to say anything before we lower the departed?"

Nobody spoke. Thinking that some of the friends would like to say a few good words about the deceased but were shy, the minister said again, "Isn't there anyone here who would like to say some little thing?" Nobody moved.

Finally, from the rear, a tall, broad shouldered fellow started moving up through the mourners until he stood alongside the minister. "Wal," he drawled, "since nobody else is going to talk, thar's a few little things I'd like to say about Texas...."

Theater

A heavy man and his wife were returning to their seats in the concert hall after an intermission.

"Did I step on your toes as I went out?" he asked a man at the end of a row.

"You did," replied the other grimly, expecting an apology.

"The heavy man turned to his wife. "All right, Mary," he said. "This is our row."

"But you don't understand," she exclaimed to the usher as he led her down the orchestra aisle. "I have a box seat."

"Just keep your coat on," the usher advised, "and no one will notice it."

USHER: "How far down do you want to sit sir?"
PATRON: "All the way, of course."

HUSBAND: "I've tickets for the theater."
WIFE: "Fine. I'll start dressing at once."
HUSBAND: "Yes, do. The tickets are for tomorrow night."

"I wish you'd wear a gown in the second act that is not quite so revealing," the stage manager told the star in the show.

"But this is the latest style and I paid a fortune for it," she pouted. "Why should I change?"

"Well, in that serious scene when your husband says, 'Woman, you're hiding something from me,' the audience laughs."

Theft

Luke's sister-in-law insists on doing all her shoplifting in the same store. Says she gets better bargains there.

A man who had his purse stolen some years previously, received the following letter:

"Sur, sum years ago I stole your muny. Remorse is gnawin' me, so I send sum back. When it gnaws me again I will send sum more."

A lady went to the governor of her state and said to him, "Governor, I want to get my husband out of prison."

The governor asked, "What is he in prison for?"

She replied, "For stealing a ham."

The governor asked, "Is he a good husband?"

She replied, "No, sir. He drinks, he beats the children and he is no good."

Then the governor asked, "Why do you want him out of jail, if he is no good?"

She replied, "Well, Governor, the fact is that we are out of ham."

Tipping

The traveler was feeling in excellent humor as the colored porter was brushing his coat. He asked the porter the amount of his average tip.

"Mah average tip, Boss?" grinned the porter. "Ah should say dat 'bout one dollah, suh, is mah average."

The traveler reached into his pocket and fished out a dollar.

"Thank you, Boss!" said the elated porter as he creased the bill affectionately. "Thank you indeedy, suh. An' ah will add dat yo' is de fust pussen what has come up to de average!"

Traits

During the great flood, Noah's Ark sprang a leak and Noah told his dog to put his nose against the hole. The water continued to rush in, so Noah asked his wife to stand over the spot. As the leak grew, Noah himself sat on the hole.

And to this day, a dog's nose is always cold; a woman's feet are always clammy—and men always stand with their backs to the fireplace.

Tranquilizers (see Doctors, Medicine)

There's a new tranquilizer called Damitol. It doesn't relax you, it just makes you enjoy being tense.

Travel

The train came to a sudden stop, shaking up the passengers more than somewhat.

"What happened?" gasped a nervous old lady.

"Nothing much," replied the conductor. "We hit a cow."

"Oh," replied the woman. "Was she on the track?"

"No, lady, we chased her into the barn."

TRAVELING LADY: "Can you tell me which platform to go to for the train to Boston?"

CONDUCTOR: "Just turn to the left and you'll be right."

LADY: "Young man, don't be so smart-alecky."

CONDUCTOR: "O.K., lady, then just turn right and you'll be left."

POLITE YOUNG PERSON ON A TRAIN: "I'm afraid, sir, you're in the wrong seat."

BURLY INDIVIDUAL: "You've got nothing to be afraid of, mister, so long as you don't try to move me."

"Conductor, does this train stop at San Francisco?"

"Lady, if it doesn't, there's going to be one hell of a splash."

A lady was riding on the train with her son. When the conductor came by, she said: "A fare for one and a half fare for the boy."

The conductor looked at the boy and said: "Lady, that boy's got long pants on."

"In that case," said the lady haughtily, "full fare for the boy and a half fare for me."

And the colored mammy in the seat behind the boy and his mother said: "Bless my soul. I goes for nuffin!"

Travel broadens one. But then just sitting at home in an easy chair does, too!

CHEERFUL WIFE (*to seasick husband*): "Never mind, dear, you're beginning to look like your passport photo."

Speaking of water, a tourist on his way to Europe was experiencing seasickness for the first time. Calling his wife to his bedside, he said in a weak voice: "Jennie, my will is in the National Bank. Everything is left to you, dear. My various stocks you will find in my safe deposit box. (*Then feverishly*) And Jennie, bury me on the other side when we get there. I can't stand this trip again . . . dead or alive."

PASSENGER: "Motorman, at which end can I get off the car?"

MOTORMAN: "Either end, lady. Both of 'em stop."

MR. NEW RICH (*touring in his new car*): "Where are we now?"
CHAUFFEUR: "Halfway between Paris and Marseilles, sir."
MR. NEW RICH: "Don't bother me with niggling little details. What country are we in?"

WIFE: "Wasn't it disgusting the way those men stared at the girl getting on the train?"
HUSBAND: "What train?"

GUIDE: "We are now passing the largest brewery in the state."
TOURIST: "Why?"

"Isn't science wonderful?"
"In what way?"
"Well, when it couldn't raise the train windows, it air-conditioned the coaches."

PULLMAN PASSENGER: "Porter, what about these shoes? One's black and one's tan!"
PORTER: "Well, if it don't beat all! Dis is de second time dat's happened dis mawnin!"

A man traveling in an upper berth in a pullman car was aroused in the night by a tapping on the bottom of his bunk. He peered over the side and found the lady below trying to get his attention.

"I hate to disturb you," she said, "but I'm cold. I thought you might have a blanket you could spare."

"Are you married?" the man asked.

She nodded.

"Well," he said, "in that case let's get warm like married people do."

"What do you mean?" she asked.

"Get your own damn blanket!" he snarled.

The two gals boarded a Pullman sleeper crowded with revelers returning from a convention. One of them was frightened and she locked herself in her drawing room. The other remained calm and cool, and collected.

Here's a scene that took place on a crowded trolley. A young lady is vainly groping for her purse to pay her fare. A young man is standing nearby with anguish written on his handsome features.

YOUNG MAN: "Pardon me, miss, but may I pay your fare?"
YOUNG LADY: "Sir!"

YOUNG MAN: "I beg your pardon again, young lady, but won't you let me pay your fare?"

"YOUNG WOMAN: "Why, I don't even know you, and anyway I'll have this purse open in a minute."

YOUNG MAN: "I really must insist on paying your fare. You've unzipped me three times."

The green car rolled to a smooth halt and the driver leaned out of the window and called to an old man with a cane. "Am I on the right road to Springfield?" he said.

The old man looked up and said, "Eh?"

The driver shouted, "Am I on the right road to Springfield?"

"You'll hev to talk a leetle louder, young feller, I'm a mite deef," the old man replied.

The driver tried a third time, then realizing the case was hopeless, continued on his way.

He had traveled about three miles when he came to a farmhouse in front of which the farmer's wife was standing.

He stopped the car and called, "Am I on the —?"

"Keep right on this road," she said, "I heard you the first time."

A pretty young secretary got tired of standing up on the bus every morning on the way to work. So one morning she tried an experiment. She got on the bus carrying a copy of a book titled "Having Your First Baby." Worked like a charm. She kept repeating the experiment. Almost every morning for eight months she was offered a seat on the crowded bus.

One night the young lady's steady boy friend finally brought himself to the point of proposing marriage. She accepted. The next morning she got on the bus flashing a new engagement ring.

The bus driver gave an admiring look and nodded approvingly. Then he pointed to a series of pencil marks on the dashboard in front of him: "I've been keeping track, sister," he said. "You're just getting in under the wire, you know."

Troubles

Funny thing about trouble—it always starts out being fun.

One of the best ways to avoid trouble and insure safety is to breathe through your nose. It keeps your mouth shut.

If you could kick the person responsible for most of your troubles, you wouldn't be able to sit down for six months.

It's best not to tell people your troubles. Half of them are not interested, and the other half are glad to hear you are getting it at last.

One of our present troubles seems to be that too many adults, and not enough children, believe in Santa Claus.

Trucking

The salesman was following a truck through heavy city traffic. At every traffic light, the truck driver would stop, climb out of the truck and pound with a sledge hammer on the sides and back of his truck; finally, after a couple of miles of this, the salesman jumped out of his car and ran up to the driver.

"I'm not normally nosy," he said, "but I've been trying to figure out why you bang on your truck like that every time you stop."

"Well, I'll tell you," said the driver. "With the license I've got, I'm only supposed to haul two tons. But I have three tons of canaries and I've got to keep one ton of them flying."

Trust

It is a real kindness to trust certain people with your secrets; they can feel so important as they pass them along!

Twins

Cuzzin Woodrow's first-born was a set of identical twins.

The only way he could tell 'em apart was by their bawls. One bawled all day. One bawled all night.

DOAKS: "My girl friend is a twin."
JOE: "How do you tell them apart?"
DOAKS: "Her brother is built different."

Unhappiness

Money makes unhappiness pretty doggone comfortable.

Unions

"Is this a union shop?" asked the labor organizer as he rushed into the "Lonely Hearts Matrimonial Agency."

"It sure is," replied the manager

After several minutes of thumbing through photos of all descriptions, the young man came up with a picture of a cute little number, age 19.

"I'll take this one," he said.

"I'm sorry, but we can't do that," the manager replied. And he handed him a photograph of an old hag who was 52.

"How come?" asked the young organizer. "What is the meaning of this?"

"She has seniority, my friend," replied the manager.

Untouchables

Untouchables are people as broke as we are.

Vacation

Some people's idea of vacation is to spend two weeks on the sands and the other fifty on the rocks.

Vacation: It consists of 2 weeks which are 2 short, after which you are 2 tired to return 2 work and 2 broke not 2.

The junior executive arrived back at the office after his vacation tired and haggard. "What's the matter," asked his secretary, "vacation too much for you?"

"I guess so," was the reply. "With the kids taking vitamins and me taking tranquilizers, it was a losing battle all the way."

Vegetarian

A tall tree in a roadside field cast a cool-looking, inviting shade. So the salesman stopped his car, climbed the fence, and stretched out to relax for a few moments. He had no sooner settled down when a huge, infuriated bull appeared, galloping at top speed toward the man. At the last possible moment, the salesman noticed the bull. He scrambled up and tumbled over the fence to safety with not a fraction of a second to spare.

"You brute!" he sputtered, shaking his fist at the angry animal. "And I've been a vegetarian all my life, too!"

Virtue

ANGRY EDITOR (*reprimanding girl reporter*): "Watch your stories. As Pulitzer said, 'Accuracy is to a newspaper what virtue is to a woman.'"

GIRL REPORTER: "Maybe. But a newsaper can print a retraction."

The girl who doesn't drink or smoke, and goes to bed every night at nine. She'll be seven tomorrow.

Walking

The man who never thought anything of walking ten miles a day now has a grandson who doesn't think so much of it either.

Water

The Army medical officer was testing the water supply. "What precautions do you take against infection?" he asked the sergeant in charge.

"We boil the water first, sir," the sergeant replied.

"Good!"

"Then we filter it."

"Excellent!"

"And then," said the sergeant, "just for safety's sake, we drink beer."

Weather

Forecaster: A guy who can look into a gal's eyes and tell whether.

A man dropped the weather bureau a card which read: "I thought you'd be interested to know that I shoveled three feet of partly cloudy from my front steps this morning."

A stranger was talking to an old-timer in a small Missouri town. "I don't like the looks of those clouds . . . look just like some we had back in Texas just before a tornado struck."

"Was it a bad one?" asked the native.

"Bad! Why, man, I didn't want to come to Missouri!"

A man living on the Wisconsin-Minnesota border was puzzled for years about what state he lived in. Finally he hired a surveyor.

"You live in Wisconsin," decided the surveyor.

The man cheered and tossed his hat into the air. "Thank heaven!" he cried. "No more of those terrible Minnesota winters!"

A visitor to a drought-stricken area was engaged in conversation at the local store about the "no-rain" situation.

"You think the drought is bad here," the merchant observed, "but down south o' here a ways they haven't had any rain for so long that the Baptists are sprinkling, the Methodists are using a damp cloth, and the Presbyterians are issuing rain checks!"

The local weatherman was wrong on his forecasts so often he was publicly embarrassed and applied for a transfer. "Why do you wish to be transferred?" came the question from headquarters. "Because the weather here doesn't agree with me."

Hurricanes are named after girls because they're spinsters.

Nine-tenths of the people couldn't start a conversation if the weather didn't change once in a while.

At the officer's club they were bidding farewell to one who was leaving for India. In the conversation a friend said: "It gets very hot in India at times. Aren't you afraid the climate might disagree with your wife?"
The man looked at him reproachfully. "It wouldn't dare."

Weddings (see Newlyweds, Marriage, Courtship)

Displaying her wedding gifts to her friends, the bride came to one from the groom's old Marine buddy.
"I just adore these personalized gifts," she told her friends. "We received towels and wash clothes with HIS and HERS on them, but (*blushing*) this is even more personal."
And she held up an olive drab blanket with the letters US stamped in the middle.

In the small country parish, it was the custom for the pastor to kiss the bride. However, one bride from another town didn't like the idea and asked the groom to tell the pastor. Just before the ceremony she asked again.
"I did, darling," replied the groom, "and the pastor said that in that case he would charge only half the usual fee."

The shotgun marriage . . . it was a case of wife or death.

"Is there anyone here who knows why these two should not be joined together in wedlock?" asked the minister. "Speak now or forever hold your peace."
"I'd like to say something," volunteered a voice.
"You keep out of this," replied the minister, "you're the groom."

Weight and Diet

A fellow we know lost 125 pounds when he left New York. She was a brunette.

Wife reading her husband's fortune on a weight card: "You are dynamic, a leader of men, and admired by women for your good looks and strength of character." Looking up, she said, "It's got your weight wrong, too."

> A little girlie whose name doesn't matter
> Found she was getting fatter and fatter,
> But she dieted so well, that now she looks like 'ell
> And there isn't a place you can pat 'er.

"I simply can't stand my husband. He has such a nasty disposition. He's made me so jittery that I'm losing weight."

"Why don't you leave him and go back to mother?" said her friend.

"Oh, I will," was the reply, "I'm just waiting 'til he gets me down to 120 pounds."

"Can you tell me what makes the Tower of Pisa lean?"

"If I knew I'd take some myself," said the overweight woman.

"You've picked up a little weight, haven't you?"

"No, I haven't. I weigh 118 in the nude and I can prove it."

The spare tire around your waist is the most expensive one you can buy.

Jane bought a reducing machine. Now she's starving herself to keep up the payments.

A stout lady in Topeka was told by her physician: "You have too much around the hips. And the weight has retreated to your rear, giving you lardosies and affecting your posture. You'll have to reduce."

She looked at the doctor's protruding stomach. He was as much out front as she was in back.

"Seems to me, Doc," she retorted, "I'd rather pull it than push it."

> If you're blest
> With strength to diet,
> Be my guest
> But diet quiet!

> You eat and eat
> I sit and chat;
> You eat, I chat
> You're thin, I'm fat

Everything is delicious to a man who's reducing.

Destiny shapes our ends—but our middles are of our own chewsing.

The girl who went on a diet found that the bottom dropped out of her life.

"I'm not saying she's exactly fat, mind you, but two or three more pounds and they'd be asking her to wear license plates."

What a lot of women would like to do with last year's dress is get into it.

Every woman expects to be met half weigh, especially when she's on the scales.

Two friends were discussing another member of their bridge club.
"What's bothering Ann?" asked one. "She looks simply furious."
"Oh, she's trying to reduce and just weighed herself on one of those scales with the new speaking attachment."
"But what happened?"
"When she stepped on the scales the voice said, 'One at a time, please.' "

There are four kinds of women: Fat, Skinny, O.K. and "Get-a-load-of-her."

"I've heard of a new sulpha drug for reducing," her husband remarked after dinner.
"You have? What is it?"
"Sulpha-denial."

"How did your wife get on with her reducing diet?"
"Just fine. She disappeared completely last week."

A Lancashire woman, wishing to lose weight, had been put on a diet by her doctor. One day a friend dropped in and was amazed to behold her tackling with great appetite a large potato pie.
"I thought you were on a diet?" asked the friend.
"Ay, so I am," was the reply. "But I've already had my diet. Now I'm having my dinner."

He can't lose weight simply by talking about it. He has to keep his mouth shut.

The girdle makers live off the fat of the land.

INSURANCE MAN: "How much do you weigh?"
PROSPECT: "One hundred and ninety-five with glasses."
INSURANCE MAN: "Why include your glasses?"
PROSPECT: "Because I can't read the bathroom scale without them."

Many a girl with a million dollar figure lets inflation set in.

And then there's the prof who is dieting—he wants to win the nobelly prize.

> Hi diddle diddle
> I'm watching my middle,
> And hope to whittle it soon,
> With those good things to eat
> I won't master the feat
> Till my dish runs away with my spoon.

Diet: Triumph of mind over platter.

"Mister, will you give me a penny? I ain't ate nothing in three days."
"What good will a penny do you?"
"I want to see how much weight I've lost."

A diet is what you keep putting off while you keep putting it on.

Widow

A widow is the luckiest woman in the world. She knows all about men, and all the men who know anything about her are dead.

A widow is a woman who no longer finds fault with her husband.

Wills

A certain old maid called in her lawyer and explained her last will and testament. "I want to give $3,000 to the art museum, $1,000 to my nephew, $1,000 to the YWCA, and $2,000 to the library."

"And what are you going to do with the remaining $500?" he asked.

"I've never had a lover," said the poor old maid, "and I'll give that to anyone who will kiss me and make love to me."

"I'll do it," said the lawyer. He hurried home and explained to his wife. That night he called at the home of the old maid.

Later that night his wife became nervous and called him on the telephone.

"It's all right, dear," he said. "She has cut off the art museum and the library and if you'll let me stay a little while longer, she'll drop the YWCA"

CLIENT: "I want to draw up my will, but I don't know how to word it."

LAWYER: "You needn't worry—just leave it to me."

CLIENT: "Yes, I suppose that's how it will turn out anyway."

The relatives were all gathered in the lawyer's office eagerly waiting for the reading of rich Uncle Herkimer's will. The lawyer gravely opened the envelope and read:

"Being of sound mind, I spent all my money."

The dying man beckoned to his wife. "Sarah," he whispered, "be sure to put David in charge of the store when I'm gone."

"David? Why not Joey? He's a smart boy."

The man nodded weakly. "Okay, but give Harry the station wagon."

"But Benny needs it for his family!"

"All right—give it to Benny. But I think the house in the country should go to Shirley."

"Papa, you know Shirley hates the country. Give it to Rosalie."

The old man finally lost his patience. "MAMA," he groaned, "who's dying—you or me?"

A woman advertised a new Cadillac for $50. A man answered the ad and the first thing he asked was, "What's wrong with the car?" She said, "Nothing. If you want it for $50, give me the fifty and take it away. If you don't want it, please don't waste my time." He asked for the keys and went to the garage, backed the car out, parked in front of the house, counted out $50 and handed it to the owner, with this comment, "Now, you have your $50, what's the catch?" She said, "My husband just died and in his will he instructed that the Cadillac be sold and the proceeds be given his secretary."

Two friends, Russ and Dick, were motoring home from a fishing trip in Wisconsin when they encountered engine trouble on a lonely road at dusk. They knocked at the door of a farm house down the road and the farmer's daughter answered their knock.

She gave them dinner, and let them stay over night. Six months later Dick received an ominous looking legal document. A frown disappeared as he read it, and then he phoned his fishing companion. "I say, Russ," he said, "did you by any chance spend a little time with that beautiful farm girl the night the car broke down?"

"Why—ah—yes," answered Russ sheepishly.

"And did you in a moment of machiavellian cunning give her my name and address?"

"Now don't get sore about that," broke in Russ. "Where's your sense of humor?"

"Oh, I'm not a bit sore," his friend assured him. "I just thought you'd like to know I've heard from her lawyer. She died last week and left me the farm and $20,000 in cash."

Wisdom

Every man is a fool for at least five minutes a day. Wisdom consists in not exceeding the time limit.

Wishes

"If you could have two wishes," said one girl to another, "what would they be?"

"Well," said her friend thoughtfully, "I'd wish for a husband."

"That's only one wish," pointed out the first girl.

"I'd save the other until I saw how he turned out."

Wives (see Marriage, Husbands, Courtship, Divorce)

WIFE: "When we were first married, you said I had a shape like a beautiful ship."

HUSBAND: "Yes, but your cargo has shifted."

Mr. Jones was skipping along the street whistling a gay tune. His neighbor, falling in step with him, remarked, "You're pretty happy this morning."

"I should be," said Mr. Jones. "I just cured my wife of yelling at me all the time."

"You did! How did you do it?"

"I convinced her that it was making a nervous wreck out of the dog."

"I can't get along with my wife. All she does is ignore me."

"Ignore you?"

"Yes, and if there's anything I dislike, it's ignorance."

ONE MARRIED MAN: "I'm very happy. I have a wonderful home, a good job, and the finest wife in the country."

ANOTHER MAN: "Who wouldn't be happy with his wife in the country?"

Sign in a tavern: "Your wife can get only so mad, so why not stay longer?"

PETE: "Doctor, do you think my wife will live?"
DOCTOR: "My man, be prepared for the worst."
PETE: "Now you've got me guessing."

"Look what I got for my wife," a proud husband exclaimed to his next door neighbor as he showed him a new Cadillac in the garage.
"You lucky dog," replied the neighbor. "Where did you make a deal like that?"

FIRST WOMAN: "Her husband was a judge, wasn't he?"
SECOND WOMAN: "Everyone thought so until he married her."

"They say brunettes have sweeter dispositions than redheads."
"That's a lot of hooey. My wife's been both and I can't see any difference."

"What did Eli Whitney say to his wife?"
"I don't know, what did Eli Whitney say to his wife?"
"Keep your cotton-pickin' hands out of my gin."

"My wife is always asking me for money," complained the husband. "Last week she wanted $200. A couple of days ago she asked me for $75. This morning she wanted $50."
"That's ridiculous," commented his friend. "What does she do with all that money?"
"I really don't know," replied the husband. "I never give her any."

If you really want to get your wife home quick from an out-of-town vacation, just send her a copy of the local newspaper with one item cut out.

One reason why Solomon's temple took 42 years to build might have been because he had 1001 wives to make suggestions.

There's nothing more exasperating than a wife who can cook and won't, unless it's a wife who can't cook and will.

On the way to work one morning, Ole told Lars, "Lars, I hate to mention this, but you should be careful to pull your shades in the evening. Last evening about 9 o'clock I walked by your house, the lights were turned down low, but the window shades were not drawn. I could see you and your wife making love very passionately."

"That's a good joke on you," laughed Lars. "I was out bowling with the boys last night."

YOUNG HOPEFUL: "Sir, may I have your daughter for my wife?"
FATHER: "Trot your wife around and I'll see."

The speaker was shouting at her audience. "Is there a man here," she asked, "who would let his wife be slandered and say nothing?"
A little mouse of a man rose to his feet.
With a frosty glare, the speaker inquired, "Do you really mean to say you would let your wife be slandered and say nothing?"
"Oh, I'm terribly sorry," apologized the little man. "I thought you said slaughtered."

A man wanted to buy a riding horse for his wife and was trying one out. The horse, however, required a firm hand and constant watching. Worried about whether his wife could handle it, he asked, "Do you think this is a suitable horse for a woman?"
The salesman was an extremely honest man, but at the same time he wanted to make the sale. He answered carefully, "Well, yes, I think a woman could handle the horse. But I wouldn't want to be the husband of the woman who could do it!"

LITTLE BOY: "Daddy, did Thomas Edison make the first talking machine?"
FATHER: "No, my son. The Creator performed the feat in the Garden of Eden, but Mr. Edison made the first one that could be shut off."

Every man needs a wife—because many things go wrong that you can't blame on your secretary.

"I haven't been able to sleep or eat since my wife left me!"
"You really love her, huh?"
"That's not the reason. She took the mattress and my false teeth."

Women

Women are to blame for most of the lying which men do. They insist on asking questions.

The husband was growling like a wounded bear because a button was missing from the shirt he was putting on.
"How helpless you men are," his wife sighed. "What would you ever do if there were no women to sew on your buttons for you?"

"Has it ever occurred to you, my dear," he replied, "that if there were no women, we men wouldn't need any buttons?"

The Kinsey reports show one thing—that some women talk too much.

Mother Nature fills some stockings better than Santa Claus does.

It isn't surprising our present-day girls are live wires—they carry practically no insulation.

Women need never expect to be men's equals until they can sport a large bald spot on top of their heads and still think they're handsome.

Toast: Here's to the women—without whom life would be impossible.

Nothing makes a woman look better than three cocktails inside a man.

Some girls have the hour-glass figure—others are the alarm clock type.

No one pays any attention to apple skins—but you should see the crowd around a peach peeling.

"Yep," said Grandpa, "newspapers are just like women."
"But, Gramp," questioned his college grandson, "I don't get it. What do you mean?"
"Well son," said Grandpa, "it's like this. They both have forms, back numbers are not in demand, they always have the last word, they are well worth looking over, they have a great deal of influence, you can't believe all they say, there's small demand for the bold-faced type, and every man should have one of his own and not borrow his neighbor's."

When a noted psychologist finished his address at a women's club meeting, one of the ladies came up to him and said, "Don't you think a woman is the best judge of women?"
"Not only the best judge," replied the psychologist, "but the best executioner."

A pair of nice pins helps a gal feel more secure.

Women are smarter than men. They have the figures to prove it.

A woman's face may be her fortune, but her legs draw the interest.

"If all the women were taken out of circulation," the professor asked his class, "what kind of a nation would this be?"

At this point a man in the back row shouted: "Stag-nation!"

"Which do you think women prefer—men who give in to them, or the other kind?"

"What other kind?"

A woman is happy if she has two things—a room full of furniture and a man to move it around for her.

More and more women are working, states a report. At long last white man is finding Indian no fool.

"Which would you rather give up—wine or women?"

"It depends on the vintage."

The old-fashioned girl who used to go to the city and stop at the YWCA now has a daughter who goes to the city and stops at nothing.

INDISCREET HOSTESS (*seeing her nephew's fiancée for the first time*): "I never should have known you from your photograph. Algy told me you were so pretty!"

ALGY'S FIANCÉE: "No. I'm not pretty, so I have to try to be nice, and it's such a bore. Have you ever tried?"

Words

If you add just five words a month to your vocabulary, in a single year your friends will wonder who in the heck you think you are.

A man with a wonderful vocabulary is one who can describe a shapely girl without using his hands.

Work—Working Hours—Working Conditions

I'm a great believer in luck. The harder I work, the more I seem to have of it.

JOE: "How long have you been working for the company?"

JIM: "Since the boss threatened to fire me."

GRADUATE: "Will you pay me what I'm worth?"

EMPLOYER: "I'll do better than that. I'll give you a small salary to start with."

BILL: "I have to earn my living by my wits."
DOTTY: "Well, half a living is better than none."

Heard in the office building elevator: "The only time I believe in reincarnation is at five o'clock in the afternoon when all the dead people come to life."

Sign in Contractor's Office: Anyone who likes work can have a hell of a good time here.

Don't itch for something that you're not willing to scratch for.

"Now don't worry, Joe," the office manager said to him in the nursing home, "everybody in the office is going to pitch in and do your work—as soon as we find out what you've been doing."

His death came as a shock for the reason that he was at work as usual on the day he died, and just passed away in his sleep.

Anyone who thinks by the inch and talks by the yard ought to be moved by the foot.

Keep your eye on the ball, your shoulder to the wheel, your ear to the ground—now, try to work in that position.

"Yes, I'll give you a job. Sweep out the store."
"But I'm a college graduate."
"Sorry, that's the easiest job I have."

ARTHUR: "So your new job makes you independent?"
ALBERT: "Absolutely. I get here any time I want before eight, and leave just when I please after five."

"Why, man, this machine will do half your work for you!"
"I'll take two of 'em!"

SERVICE MANAGER: "Been to the zoo yet?"
NEW DELIVERY BOY: "No, sir."
MANAGER: "Well, you should. You'll enjoy it and get a big kick out of watching the turtles zip by."

The city had hired a high school student to work during vacations collecting coins from parking meters. For two weeks after he started he didn't appear at the office. Then one day he walked in nonchalantly to report that he had lost his key to the meter coin boxes.

"Where have you been?" asked his supervisor. "The cashier has been holding your salary for you."

"What!" exclaimed the amazed beginner. "You mean that I get a salary too?"

When an old Negro walked into the local employment office to file an application for employment, he signed his name laboriously: "George Washington."

"Well," said the clerk with a smile, "are you the George Washington who cut down the cherry tree?"

"No, suh," answered the colored man quickly, "I ain't done no work for nigh onto a year."

We'd shorten our working hours if we could think of anything to do with our leisure that was as interesting and inexpensive as work.

The executive was on his way to the country club one Sunday morning for a game of golf, when in a field he noticed an elderly farmer whom he knew.

"Say, John," he asked, "don't you know that the Creator made the world in only six days and that he rested on the seventh?"

"I know all about that," said the farmer as he glanced at the darkening clouds. "But he got done and I didn't."

"Do you mean to say that you worked all night? I wouldn't have dreamed of it."

Neither would I—the boss thought of it."

"I can't understand why you're leaving us. Is it working conditions? hours? the pay?

"Conditions are wonderful and enjoyable. The hours are just right. The pay is good."

"Then why—why—why are you leaving?"

"Because you allow so many coffee breaks that I can't sleep nights!"

An attractive young employee made a practice of coming in late every day. Repeated warnings by her superior had no effect. Finally, in exasperation, he announced: "Miss Brown, I am tired of talking about your tardiness. I am, therefore, suspending you for one day without pay. When would you like to take the day?"

"Well, if it's all right with you," she replied, "I'd like to use it up being late."

"So you want another day off," snorted the office chief to his small office boy. "I'm anxious to hear what excuse you have this time. You've been off for your grandfather's funeral four times this year already."

"Today my grandma's getting married again," said the youngster.

"I'm very sorry," said the personnel manager, "but if I let you take two hours off for lunch today, I'd have to do the same for every employee whose wife gave birth to quadruplets."

"I'm sorry we won't be able to use you any longer," said the boss to one of his employees, "but it should give you a great deal of satisfaction to know that it's costing us $275,000 to replace you with a computer."

Worry

One good reason for not worrying is that you feel like a fool when things turn out all right.

Writer—Writing

A writer decided to submit his material to company magazines or so-called "house organs." He called one large firm in Cincinnati, and inquired, "Could you please tell me if your firm has a house organ?"

"Oh, no," the telephone operator answered, "we don't even have a piano!"

Youth

Puffing and blowing, the sailor just managed to jump into a coach as the train left the station.

The middle-aged man in the corner eyed him with scorn.

"When I was your age, my lad," he said, "I could run a half mile, catch a train by the skin of my teeth, and still be fresh as a daisy."

"Yes," gasped the young fellow, "but I missed this one at the last station."

INDEX

A

C

F

G

H

I

N

O

P

T

W

Y